Pocket Money

Gordon Burn is t   y
acclaimed books of r   *oney*
and *Somebody's Husband*   *Son: The
Story of the Yorkshire Rip*   well as a best-
selling novel, *Alma Cogan*, which was short-
listed for the Whitbread Book of the Year in
1991. He was named Columnist of the Year
in the 1991 Magazine Publishing Awards for
his sports column in *Esquire*. He was born in
Newcastle in 1948 and lives in London.

GORDON BURN

POCKET MONEY

*Bad-Boys, Business-Heads
and Boom-Time Snooker*

Mandarin

A Mandarin Paperback
POCKET MONEY

First published in Great Britain 1986
by William Heinemann Limited
Revised edition published 1987 by Pan Books Ltd
This edition published 1992
by Mandarin Paperbacks
Michelin House, 81 Fulham Road, London SW3 6RB

Mandarin is an imprint of Reed Consumer Books Limited

Copyright © Gordon Burn 1986, 1987
Illustrations copyright © David Bailey 1986

The illustrations in this book were first published
in *The Sunday Times* colour magazine, 16.11.1986

A CIP catalogue record for this title
is available from the British Library
ISBN 0 7493 1333 1

Printed and bound in Great Britain
by Cox & Wyman Ltd, Reading, Berks

Contents

Illustrations

For Jimmy Fisher

Acknowledgments

The author and publisher acknowledge with thanks the use of extracts from the following:

This Sporting Life, David Storey, Longmans, 1960;

The Autobiography of Billie Jean King, Billie Jean King and Frank Deford, Granada Publishing, 1983;

'Hawthorne', Robert Lowell, in *For the Union Dead*, Faber, 1955;

'At Thurston's', J. B. Priestley, in *Self-Selected Essays*, Heinemann, 1932;

English Journey, J. B. Priestley, Heinemann, 1934;

What They Don't Teach You at Harvard Business School, Mark MacCormack, Collins, 1984;

Frame by Frame, Dennis Taylor, MacDonald/Queen Anne Press, 1985;

'The Commercial', Tom Wolfe, in *Mauve Gloves and Madmen, Clutter and Vine*, Farrar, Straus & Giroux, 1972;

Steve Davis: Snooker Champion, Steve Davis, Arthur Barker, 1981;

The Loneliness of the Long Distance Runner, Alan Sillitoe, W. H. Allen, 1959;

The Profession of Violence, John Pearson, Granada Publishing, 1984;

The Hustler, Walter Tevis, Michael Joseph, 1960;

The Kingdom by the Sea, Paul Theroux, Hamish Hamilton, 1983.

I wasn't sure which pocket I should put the cheque in. It was like the pre-title weigh-in, with all the fans and backers milling round. They watched me switch the cheque about, then Weaver said, 'Aren't you going to read it?' 'Oh yes,' I told him, and glanced at the words and numbers . . .

'Don't spend it all at once,' he said, and laughed. For a minute I hated the stinking money. It burnt a hole in my pocket. Then I remembered it was mine, and I was smiling.

This Sporting Life, David Storey

1 'To get rich is glorious'

Sha-Tin looks like a pair of trousers that have been removed in a hurry and left lying inside out. Sha-Tin is a satellite town in the New Territories, between Hong Kong and mainland China. Apart from the 38-storey monoliths in which the entire population lives, it is indistinguishable from the nearby Goodluck Industrial Estate, where a large part of the population works. The whole town looks like the backyard service area of any modern shopping centre anywhere in the world.

The only thing that makes Bun's Amusements ('Roller Disco, Snooker, Video Games, Boom Boom Car') any different from the other raw-brick bunkers that constitute downtown Sha-Tin is the reception committee waiting to welcome Steve Davis, Dennis Taylor and their party when they arrive. This is made up of a small army of broad-shouldered and – in spite of the dripping heat – tuxedoed Chinese, and the youths who seem to be the main reason for the shortwave radios crackling impatiently in their hands. With their streaked hair and baseball boots and painstakingly 'distressed' leather and denim, the paying customers at Bun's immediately identify themselves as hardcore Alex Higgins and Jimmy White fans.

'Stand up, Poon,' Bruce Donkin says to Mr Poon, the proprietor of Bun's, when the bus that has ferried Davis, Taylor and the accompanying 'foreign devils' from the Hong Kong Hilton finally judders to a halt. 'Oh you are standing,' Bruce says as Poon alights from the bus and begins clearing a path for his guests through the now urgently babbling security presence and the enthusiastically applauding crowd.

Bruce Donkin is the export director of E. J. Riley Ltd, the snooker table manufacturers in which Steve Davis and his manager, Barry Hearn, both have a substantial holding; Mr Poon is one of Riley's major customers.

Eight months earlier, there had been an estimated two thousand snooker tables in Hong Kong. Now, in early September, there are probably three times that number, and several hundred of those are in clubs controlled by Mr Poon. One of the reasons Poon likes spending his money with Riley's is because of their Unique Selling Point: every time he opens a new club, he is guaranteed a local-headline-hitting visit from Steve Davis or one of the other three players in the 'Matchroom' team. Another reason is that, in Bruce Donkin, he has a safari-suited, fiery-faced Englishman of the old school whose ways he understands.

'Gin-tonics, Poon!' Bruce calls ahead to Mr Poon, who is leading his guests anxiously through the crowds packing Bun's. 'Onetwothreefourfive gin-tonic! No drown! Plenty gin!'

Bruce Donkin has been coming to Hong Kong for ten years. But it is only in the last year or even less that he has started to see any return on the investment of his time. A year earlier, one of the main Hong Kong television stations had shown the Hong Kong Masters, an invitation tournament in which some of the top local players had been seen playing some of the top players in the world. The demand for tables exploded overnight.

Riley's factory in Lancashire had been put into round-the-clock production and tables were arriving in Hong Kong by the containerload every week. New-style establishments like Bun's, with upwards of a hundred tables, were typical of the 'amusement centres' which were starting to replace the backstreet snooker parlours with their inescapable 'triad' and underworld connections.

After a tour of the facilities, including the bowling alley and the roller disco, where Dennis Taylor asks the disc-jockey to play 'Everybody Wants To Rule The World', followed by a trek through a maze of steamy subterranean tunnels, whose sides are hot to the touch, Mr Poon finally opens the door onto the room where the exhibition is to take place. It is cool and dark and full of families who applaud respectfully when Davis and Taylor are introduced. The women are wearing crisp, plain dresses and the children are well-scrubbed: they make a nice backdrop for the photographers who are happily snapping away.

Outside the hall, however, something is going on which has the heavies jabbering excitedly into their walkie-talkie sets. The quality control introduced by Mr Poon for the occasion – prompted by a serious stabbing in one of the colony's new snooker centres the day before – has ensured that all 'undesirable elements' have been kept out. But now they are on the other side of a pair of buckling glass doors, banging and chanting in their hundreds and demanding to be let in.

'They are the regular customers, but some I do not know them,' Mr Poon's personal protector, a big Chinese called Malcolm, explains. 'We are afraid unless some damage or disturbance comes to Mr Davis or Mr Taylor. Some of them are uneducated persons, you see.'

'Let 'em in!' Bruce Donkin bellows when the reason for the commotion reaches him. There's another club to open in an hour. 'We've got plenty of them at home.' Sitting quietly by the table on which he is about to demonstrate the art and mechanics of snooker, Steve Davis tips a paper cup tentatively towards his lips and then away again before the water in it has had a chance to touch them, a gesture which is familiar to television viewers all over the world.

The first commercial contract Barry Hearn signed in Steve Davis's name was with E. J. Riley. It was signed the morning after Davis won his first major title, The UK Championship, in 1980 and it was for a cue endorsement worth £25,000. Now Davis, together with Hearn's three other players, have endorsement and promotional contracts with Riley worth £350,000 a year. Davis reportedly earns 3 per cent commission on all sales, and Hearn consistently reinvests on Davis's behalf in the company – of which he himself is a director.

On top of what they were earning from Riley in the Far East, the Matchroom players were also being paid to endorse Goya 'Matchroom' aftershave and men's toiletries, Cathay Pacific and Camus Cognac. Camus were the sponsors of the tournaments in Singapore and Thailand as well as in Hong Kong which, for the past two years, Barry Hearn had packaged as a Far East summer tour.

This year, for the first time, the tour was to include an exhibition match in communist China, where the slogans epitomising the new age of individual enterprise ushered in by the Chinese leader, Deng Xioaping — 'Go first in achieving prosperity', Mr Deng urged the toiling millions: 'To get rich is glorious', he assured them — were words that gladdened Barry's heart. They also reminded him of a slogan of his own. 'If you're a top player, you must earn lots of money,' Barry likes to say: 'The cream on the cake is, if you're with us then you earn fortunes.' Once more with feeling. *'Fortunes.'*

There was no better demonstration of the gulf that has opened up between Hearn's Matchroom team (Davis, Taylor, Terry Griffiths and Tony Meo) and the rest, than the two players who had accompanied Barry's 'boys' to the Far East to make up the numbers. While the Matchroom players were being 'limo-ed' around Hong Kong, Kowloon and the New Territories giving demonstrations, making speeches and opening new clubs (often as many as six a day), Tony Knowles and Willie Thorne languished in the jacuzzi at the Hong Kong Club or lay in their beds at the Hilton, sleeping off what they and everybody else regarded as dead time, because it was time when they could have been out earning, and weren't.

Neither Knowles nor Thorne are so stretched for cash that they have to worry where the next Rolex is coming from: Knowles had won £91,000 and Thorne £74,000 in the previous season. In addition they both have large houses, large cars and thriving snooker centres to their names. But, compared to the players in the Hearn camp, they are struggling in a distinctly minor league. Barry Hearn finds this particularly gratifying in the case of Tony Knowles.

Knowles made his name thrashing Steve Davis 10–1 the first time Davis defended his world championship, at Sheffield in 1982, and was expected to capitalise in a spectacular fashion on his youth, his talent and his striking, Italianate good looks. That he didn't was only partly because he wasn't sharp enough. 'I don't think Tony Knowles is ever going to go on "University Challenge",' as Barry Hearn says.

Knowles was stopped in his tracks by what was later described as 'a tawdry three-part extravaganza of sexual boastings' which appeared in the *Sun* at the start of the 1984 world championship fortnight and for which Knowles was paid £25,000. It proved as damaging to Knowles as a commercial entity as Billie Jean King's admission to a lesbian affair with her secretary had been to her business career.

Mrs King has itemised what this cost her in hard cash: 'Illingworth-Morris were bringing out a tennis clothing line by the name of Wimbledon, and I was the logical American to represent them as a spokesperson ... Wimbledon cancelled it when the news broke, and that cost me half a million dollars. I also lost an existing contract with Murijani jeans — $300,000 gone. I lost a $45,000 deal with Charleson Hosiery, a $90,000 Japanese clothing contract, and my business managers estimate that for the next three years I shall forfeit $225,000 in various television commercials, $150,000 in corporate appearances, and $150,000 for coaching and training. That means, in a very conservative accounting, I have lost $1,500,000 on account of Marilyn's suit.'

Only five years before it would have seemed fanciful to talk about men who earned their living playing snooker in the same breath as the super-rich of the international tennis circuit. But Tony Knowles's estimate of £250,000 as the cost of his 'Why They Call Me The Hottest Pot in Snooker' indiscretions is not one with which Barry Hearn would take issue.

'Knowles, at the time of the articles, was approaching a good following. He'd won a couple of tournaments, he'd beat Steve in the world championships, good-looking feller ... No brain but, even so, you could've got over that. The way it was working out, he could've been used by the big boys. Someone could've got behind him and done something. And then he sold that story an' it just ... I mean, good news for us, because it effectively eliminated another *potential* competitor in our marketing world. But for him, it was a disaster. I mean, we fined him five-thousand quid for bringing the game into disrepute and a lot of people on the board [of the World Professional Billiards and Snooker Association — WPBSA] were in favour of slinging him out. There was high feeling. It *definitely* would've cost him quarter-of-a-million in lost earnings. It cost him his reputation.'

Although he couldn't know it in Hong Kong, Knowles was only two weeks away from the second major scandal of his career, and it was a scandal that was going to hit him somewhere even more painful than his pocket. In the coming months, it was going to undermine his confidence, ruin his health and leave his game in tatters.

At the time Hearn invited Knowles to join the 1985 Far East summer tour, however, he was two-and-a-half years away from the original uproar, which was far enough away, flying media-time, for him to be regarded as 'clean'. It had only been about sex in any case — unkinky, heterosexual sex — which, as far as Barry was concerned, could almost be regarded as a plus. It wasn't as if you were talking about a Kirk Stevens here or, even worse, a Higgins, whom Hearn absolutely, *completely* refuses to touch. He has a reputation to protect.

'The imagery', Hearn says, 'would, to put it mildly, be totally wrong. The tour would be tainted with the wrong brush and, in all honesty, after the time I've spent building up the area, I couldn't afford that.'

Less than a month earlier, Higgins had been obliged to play his matches in the Australian Masters twenty-five miles away from where all the other competitors were playing theirs, because he was barred from entering the club where the tournament was being held. On his first visit, as the youngest ever world champion, he had been shown the door for calling a distinguished senior player 'an old no-hoper', and evicted from his hotel for wrecking his room. Over the years, this had become something of a signature activity: Higgins, who, like W. C. Fields, never tasted liquor before he was six, is probably more unwelcome at more hotels in every part of the globe than any other person in Britain.

Barry Hearn had only been in Hong Kong a few days when news of the latest Higgins 'outrage' reached him: 'Filthy Higgins groped me in front of my mother' was the story that had run in banner-headlines across the front page of that morning's *Daily Star*. The same story had also made page one of the *Sun*. 'How to ruin the image of snooker in one easy lesson,' Hearn groaned as the coach taking the officials and players to the Queen Elizabeth Stadium merged with commuter traffic splashing through the central business district of Hong Kong.

Barry Hearn decides who, besides his own players, gets to go on the lucrative Far East tour and who doesn't. And he had decided, even before the 1985 World Championship had been contested, which of the top players weren't going to receive an invitation. Stevens and Higgins obviously weren't; Jimmy White wasn't, apparently because of legal/management problems; Cliff Thorburn wasn't, because Hearn considers him 'too dull' and therefore box office poison; Ray Reardon *was*, although the invitation would subsequently be declined.

Dennis Taylor was one player who was always going even before his black ball victory over Steve Davis in the 1985 World Championship final turned him into an instant, human made-for-television special. What made Taylor an automatic choice, apart from the bargain–basement fees he was then charging, were the qualities which had led 'Cueman' in the *Accrington Observer* to dub him 'Mr Nice Guy' almost a decade and a half before.

Taylor turned professional a few months after Alex Higgins won the 1972 world championship at his first attempt. Taylor and Higgins had known each other as teenagers in Ireland: Higgins, to the Taylor family's horror, had once proposed to Dennis's sister, Molly. In 1972 they both found themselves living in Blackburn, in Lancashire, but their approach to life could hardly have been more different. Taylor was steady, shy, happy to ease his way into the professional ranks by managing a snooker club in Preston. Higgins, who had overdosed on *The Hustler* – the film, not the book; he was never very big on reading – was unpredictable, arrogant, and apparently hellbent on self-destruction.

In those days, Taylor was already married with a modest mortgage and two children. Higgins, by his own account, was still happy playing money matches, doing the horses, ducking and diving and sleeping rough. At one point he was dossing in a row of derelict houses in Blackburn where, he claims, he kept just ahead of the bulldozer, with five addresses in one week: 9, 11, 13, 15 and 17 Ebony Street.

Taylor encapsulated the different kind of people they are in the autobiography published during his year as champion: 'I've seen Alex abuse [vulnerable young kids] and even threaten them with physical violence – just because they've asked for his autograph at a moment he found inconvenient.

'These are the people who, in the end, are paying for his food and drink. The time to worry about autograph hunters is when they stop. Alex gets more fan mail than any other player, but I doubt if he answers all or even most of it. He has been known to throw some of it away unopened.

'Trish and I sit down at the dining-table and deal with mine. It's sometimes a chore ... but it has to be done. After all, it's a human contact you've made with someone, a living relationship – you can't just deny it like that.'

The one thing Higgins and Taylor did have in common was that, at the end of thirteen years on the professional circuit, they had very little of any substance to show for it. In Higgins's case, this was because, in addition to his natural fecklessness, he carried too many 'downside risks' to be considered seriously merchandisable. The £200,000 or thereabouts that Steve Davis earned from tournaments represented no more than about 25 per cent of his annual income. The £100,000 or so that Higgins won in a good year, on the other hand, was only supplemented by meagre off-the-table earnings. Where Davis could command £4,000 for a personal appearance, Higgins – 'a living rebuke to everything clean, corporate and prime time', as somebody once wrote of the mafia-controlled world heavyweight champion, Sonny Liston – was still turning out for £300 or £400 a night. *When*, that is, he bothered to turn out.

This wasn't Dennis Taylor's problem. Taylor's problem was that his achievements at the table didn't merit high fees and he was therefore obliged to keep touring the country between tournaments, performing the variety act that he'd worked up over the years. In the season before he became world champion, his prize money had totalled a little over £15,000.

As world champion, however, Barry Hearn immediately grasped that a lot could be done with Dennis. His first task was to triple and, in some cases, quadruple his fees. Barry flipped through the pocket diary that Dennis's wife handed over to him, along with all Dennis's other papers, and he couldn't believe what Dennis had been going out for just three months earlier: Preston Cricket Club, £800. Chalkies, Southampton, £1000. Colerain, £400 ... He cancelled the contract with Matthew Brown, the northern brewers, which Dennis had had for eleven years. He let it be known that Dennis no longer talked for nothing: anybody wanting to interview the world champion from now on would be expected to pay.

He got Dennis a two-book contract with a hardback publisher, for a 'biography' and a book of jokes. Plus – and this was where Dennis was really going to start earning – he was now a member of the Matchroom team, with all that that entailed. This meant an endorsement and promotional contract with Riley, plus some shares, plus a cut of all the other contracts in the Matchroom team portfolio, which had grown to be one of the fattest in British sport.

The conditions of membership had been laid out in advance, and Dennis readily accepted that 'total management', Barry Hearn-style, meant handing over not only the running of his business life, but most of the running of his domestic life as well: from now on everything, down to and including household bills, would cross Barry Hearn's desk in Romford. Dennis's cheque book would join Davis's, Griffiths's and Meo's in Hearn's top drawer.

'Their cheque books are all in *there*,' Barry would assure visitors, swivelling back in his chair and indicating the desk drawer with his knees. 'They don't have their own cheque books. When they want anything, they ring me. They've got their credit cards for their day-to-day, but y'see they're working all the time. All they need is hotel and petrol. It works very well.'

When, a few days after the World Championships, Barry decided he could do a job for Dennis, he had sat him down and let him have it straight: on the table they were the guvnors; off the table his word was law. 'We meet on common ground on image, on future planning, on how we wanna work with different people, on the type of products we endorse, where we wanna be in the future, what our medium-term and long-term objectives are,' he told Dennis. 'There's our common ground. But anything on the table is your responsibility. I don't involve at all. There's no way I'm qualified. Just as I don't expect you to do a lot of your own tax planning either. At the end of the day, the individual's gotta rule. But we are a very tight, a very closely-knit group. Nearly all our work now is companies. Everything is corporate. Everything is premeditated here. It's extremely organised.'

The Far East tour, neatly scheduled to end just as the new season back in Britain was about to begin, was Dennis's first time in harness with his fellow Matchroom Professionals, and

Barry was pleased with the way he was shaping up. The man was performing. He was proving himself to be a genuine asset in a team whose star member had long ago earned himself the nickname 'Personality Minus'.

Take Thursday at the Foreign Correspondents' Club in Hong Kong. Dennis stood up after lunch and did his bits about Higgins should've been there only he was asked to launch a ship the day before in Bangkok and wouldn't let go of the bottle, and about Steve Davis being so rich now that when he signs cheques the banks bounce. He even managed to say what they were all thinking, which was that the food was lousy, without causing any offence. 'Steve was here last year,' he said, 'and I think we're having the same duck.' Afterwards, he invited questions from the floor ('about anything but Bangkok') and performed half an hour of trick-shots in the pool room adjoining the bar.

Barry thought the key to it was that, after all those years as an also-ran, Dennis was now world champion and he wanted people to know he was world champion, which Barry thought was good. Dennis's view was that if he didn't remind audiences himself that he was now the holder of the title, nobody else would.

'Colleague' was what the rest of the party had started to call Dennis because of the signs that greeted them – 'Welcome Steve Davis and colleagues' – wherever they travelled in the Far East. The knowledge that Davis was on a guaranteed income three times bigger than anybody else's also did little to soothe a number of badly bruised egos. But to Barry Hearn this seemed no more than fair because, without Steve Davis, there would have been no tour: if Davis was to pull out tomorrow, for whatever reason, the sponsors reserved the right to cancel the whole shebang. The trouble was that some of the other players didn't have the commercial experience to realise that Steve was *entitled*. He was still far and away the highest ranked player in the world.

'Dennis is a world champion. Davis is a legend.' In Barry's book, that said it all. 'In the four months or so Dennis has been with us, we've moved a tremendous amount of work for him, which will make him a *great* deal of money this year. And if he can knock in another season as good as the last one, they might then look at Dennis as being "Mr Consistency", the way they now look at Davis. If he can go through that barrier of just being a winner into being something a little more than a winner, then we might start to see things turn around.

'But, right now, the diaries tell the difference. Dennis's work is personal appearances, trick shots, that sort of stuff. Davis's work is endorsements, company days, promotion back-up. If you've got a product you want to be a winner, you go with a winner that's consistent. If you wanna entertain people, you go with an entertainer.'

As Dennis worked through his routine at the Foreign Correspondents' Club, Steve Davis wandered listlessly among the deserted tables at the back of the crowd. As he stood weighing a pool ball contemplatively in each hand, he was buttonholed by a member dressed, as everybody else in the club was dressed, in a dark business suit and a dark silk tie.

'It must be strange for you . . . er,' the man started, hesitantly. 'Well . . . erm . . . having to step back. As it were.'

'Sorry?' Davis was now examining one of the balls minutely, as if it was the ball that had suddenly started to speak.

'Now that you're no longer . . . you know . . . champion.'

'Oh I'm not jealous at all, if that's what you mean.' He smiled at the man sweetly. 'Dennis is much better at all this than I am . . . No, it's just made me realise how important it is and want to win it much harder.' He spun the pool ball on the table, stopped it spinning with the tips of his fingers, picked it up and spun it faster.

'Who was it could burn a hole in the cloth doing that, Steve?' The speaker now is a plump woman with a cigarette smouldering in the fingers of her raised right hand. Janice Hale is writing up the tour in her 'Diary' in *Snooker Scene*.

'Oh come on, Janice,' Davis says, sinking to his elbows on the table. But Janice, on the scent of what has all the makings of at least a small 'par', is not to be deflected.

'No,' she says, 'wasn't it Norman Squire?'

Davis sighs, and cradles his head in his hands. 'I've no idea,' he says. And then, inconsequentially: 'I'd like to see him pick his nose.'

The pattern in Hong Kong is that the Matchroom players perform exhibitions and officiate at club openings in pairs. Davis and Taylor are the 'A' team obviously, with Terry Griffiths and Tony Meo bringing up the rear. Only four months earlier Terry Griffiths had been the team number two.

Griffith's attitude is that it doesn't bother him that Dennis, so long relegated to the sidelines, has suddenly leapfrogged him in the rankings. What does bother him is that people keep insisting – or, worse, insinuating – that it must be eating him up inside.

Arriving in Hong Kong from Thailand, Griffiths had been coralled into a room at the airport for the obligatory press conference, along with the other five players – 'Welcome Steve Davis and colleagues' – on the tour. He had been dragged away from two friends he hadn't seen for some time and who had come to meet his plane, only to stand around and mouth the usual, yes, he was looking forward to Hong Kong, yes, he was sure it was only a matter of time before Hong Kong produced a world-class player, blah blah.

So he's standing there listening to the others saying how, oh yes, they'd really enjoyed Bangkok, and watching the interviewer nodding – doing 'the noddies' – sympathetically, and suddenly the microphone's there and the camera's turning and the noddies are being directed at him. And he thinks: Wait a minute. What's this all about?

'So how did you enjoy it in Bangkok, Terry?'

'I didn't enjoy it at all,' he says. 'I lost,' he says. 'How do you enjoy it when you lose?'

'Oh . . . I see you've got a new hairstyle these days. Where'd you get that then?'

'In a butcher's shop.' Just like that. No smile. Not even a flicker. There's no going back now.

'Dennis Taylor's up there with Steve Davis having an interview. Do you find any animosity between you because they're up there in the limelight as a result of them being in that classic world championship final that everybody's still talking about, and you're down here? Do you *feel* anything about that?'

'I hate Dennis. I've always hated him. I just put up with him for three weeks because we're on the tour.' Cut.

Terry doesn't hate Dennis. Ever since he came from nowhere to beat Dennis in the 1979 world championship final, they have been the best of friends. They have taken their families on holiday to Disneyland together. But increasingly lately – in fact over the last couple of years – Terry has stood around in amazement listening to himself saying these sorts of things. Stupid things. Being lippy. Putting people down. Putting them on. And he has decided that it isn't good for him and it isn't good for his game. He has decided, as soon as this tour is over, that he is going to try to get back to being how he used to be. 'What did everybody used to say I was like, now?' Terry wonders aloud. 'They used to say I was a very easy-going person. Happy-go-lucky. Even though I was burning inside to play and to compete and to win. I always seemed so relaxed and easy-going. And, really, that's the type of person I've been all my life, and I've just changed the last few years. Possibly because I hadn't had any success for a while, which is something I'd never really experienced in my career before, even as an amateur player.

'I found I was too tense when I was playing. I found I was having all these strange feelings. I wasn't being able to think clearly under pressure, which I'd never experienced before. Freezing when you can't see the simple things that you normally see straightforward. I was the type of player before that, when I was under extreme pressure, I always was a better player. I thought clearer, my adrenalin started flowing and I normally performed that bit higher. But the last few years it'd changed. So now I've got to try and get that back. Because, at the end of the day, when you're under pressure, no matter what walk of life you're in, the type of person you are will come out then. Which is why I've decided to try and change my life overall as a person.

'I just feel that I haven't been treating people the way I used to treat them, you see. I mean, I don't talk to people the same as I used to. I dunno why. It's just the way you go in life somehow. But I think it's obvious it has to do with my relationship with Barry and the boys. I mean, every time you see them, it's a leg-pull. Everything's a leg-pull. Everything's a send-up. All the time, you know.

'They're all good boys. It would be wrong to say I don't like them, because I do. But I think that being with them a lot has changed me as a person. Because Barry is an East End Londoner; Steve is an East End Londoner, and I'm from West Wales and we're completely opposite people, you know. I mean, we've got different views on so many things. Our *lives* are so different. I tried to mix the two lives up together as best I could, and I found it very difficult.

'In the beginning, Barry took me on for my skill as a snooker player and, hopefully, as a professional person. He was going to manage me, he was going to make money out of me, he was going to make money *for* me, it was as simple as that. But Barry's a very dominant sort of a person. Very aggressive. Steve's a very aggressive person when he plays snooker. They are very cynical in many ways. I mean, I don't see anything *wrong* in it. But it's just not the way *I* am, you know. I wanted to stay as I was. But then you just get carried along with what happens. You just sort of get hooked up in it.

'All of a sudden you're going up to people you've never met before and who are possibly not too comfortable in your company anyway, because you're a known person, and you're putting them on; pulling their leg. It's just a continual piss-take. If you want to sum it up in one word, it's that. And *really*, I dunno, it doesn't seem the right thing for me . . .

'I just feel I used to be more of a giver in life, if there was such a thing. I used to enjoy people's company. I could chat to people, have enjoyment with them, and people used to feel comfortable in my company. That's what they used to tell me always. That's because I'm pretty much of an open person. And I used to find, by being nice to people and possibly giving more than taking, emotionally I used to feel a lot more secure. I used to feel very comfortable inside for it, and therefore my mind was peaceful at all times.

'Since I've gone the other way, I'm the complete opposite. I'm blanking people out and I'm saying things to people . . . not *nasty*, but that type of thing, setting people up like that all the time, taking away from people instead of giving. And I think that's one of the main reasons why my snooker has gone bad, because my mind was never at peace with itself. And if your mind's not at peace you can never play snooker or do anything else, if it comes to that. And the more I think about it, the more and more I'm going to change.

'I'm very lucky in some respects, in that I've got videos at home of every television appearance throughout my whole career. And I watch those and I think back, not to my actual play, but to my emotions and feelings at the time. I think a lot about it and I've changed a great deal over the last few years. And really, being truthful, I don't really like the kind of person I've turned into. It's difficult to put into words, but I really want to be the same person as I was before I turned professional. I've got to try and be more like I used to be.'

Terry Griffiths went from being an insurance salesman in Llanelli to being world champion and a national celebrity in the space of just eight months. In those days, in the late 1970s, he was pink and jolly and almost beefy. He quickly became a favourite with the television audience for his unaffected, unapologetically provincial charm.

The player who stepped off the plane in Hong Kong was pale and harrowed, off on his own and singing and talking animatedly to himself. If it hadn't been for the fact that his face was famous from the television, people would have moved out of the way when they saw this strange, mumbling person approaching.

Even Barry Hearn admitted that Terry looked ill, but he attributed it to the homesickness that Griffiths quickly learned was one of the penalties which offset the rich-pickings of fame.

Griffiths was 31, a family man with two children, still collecting insurance money 'on the knocker', when he decided to turn professional. It wasn't for the glory. All his instincts told him that the life of a successful snooker player wasn't any real life. His problem was, he had a question and it needed an answer: he had to know if he could play against the best players in the world and beat them. He wanted to know if he could stand up to that kind of pressure. He didn't want to spend the rest of his life regretting that he hadn't taken his chance.

He agonised. He made up his mind and changed it again. He was constantly forcing himself up to the brink, only to pull back. His wife was always particularly unkeen. And in many ways the six years since he won the championship had been a period of proving what he anyway always suspected: he didn't want the life as a professonal if he was going to be successful, and he certainly didn't want the life if he wasn't going to be. He was in a double-bind.

'When I became world champion the first year,' he says, 'I suppose all my questions had been answered for me. Then I just got caught up in the life, in the snooker circus: I was working all the time and I was earning a lot of money. I was earning a fortune. I was bringing money home I'd never seen in my life before. And it was all very nice. But that soon wears off.

'All of a sudden my kids were saying: "When are you coming home again?" you know. "You're not going away again." All this. And really, after a year, it got to me bad, mentally. Oh Christ. Because your diary just fills up. I mean, from a man who had worked all his life, all of a sudden I'm out in the bloody glamour world seven days a week, and I found it very difficult, people coming on to me all the time. I found it very hard to handle.'

He had been given his first taste of what life was going to be like as a celebrity on his first day back in Llanelli after hardly ever being off the television for two weeks on his way to winning the world championship in 1979.

'I went into my local club when I got back home, somewhere I played every day, and did what I always did, put my name up on the board. And they go: "Oh look at this, boys, the world champion here's put his name up on the board. I'm not coming off the table to let the world champion on." And it just went straight through my fuckin' heart. I never went in the club again. Ever. Although it's still in my town. I couldn't accept it, you see. They all just changed towards me in a day.'

Griffiths either won or came close to winning every tournament he played in during his year as champion. But then, defending his title at the Crucible in Sheffield, he was eliminated in the second round by a young player whose concentration, competitive spirit, and fluent, flawless technique were to haunt him. Griffiths' rivalry with Steve Davis over the next few years was to develop into almost an obsession.

After beating him in the world championship, Davis went on to whitewash Griffiths 9-0 in the 1980 Coral UK semi-final, and the following year inflicted a humiliating 16-3 defeat on him in the final. Asked to give his opinion of Davis's abilities on television after this match, Griffiths said simply: 'I think he's the best that's ever played the game.'

Davis and Griffiths completely dominated the 1981-2 season and, when it was over, Griffiths – against the advice of everybody whose opinion he respected – signed a management contract with Barry Hearn and became a member of the Matchroom team. In the first year, Hearn tripled Griffiths' income and halved his work. But, almost perceptibly, Griffiths stopped being the player he was. He stopped getting the results. He started the slide down the rankings that would take him from number two in the world in 1981 to number eight at the beginning of the 1985–6 season. By the end of it, he would have dropped a further two places to number ten.

Ray Reardon, world champion from 1973–6 and again in 1978, isn't alone in tracing the beginning of Griffiths' decline to his signing with Barry Hearn. 'Griffiths when he went there was a *natural* player. But you see Terry's doing things that he didn't used to do. He's altered his cueing. He's made it longer. Why? He's getting shorter or something? And he *stands* differently. And he's staying down longer after each shot. So where's the natural flair? Because Welsh players do have a natural flair. All gone.'

Griffiths' tinkering with the mechanics of his snooker is one of the symptoms of the self-consciousness which descended with the realisation that there was a player in the world who was not only better than him but *so* much better that, to ever have any chance of beating him, he would have to raise the entire level of his game.

'I don't care what anybody ever says about the past greats,' Griffiths says, 'I don't think anybody has ever played to the standard that Davis has played, given today's pressures in life. I just found it difficult to accept that there was a player better than me in the world. I couldn't really accept that as a person. So I've tried to learn from him and perhaps tried to do different things that he does. Perhaps looked at Steve and thought: I should be more like that. I've tried all different things over the last few years to try and better my game. And, of course, what happened was that, instead of staying second-best and trying to go first, I went the other way down. I tried to alter so many things I went the other way and I wasn't even getting at Steve Davis because all the other players were beating me first.'

To many of the other players, Griffiths' introspection is taken as evidence that he doesn't enjoy playing any more. 'He's not happy. He's not enjoying life and he's not enjoying snooker,' Tony Knowles said late one night, sitting in the cocktail bar at the Hong Kong Hilton. It was Knowles's opinion that Terry

Griffiths is the most knowledgeable player in snooker, but that at that moment he couldn't beat a blind man.

'Before, Davis was the one he had to beat. He had to beat Davis,' Knowles continued. 'That's all there was to it. Now there's two players. Davis and Taylor. He's concentrating. Concentrating all the time. It's stress. He's grey. His face is gaunt. His eyes are set right back. His eyes are out of the back of his head. Big black circles underneath them. His brains are scrambled. Somebody should tell him to take a holiday. Go away for a few weeks and forget about it.'

Knowles had spent the evening with other members of the touring party 'yam-sing-ing' on a junk in the harbour. They had challenged a group of local policemen to see who could down the greatest volume of the sponsor's cognac (retail price £40 a bottle) in a single swig. Yam-sing-ing is not something you would expect to find Terry Griffiths doing, any more than you would expect to find him in a cocktail lounge in the early hours.

Griffiths isn't only teetotal. He's a loner who, much to Barry Hearn's distress, refuses to go along with many of the 'corporate' decisions of the Matchroom team. Some time ago it had been decided that keep-fit – swimming, executive treadmills, Nautilus machines – was the thing. But after a year of it Terry pulled out. Not only that, he took up smoking again, which Barry thought was just diabolical. Terry felt that not smoking was affecting the way he was playing, which Barry knew of course it wasn't. It was psychological. But he thought that perhaps Terry wasn't strong enough to get over that, and gave in.

Apart from an 1100cc Yamaha motorbike which, again, Terry insisted on buying despite disapproving noises from Barry, smoking is his only vice. In Hong Kong, he was only ever seen at exhibitions and matches; the rest of the time he kept to himself. 'You haven't spent that twenty quid I gave you in Singapore, have you?' Barry ribbed him one morning at a players' briefing in his suite at the Hilton. He had asked Terry if he needed any more 'spending', and Terry had said no, he was alright.

Part of the reason for the distance Griffiths had put between himself and the rest of the party was the fact that he was home-sick; partly it was because, being a veteran of these Far East trips, he had seen it all before, and partly it was to dissociate himself from what he regarded as the inappropriate behaviour of some of the other players.

'Out in Hong Kong I didn't like some of the things that was happening with some of the other players,' he would say, once he was home. 'There was different things happening there with some of the players which I didn't really want to be part of. Off the table, I mean. *On* the table, of course, it's quite straight-forward: we all hate each other and we all want to win. It's that simple, really: there's no "ifs" or "buts". But off the table, it's very difficult to go on tour with other top players for three weeks and become friends. There's a lot of things that happened there which weren't really what I thought should be happening. There's a few players that clashed out there and I found it very uncomfortable being in their company.

'The type of person I am, you see, I just wanted to tell the people. But I found it very difficult, because they're snooker players and if you say things they take it in the wrong way: they think it's because of snooker, whereas I really wanted to tell them what I thought they should be doing, because I thought they were doing wrong. But if you do that they take offence, you know. So what I did then was, I just kept away from it as much as possible. I mean, the other boys didn't like it, because they think I should be doing all what they're doing. But I do what I want to do.'

For the four nights of the Hong Kong Masters, Griffiths was a shadowy presence in the partitioned area backstage at the Queen Elizabeth Stadium in which Camus entertained their guests. He let himself be glad-handed, and tried to smile and party-chat politely, but never for a second stopped exuding a puritanical Welsh disapproval of all the free booze, free food and free cigar-ettes. He has made an effort to acquire the silken, snaggle-free technique which commonsense tells him is the only way to deal with gatherings of this nature, but it is yet another part of being a 'known person' with which he is still struggling to come to terms.

'You go into a packed room now', he says, 'and you do a Steve Davis. You go round and you say hello to everyone, you smile and your mouth opens and closes and you just sort of . . . shut off. Well I just can't accept that, you know. As a person, I can't accept it. I like to go in there and *talk* to people and be with my mind at peace. But I mean, it's very, very difficult. No wonder people get caught up in bloody drugs and what-have-you in this world. I'm not surprised . . . I never criticise. I know there must be reasons for it. I feel sorry for them more than anything else.'

One night, hanging around the hospitality area, Bruce Donkin tried to encourage Terry by reminding him that the exhibition he was stopping off to perform with Tony Meo on their way to the airport marked the end of his commitments in Hong Kong. Eighteen hours later he'd be back in Llanelli with Annette and the kids. 'Is that for Riley Leisure as well?' Terry said, and smiled his pale, piercing, unambiguous smile.

On the afternoon of the next-to-last day of his visit, a Saturday, Griffiths gave a coaching session at the stadium. A handful of enthusiasts had been expected; twelve hundred — mainly Chinese boys aged fifteen and under — turned up. The irony of a player who hadn't won a major tournament for six years telling others how to play perfect snooker wasn't lost on him. But then neither was the humour of having to have everything he said translated into Chinese.

The simple exercise of striking the cue ball perfectly in the centre so that it travelled over the spots to the top of the table and then back to the tip of the cue, seemed, in its purity and inevitability, to hit an especially responsive chord in his audience, who appeared as wonderstruck as if he had just provided them with the clue to some great truth. It is the sort of simple stroke every club player can achieve in practice but only those at the top of their game can achieve consistently under conditions of extreme stress.

The distance between perfect execution and the flawed motor action that is the result of anxiety, lapses of concentration, over-confidence, nerves and a thousand other unfathomables, is one that every player of the first rank is constantly striving to close. Terry Griffiths knows enough about Zen theory and the principles of yoga to know that it is only a thin line that separates victory and defeat. He does meditation at home and before a match. 'Everybody wants to win. That's what we're all playing for. Everybody wants to win all the time. But sometimes you play bad and you lose and the disappointment can be . . . well it can be pretty bad, you know. You can't really put it into words.

You get a very empty feeling inside. You feel you've let people down.

'But if you look at me after I've been playing, you can't really tell if I've won or lost. People find it difficult to see the difference. My feelings are my own, you know. I'm not really the type to jump about, because I know what the other side is like, and I've tried to balance them out. Next day you're going to be somewhere else and you may be down at the bottom of the pile again. It's a hell of a long drop once you get yourself up high, and then when you drop down . . . I've found it's better to try and keep more of an even-keel.'

Griffiths also knows that there only has to be one brick unsound or missing, only one joint weakened, for the whole edifice to come tumbling down. 'When you're wrong in your attitude', he has said, 'everything's bloody wrong then. The cameras keep moving all the time. The table's hopeless. People keep moving up and down the steps. The other player is getting in your way. The referee keeps getting in your way. Everything's wrong. It all goes then. Of course there's nothing wrong in all these things. It's you who are wrong.'

He qualified for the final of the Camus Masters by beating the Hong Kong player, Stanley Leung, and his own team-mate, Tony Meo. The final, in which he was to face Steve Davis, wasn't played until Sunday evening and, in the hours leading up to it, everything, as far as Griffiths was concerned, was going wrong.

Some see it as being symptomatic of the anxieties that have plagued him that he has become obsessive almost to the point of neurosis about his hair. It is tempting to read symbolism into the fact that what was once worn long and floppy is now chopped, blown and lacquered into something stiff and solid that seems to balance precariously on the top of his head.

Predictably, it was on his hair that most of Griffiths' anxieties seemed to focus on the Sunday that the final was to be played. Trevor East, the executive producer in charge of snooker at ITV, had flown in intending to take a few days' holiday. But he had decided to get a crew together at the last minute and grab some 'colour' footage of the players out and about in Hong Kong. They strolled up and down picturesque alleys and along the harbour on a Sunday morning that combined dense, dark heat and lashing rain, and all the time Terry worried about his hair. He also worried about the fact that he had promised to give some coaching to the son of a friend and all this was making him late.

'What am I going to do now, look at the boy, is it?' he said distractedly when his friend eventually arrived to pick him up at the hotel. The friend, John, a successful architect, was a non-smoker and Terry immediately realised that he had forgotten his cigarettes. He patted the pockets of his shirt and his trousers repeatedly on the way to the Hong Kong Cricket Club as if the cigarettes were going to miraculously reappear.

When they arrived at the club, John ran to fetch an umbrella and Terry decided he was getting a chill. He hadn't slept all night. There had been a disturbance in the corridor at four in the morning with some of the boys. Then he had woken ten minutes before the filming was due to begin. Not eating, not sleeping, that had been the story of this tour. If he didn't get some sleep, he said, he was going to die tonight.

John's son, and a group of his friends — all Chinese — hung back shyly when Terry asked which of them wanted to be first to have a go. None of them, it seemed, had played snooker more than a few times. For two hours, as the boys took their turn at the table, he demonstrated the rudiments of the game: hit the ball on the centre line; never hit the ball hard when you can hit it soft; always keep the cue straight; relaxed muscles, relaxed body, a slack grip and a smooth cue delivery; the secret of steadiness is the bridge hand.

'Stillness . . . relaxed but solid . . rhythm of your mind . . . no tightening up . . . you keep smooth and slack in the back . . . the main thing is, don't go quick at it.' And in the act of telling it, he relearns it.

'I started at fourteen,' he tells the boys. 'It's taken me a long time to get bad.' An hour and a half later he goes out and makes two breaks over 90 on the way to beating Steve Davis 4 frames to 2.

The crowd at the Queen Elizabeth Stadium is made up one hundred per cent of the 'civilised populations' who would never have darkened the doors of the old snooker parlours in the bad parts of town but who have responded enthusiastically to the new family image of the game.

Among them is Mr Ivan Au whose new 88-table, 50,000-square-feet snooker centre in outlying Kwai Chung Davis and Meo had opened the previous day. There had been banners and Buddhas and red ribbons for the honoured guests to cut with ceremonial scissors that had been presented to them on cushions covered in plum-coloured velvet. There had also been enigmatic warnings, such as 'Youth no dusty white chalk' and a larger-than-lifesize, giltwood-framed photograph of the Matchroom team, in which a wad of chewing gum as big as a tennis ball gleamed on Tony Meo's tongue.

With the Davis-Griffiths final duly completed, the audience at the stadium are treated to a Barry Hearn special. All six players, he announces, with exaggerated winks to where the people from Camus and the other VIPs are sitting, will now make an attempt on the world record for the machine-gun shot – a trick shot in which the white ball is played slowly towards a pocket and a series of red balls are fired off in the direction of the same pocket before the white has had a chance to drop.

Very quickly five players are eliminated until there is only Tony Knowles left. Twice he goes for nine reds, and twice he misses. Barry Hearn, meanwhile, whips the crowd up into a frenzy. Knowles gets the nine reds at his third attempt and – 'Will he do it folks?! If he gets this, Tony Knowles will be the holder of the new world record!' – goes on to take ten. Pandemonium ensues.

'Is he pie-and-mash, or what?' Willie Thorne asks nobody in particular, as 'Flash' Tony stands centre-stage, basking in the cheers and the applause.

'*Snooker Scene* would be interested to know if this is a world record for the machine-gun shot or not,' Janice Hale will later note sternly in her *Snooker Scene* 'Diary'. 'Have any of our readers seen it with more than ten reds in an exhibition in front of a proper audience? Practice efforts do not count.'

As luck would have it, she need search no further than Dennis Taylor's autobiography, published that same month. 'I once potted thirteen reds at this trick, which is some sort of record,' Dennis writes on page 15.

'The man who brought humour back to hairdressing,' Barry booms, as Terry Griffiths surfaces from a crowd of autograph-hunters and finally boards the bus which has been waiting to take the players back to the hotel. 'The only man in snooker who thinks a blow-job means a hairdryer and three brushes,' he continues, as the bus begins to leave the stadium behind.

'I don't necessarily believe in all this "heavy pressure". I think bollocks to it,' Barry will say when he is asked about Griffiths' mental attitude and state of mind.

'I think I'd like that type of heavy pressure for that type of money. I find it very difficult to believe that people can't get motivated in our world, because God has decided to give us a living of enormous magnitude. I mean, we're a very protected sport. *Very* protected.

'Terry gets homesick. He's always got homesick. But it's no problem. 'Cause he promotes now the same as he's always promoted. Now, should he at some point in the future decide that he doesn't want to go on being away from home the way he has to be if he's going to do the job, that would have to mean goodbye. Of course. Absolutely no question about it whatsoever. No question *what*soever about it. Because, any player, whether it's Steve Davis or no matter who it is, it wouldn't be tolerated. If they expect to be managed properly, then they have to behave properly. And if they *don't* . . .

'I mean, everybody always has the choice to say "I don't want to do that". But the moment they do means they're in breach. And the moment they're in breach means they're not managed by me. Simple as that. It's a very black-and-white situation.

'It's entirely possible that as the game gets more and more international, Griffiths is going to have to be away from home more often and for longer periods. It's more than likely, in fact, that this is exactly what's going to be the case. But wherever they play, and whatever they do, is my decision. And the day it's not my decision . . . I mean, I know Griffiths gets homesick an' all the rest of it, but I have to be realistic.

'He's quite a complicated person anyway, in his own right, is Terry. But having said that, we're on the merry-go-round, an' if you wanna get off, that's fine. But you can't sit on with one foot on the ground. You're either going to be totally there, or you're not there. And, in our own way, we've set new standards for British sports, in the way we've gone about it. It's never been as professionally done'.

First Watford F.C. Then Wham! Now, thanks to the 'open door' policies of Mr Deng, its leader, China was about to get its first taste of another elaborately codified, highly ritualised Western craze. Like the other capitalist ventures that had preceded it, the voyage of Steve Davis and Dennis Taylor into the heart of 'Red' China had been hyped into a fully-fledged media event. Teams from BBC television and ITV news, Chinese and Hong Kong television, battalions of photographers, radio and print journalists were all ready and waiting in Canton.

There was nobody, however, at Kowloon station to record Dennis haggling with an elderly tramp-like figure over a few bits of wire strung between two wheels, or catch him singing 'Me and My Trolley' as he waltzed his rawhide orange dress-suit-carrier through passport control. He was still singing as he bowled it down the aisle of the train – until, like everybody else, he plugged in his 'Walkman' for a journey that was to prove as uneventful as the foreign country flying past outside: paddy fields, water buffalo and ramshackle rural settlements for all but half a dozen of the 140 miles.

Nobody risked any of the contents of the trolleys that sprucely uniformed young women constantly steered up and down the train, guessing that it was probably chopped dogs' eyes or stewed cat.

At the Canton end there was a long delay in the fetid heat of the customs hall, which Bruce Donkin filled by distributing glossy give-aways of Steve and Dennis to the tireless young wielders of the rubber stamps. They excitedly devoured the images of the pale, thin young man with the long, pale stick, and the rounder, older man with the bow-tie and the fisheye welding-goggles, and maybe some of them, the more con-scientious party members, even recalled what the American economist, Thorstein Veblen, writing in 1915, had to say about the relationship between sport and Britain's industrial stagnation – 'Sports', he wrote, 'have been a very substantial resource in this gradually maturing British scheme of conspicuous waste . . . all this superfluity of inanities has in the course of time been worked into the British conception of what is right, good and necessary to civilised life' – and pondered then on why it was that only seventy snooker tables had survived the Cultural Revolution.

When he was finally cleared, Bruce Donkin slapped a Riley sticker on a government display board near the exit and gave a thumbs-up to the grinning official standing guard over it. He, rather tentatively, returned the compliment.

Davis and Taylor had less than half an hour to change at their hotel before taking their places under the lights and in front of the cameras that were to beam them into the consciousness of an estimated 300–450 million people. Their opponents were Suen Luen Pak and Yan Jing Jing, who had cheated Madame Mao and her goon-squads and gone on developing the playful and decorative pastime of snooker at the expense of more useful social habits.

Davis and Taylor were wearing traditional snooker evening wear; Pak and Jing were in baggy trousers and plimsolls. 'The clash of cultures is thus epitomised', as Janice Hale would note in her *Snooker Scene* 'Diary'.

The clash of cultures was also being epitomised just off-camera where Bruce Donkin, scorer for the evening, was smoking like a chimney and downing the gin-and-tonics which arrived at his scorer's position in a never-ending stream. The contents of his glass only had to drop to within an inch of the bottom for a boy to appear mysteriously at his shoulder with a silver tray containing the next one. Pressed afterwards to explain how he had achieved this feat of organisational genius, the foreign devil would only tap the side of his nose with his finger and wink inscrutably.

Although the highest break they made between them was 28, Pak and Jing performed creditably. It was a non-player, however, who proved the hit of the evening. Len 'Ballcrusher' Ganley is the 'personality' referee who is as famous with British television audiences for his lager commercials as for officiating at the major tournaments. He is an enormous man and often acts as a stooge for Dennis Taylor, who likes to announce that he is going to send Ganley back to his day job, kick-starting jumbo jets at Heathrow airport.

To round off his act, Dennis always invites a member of the audience to lie on the table and balance the black ball on a cube of snooker-chalk clamped between their teeth. He then launches the cue-ball at the black ball, which disappears into one of the baulk-end pockets. The 'volunteer' for this trick is invariably a young woman. In Canton, however, it was Ganley who heaved his huge bulk onto the table. In his white gloves and patent shoes and 1950s-style tuxedo, it looked like the lying-in-state of some great world leader. It brought the house down, therefore, when Dennis Taylor stepped up and took the liberty of placing a snooker ball in the mouth of this grave and distinguished figure. So it was that Ren Ganrey, born in Northern Ireland, domiciled in Burton-on-Trent, reprobate (reformed) and grandfather, became the talk of communist China.

The White Swan is one of three recently built, luxury-class hotels in Canton. But, despite the 300-foot stainless cocktail bar and the 40-foot waterfall splashing down a cliff-face into the foyer, it didn't stand comparison with the Ramadda Inn in Reading or the Crest in Preston, as far as most of the party were concerned. And nowhere was this more true than of the food.

Halfway through the first frame of the evening, Steve Davis had asked for the customary pitcher of water and had been taken aback when a trestle table containing coffee, toast, butter and marmalade — breakfast for twenty — arrived. Afterwards there was a traditional fourteen-course Chinese banquet and the television cameras were there to see how the snooker VIPs negotiated this ordeal.

Davis, who earlier had told reporters that he was here 'to spread the gospel of snooker, a great game which has been my first love for fourteen years', got by by mimicking cueing actions with his chopsticks whenever he spotted the cameras moving in. Taylor, however, sat as rigid and purple as a painted Buddha, waggling his chopsticks over whatever was put before him, and closing his eyes whenever a piece of duck's web or a sea-slug chanced to lodge between them and started travelling in the direction of his mouth.

Afterwards, Ren Ganrey was alone in saying that he had enjoyed his meal. On production of a doctor's certificate, he had been allowed to get away with a quadruple hamburger, from which he had carefully removed any trace of greenery or other foreign jiggery-pokery before slipping the discs of meat back into their plain, de-sesamed sesame bun.

Dennis Taylor was one of the first down the following morning, impatient for the train out of China and the aeroplane home. It was barely seven but already hundreds of people of all ages were exercising on the banks of the Pearl River, which flows past the White Swan Hotel.

Dennis watched the exponents of the ancient discipline which Cathay Pacific's in-flight magazine on the trip over had called 'the Chinese dance of life' and slowly shook his head. 'I can't see the sense in sweating your cobblers off before you go to work,' he said, and headed back to wait inside where it was cool.

2 'For men who play to win'

> Leave him alone for a moment or two,
> and you'll see him with his head
> bent down, brooding, brooding,
> eyes fixed on some chip,
> some stone, some common plant,
> the commonest thing,
> as if it were the clue.
> The disturbed eyes rise,
> furtive, foiled, dissatisfied
> from meditation on the true
> and insignificant.
>
> from 'Hawthorne', Robert Lowell
> (*For the Union Dead*, 1965)

Snooker could have been invented for television. In fact it *was* largely re-invented to suit the medium that, in the space of a little over seven years, was to turn it from a marginal activity, capable of supporting no more than a handful of professionals, into part of the fabric of the national life.

Day-by-day coverage of the World Championship at the Crucible Theatre, in Sheffield, didn't begin until 1978. That year 35 hours of snooker were shown on television. In 1985, the year when 18.5 million people, more people than had watched any sporting event in the history of television in Britain, sat up into the early hours of a Monday morning to see the conclusion of the epic Taylor–Davis final, 130 hours of air time were given over to the world championships alone. Snooker, by then, was already the most popular sport on television.

Its popularity was reflected in the amounts sponsors were prepared to pay to have their products associated with what their marketing people now assured them was a thoroughly 'socially hygienic' pastime. Embassy, who had offered a total of £24,000 in prize money at the World Championship of 1978, had upped this to £300,000 by 1985. But even with the additional £250,000 or thereabouts that it cost them to provide back-up facilities every year — press rooms, hospitality rooms, transport, sets etcetera — Embassy were still getting what has been called 'the media buy of the century'. For a little over half a million pounds, they were gaining the sort of advertising exposure that, at average television commercial rates, would have cost something in the region of £75 million. And this was on the supposedly commercial-free BBC.

Since conventional cigarette advertising was banned on television, this form of marketing strategy has become the only alternative open to the tobacco manufacturers. Embassy and Benson and Hedges are two of the longest-established sponsors in televised snooker. Second in the national sponsorship league-table after the tobacco industry are the brewers. The Jameson International had been launched as the first major tournament of the snooker season in September, 1981; but, claiming to have achieved their original objective of increasing brand-awareness among whisky drinkers, Jameson announced that they were pulling out of snooker at the end of their fourth tournament, in 1984. Spotting an opportunity to increase his company's credibility and strengthen his own power-base, Barry Hearn immediately stepped in.

The son of a bus-driver, brought up in the shadow of the giant Ford motor factory at Dagenham, in Essex, Hearn has always had an eye for the main chance. He likes to tell the story of the day he went to take his chartered accountancy exams and saw the man next to him faint. 'My first reaction was: they pass fifty per cent. I'll have his spot.'

'Look at it this way,' he often says. 'There's so many opportunities, an' if you can take 'em, why not take 'em? 'Cause some other bugger's gonna do it.' The competitive instinct was bred in the bone.

Characteristically, it was Barry Hearn who had first had the idea for a line in mass-market, 'masculine', toiletries to rival the long-established British market-leaders, 'Old Spice' and 'Brut'. The advantage as far as he was concerned would be twofold: it would add a valuable account to an endorsement portfolio which, regardless of his on-the-table earnings, had established Steve Davis as easily the highest paid sportsman in the country, and set his stablemates well on their way to millionaire status; at the same time, it would enhance the 'sanitised' image on which Hearn had had the foresight to see the future of the whole sport depended.

He had taken the idea in the first instance to ICI, owners of Goya, who had made encouraging noises. ICI then sold Goya to Rigease Ltd, a perfumery manufacturing, sales and marketing company who, as luck would have it, were just beginning to think about getting into the highly competitive but potentially lucrative men's fragrance market.

The Goya 'Matchroom' range was launched in October 1984 with a 'heavyweight' television campaign featuring the Matchroom players, backed up with posters in the Underground and panels on buses, and product performance exceeded even the most gung-ho projections. They may not quite have captured the 5 per cent of the market that Barry was going round claiming, but they were on their way.

Late September/early October was the time of year when Goya, in common with all their rivals, were preparing for their assault on the Christmas market. This also happened to be when the Jameson International had always been held. To have a tournament named after their product with a minimum of thirty hours peak-viewing on it guaranteed, prior to Christmas, would be far more beneficial, Barry Hearn argued, than any straight TV advertising campaign could possibly be.

The single statistic that was more effective than any other in finally making the Goya Matchroom tournament a reality, however, was the one which showed that snooker was unique in the history of sport on television in attracting more female than male viewers. The significance of this was that, once you got away from the 'fine fragrance' end of the market, women still tended to spend much more on men's toiletries than men.

A year on, Stuart Chambers, in charge of marketing the

'Matchroom' range at Goya, seemed to glow, his pate winking in the sun streaming in through his office window in Brentford, at even the mention of Barry Hearn's name. 'The whole idea', he said several days before the first ball had been struck in the inaugural Goya Matchroom tournament, 'the whole idea was Barry's concept.'

The concept, as originally conceived, had been to project the positive aspects of Steve Davis, who Stuart considered to be a marketing man's dream. 'I mean, I think it's a fact that, other than newscasters, Steve Davis was on television more last year than any other single person in Britain. Which is a mind-blowing statistic.

'You can take Steve Davis *anywhere*, any time, and he will only say things that can be construed as being positive. Whatever situation you put him in, the man's intelligence and very sharp brain is immediately observable. He has an enormously tight control on himself. He is, in quotes, professional. And you just don't get people like that very often. They're a very rare breed. You can liken it back to Kevin Keegan. The job Barry has done there is phenomenal.'

On top of all this Steve Davis was, in Stuart's professional estimation 'a particularly well-groomed person'. But then the inconceivable happened: Davis lost his world title in the most dramatic way possible to an equally well-groomed but undeniably small, round, ruddy and bespectacled person.

Stuart and his colleagues at Goya were, as they say in Romford – and what they say in Romford they are soon saying wherever snooker's very long tentacles extend – 'well gutted'. But Barry as usual saved the day: he strode in and dangled an irresistible contract under the nose of the new champion. 'We were absolutely delighted', Stuart said, 'when Dennis Taylor was taken into the team. Because the people that Dennis appeals to are probably slightly different to the people who go for Steve. Dennis is also a very presentable, very articulate person, albeit that he is a little bit ... you could almost use the word "fatherly". A *cosy* individual is, I think, a good way of putting what Dennis is.'

Barry Hearn hadn't been thinking about taking on another player. He certainly hadn't been planning to sign up Dennis

Taylor when he did. But once he had, it was entirely in character for Barry to start going around saying that Dennis was just the ingredient he had needed to complete his perfect 'marketing mix'. 'You've got Griffiths,' Barry would begin, with barely a nudge. 'Nice clean-livin' feller. Well-established. Family man. He fitted into a marketing plan for the three. Because, like, Meo is the young crazy guy. Davis is the Mr Cool, sophistiqué, man-about-town aspirational sportsman. Cavalier. Devil-may-care. And now we have Dennis, who's more slapstick. The entertainer. I mean, for a company entertainment day, who better than Dennis Taylor? Number one. Super. And working on the principle that everybody's bound to like one of 'em, it's obviously better to stick four up. That way I can hit every area of the market.'

Stuart Chambers loves it when Barry talks like this. He's in the business but even he's a sucker for this kind of talk. These kind of *verbals*. To Stuart, Barry's a 'man-manager' – a *communicator* – par excellence. Take Stuart's own salesforce, the reps out in the country whose job is getting bottles onto shelves. Barry organised a surprise Christmas party for them at the Matchroom club in Romford at his own expense. Shut the entire club down for the evening and had Steve, Dennis, Terry and Tony along playing host.

Every time they have a meeting in London for the reps, you can bet your life that Barry and one of the boys will just 'happen' to drop in, although Goya is hardly on their – or anybody else's – doorstep. Ask him if he'd care to say a few words and it's difficult to get Barry to stop. Stuart was so impressed by what Barry said the last time he stood up that he can still recite it off the top of his head:

'"I'd just like to say one thing to you" – I can't do a Barry Hearn impression', Stuart decides wisely, 'so I won't bother – "I would just like to say one thing to you all: I would admire you *more* for failing. Because what we have done together, with the product, the price, the packaging, the support of my players, store visits, competition packs – *it will be harder to fail*." And off he goes.'

The signing of contracts and the circulation of a press release announcing total prize money of £175,000 for the 1985 Goya

Matchroom trophy had only marked the beginning of Barry's creative in-put. When, one night in the week immediately prior to the tournament, Stuart Chambers' telephone at home rang just as he was going to bed, he knew it was going to be Barry. It was. He was concerned about Goya's arrangements – or rather lack of them – for having somebody on hand at the tournament venue to encourage the punters to sample the product.

Most of the big sponsors – Embassy, Benson and Hedges, Hofmeister – employed battalions of girls to work front-of-house. He wasn't talking about anything on that scale, but he really did think a degree of sampling was vitally important, and his feeling was that Roger Whitehead, the managing director at Goya, was dragging his feet on this.

'What I'm going to do is, I am going to twist Roger's arm,' Barry said. 'I'm going to say, right, we're gonna do the tee-shirts, we're gonna do the stock, we're gonna do everything ourselves an' it's gonna cost you "x" amount. I can get girls there and they're gonna walk around, spray everybody with "Matchroom", everything,' Barry said. 'Just leave it to me,' he said. 'Because I know now what's gonna happen if you involve anybody else. They're just gonna get under my feet . . . It's not even the profit. I'm not even bothered about that. It's just the fact that I wanna do it properly, awright?

'I mean, I'm gonna do it. I'm gonna do it if he says no, so what's the difference? . . . It doesn't make any difference, does it? What is important, *I* think, is that your *customers* that you invite see that you're doing it. The Boots people an' those types of people, they wanna see you getting behind it . . *Don't* worry about it. Trust me . . . Leave it *entirely* to me. Because if he says no, I'll just bash on and do it anyway . . . It'll be done. And, hopefully, by the time I've finished, it'll be done out of your budget . . . No problem. *Nothing is a problem*, Stuart. Awright mate? Lovely. Ta-ta.'

The air at Trentham Gardens, the setting for the Goya Matchroom, the first tournament of the new season, is heavy not with the clubby aroma of Old Holborn and beeswax or with anything else that the first-timer may have been expecting from snooker, but with the sweet and heady smell of what the promotional literature — everywhere in evidence — describes as 'an international fragrance'.

Fir needles, estragon and eastern spices, such as pimento and nutmeg. The exotic aromas of patchouli, sandal and other woody long-lasting materials. Oakmoss, tonka beans, Spanish cistus and musk. Caribbean limes and other citrus notes. All of these things, according to the bumf, should be easily detectable in the range of men's toileteries which have the 'Matchroom' corporate name. 'For Men Who Play To Win' is the slogan splashed all over the display material in the foyer and the thousands of glossy, full-colour fliers which, during the two weeks of the tournament, the Matchroom players will patiently sign.

International and exotic 'Matchroom' may be, but subtle it is not. Sooner or later the tangy top notes and aromatic background characters can be tasted in the pork-pies and quiches and fricassees which make their way in endless procession into the sponsor's room; they descend unseen onto the score sheets and smart made-to-measure uniforms of the officials, and drape themselves around flagstaffs, doorknobs and banisters before finally being absorbed, probably forever, into the fabric of the building. 'A pint of Goya, please' becomes the running joke among the reporters from the national dailies (known affectionately as 'the reptiles' within snooker's inner circles) on their occasional trips to the bar.

It is a tribute to the power of the fragrance that the people at Goya have created that the source of all this smell is a single sculpted long pink nail and the spray-nozzle of a single 100ml can of Matchroom aftershave. The finger on the button belongs to 'a flame-haired cutie' called Sharon, as she is no doubt used to being described, who travels in daily from Manchester and is not to be confused — is under no circumstances to be confused — with the other Sharon, who is not only part of the Matchroom 'family' but part of the wider snooker community who, for eight months of the year, keep the show almost permanently on the road.

There are not many women in top-flight snooker. Probably, in fact, only three. There's Janice Hale, diarist of *Snooker Scene*, co-owner of *Cue World*, toiler in the archives and dedicated keeper-of-the-flame. There's Ann Yates, press officer of the professional players association, the WPBSA, imperturbable, sparky, Irish. And there's Sharon Tokley who is paid by Steve Davis Ltd to drive the 'Stevemobile' to tournaments up and down the country and set up a stall selling keyrings, posters, videotapes and ballpoint pens when she gets there.

Often to be seen de-rigging and re-loading when everybody else is enjoying the last of the complimentary sherbets, 'Stevemobile' Sharon is an attractive, if enigmatic, figure. She has, like everybody connected with the Romford 'Mafia', a sixth sense where the reptiles are concerned and, as a result, tends to be circumspect to the point of muteness.

Obviously she has carried the full range of 'Matchroom' toiletries since their launch by Goya twelve months earlier. But she is not a squirter. The plastic tubes and bottles just sit there in their dun-and-red 'livery' at the end of the stand, between the copies of Steve Davis's *Successful Snooker* and the racks of 'Steve Davis' cues. Squirting isn't 'Stevemobile' Sharon's style. And neither, her expression suggests, are the shiny black ciré stretchpants and clingfilm tee-shirt being sported fifteen feet away in the centre of the foyer by the temporary hired help.

'You can have a natural spray like this. Or do you like splashing?' this Sharon says, aiming a small puff of aftershave at the back of a big, squared-off, heavy-duty-looking hand. Sharon is wearing a red satin bow-tie on a piece of elastic around her neck and a matching sash, beauty queen style, across her chest. After a year at the Palace Hotel in Hong Kong and a seven-year stint in London, she is back living in the North with her husband, which is where Sharon feels she belongs. She's done a couple of 'Albion Markets', she says, and a couple of 'Juliet Bravos' since coming back, but sponsor-promotions are her bread-and-butter, which is how she came to meet Steve Davis and his manager, Barry Hearn.

She first met Steve at an in-store appearance at John Lewis in Manchester, and then at another couple of jobs in London, and was photographed planting a kiss on his cheek in traditional fashion once in the pages of the *Sun*. But Sharon's too busy pumping aftershave into the atmosphere to have a lot of time to talk. 'Poo, I'm smothered in it,' she says, as another bunch of citrus notes explode on-target, creating a little splashback. 'It goes really well with the Cartier I'm wearing,' Sharon adds, allowing an uncharacteristic note of sarcasm to slip in to her voice.

According to Barry Hearn, 'Matchroom' is what is known as an 'acceptable fragrance'. And Barry has been telling people (mainly reporters) that it speaks volumes abut the new age of sports endorsement that he has personally pioneered that, once it was decided to do the range, 'the boys' selected the actual fragrance themselves.

'Everywhere we went we had these little tiny capsules that we would literally put on every day. I remember we was in a lift in Dallas once an' we was all sniffin' Griffiths because he had a new one on an' there was this old gel who must have thought we was raving homosexuals. But the fact is, if you get involved in a product these days, you're involved in design, selection, promotion, point-of-sale material, advertising, TV, major-customer sales-drives, overseas markets . . . Too many sports endorsements have just been like the old Dennis Compton in the 'fifties with the Brylcreem: "I've used it and I like it. Signed, Dennis Compton." Whereas all of a sudden now, you're turning a simple endorsement into a thriving business. And that's the way we work on all our big customers. I mean, It's a whole spectrum of services.'

Barry's guiding principle in these matters has always been the same: you want it tasteful but you want it volume. He knows his market. Working-class 'aspirational'. 'For instance, we could've done an aftershave that retailed at twenty-five quid a bottle and sold three-hundred quid's worth and it would have been beautiful. But that's not our scene. We're in a *volume* business. Our sport is the number one participation sport in the country, and it's mainly C2 people who, with three and a half million unemployed, want to look up to someone who's perhaps come from their own environment. In other words, you don't wanna pick someone who is untouchable. Because the idea is that, if you wanna *be* these people, start off by smellin' like 'em.'

The fact that his players never fail to carry at least one item from the 'Matchroom' range in their toilet-bags when they travel (chambermaids are not to be underestimated when it comes to word-of-mouth), and can be relied upon to arrive with the stuff rolling off them in waves whenever they attend meetings with executives of the Goya company, Barry Hearn volunteers as examples of the new standards of professionalism which he feels the 'Matchroom' team have set for the sport.

'I don't say they think it's the greatest thing since sliced bread,' he says. 'But it's *their* product, it's got *their* name on, and it's a product from which they stand to make considerable amounts. Con-*sid*-erable amounts. Because rule-one: we always do royalty. We always take percentages of a success.'

Trentham Gardens – the 'Trentham Complex', as it is known – is a country house affair in a sylvan setting just far enough away from the 'Kwiksave' and 'Bi-wise' and 'Wisebuys' discount stores to make the visitor forget that he is on the outskirts of the once-thriving industrial centre of Stoke-on-Trent. The real world is kept even further at bay by the sense of unreality which exists inside the Goya hospitality room: claymores, old-Master reproductions and antiqued and handtooled books-by-the-yard – not to mention, of course, the bar which is non-stop, day-and-night – all add to the strangeness and disorientation.

Lavish living of this sort is naturally as foreign to most of the players as it is to nearly everybody else who is issued with a privilege pass and allowed to enter. Although £2,000,000 in prize money had theoretically been up for grabs in the previous season, the top fourteen players had carved up the lion's share of it between them. Nobody outside the top eighteen had won more than £25,000, and most of the other one hundred-plus professionals on the WPBSA's books had earned a great deal less. There were, in addition, hundreds of young aspiring professionals all over the country scraping by on next to nothing.

But Trentham Gardens represented the image that snooker people were keen to show the world at large; it fitted the image that the sport was increasingly coming to have of itself.

It had been chosen as a venue by Goya in consultation with officials of the World Professional Billiards and Snooker Association, who themselves had just moved from cramped accommodation above an amusement arcade into a handsome, double-fronted property in Bristol. The new headquarters of the WPBSA are sumptuous by any standards and are clearly intended as a statement of arrival. The boardroom in particular, with its clever juxtaposing of the old and the new, chrome-and-glass with expertly restored and hung still-lives; angular sofas and seating-modules in pea-green velvet offset by richly glowing reproduction antiques, offers eloquent testimony to the current state of the game: get-up, go-ahead and modern, but burnished with that subtle hint of history to bottom it out.

It would be a mistake, however, to see this as no more than a bit of window-dressing designed simply to separate sponsors from their money. It is how the people at the top of the sport in the second half of the 1980s genuinely tend to see themselves: as enterprising, with-it and micro-wise, but deeply rooted at the same time in a long and honourable tradition.

Trentham Gardens – a conference centre and leisure complex carved out of a stately home and 800 acres comprising landscaped gardens, sculpture gallery, tinkling stream and wishing-well – is the perfect emblem of snooker's new, enhanced self-image. The Goya Matchroom tournament, starting at the end of September, coincided with a late Indian summer. And with the sky pink-ening, the birds singing and floodlit fountains dancing in the near-distance, the stray visitor could have been forgiven for thinking he wasn't at a snooker tournament at all but at the Palm House at Kew on the occasion of an evening recital by Yehudi Menuhin.

Even the Grand Hall, where the matches were taking place, was hung with acres of baby-pink ruched tenting, so that it looked like the Veuve-Clicquot marquee at Henley. 'I ♥ snooker' it said on stickers in the backwindows of several cars in the car park. It was a sight which the managers and administrators of British football would have given their eyeteeth to have seen duplicated at their grounds.

'Women have a bigger say in how the family spends its leisure time. We've got to try to attract families, because that's the way entertainment is going,' the secretary of the Professional Foot-ballers' Association was quoted as saying in the aftermath of the disaster at the Heysel stadium in Belgium and the fire in the stand at Bradford City's ground which had resulted in the deaths of 91 people and brought British football to its knees by the close of the 1984–5 season.

It was no accident that fewer people would pass through football turnstiles in Britain in the whole of the season then just beginning than had watched Steve Davis lose his world title to Dennis Taylor on television in the early hours of April 29, 1985. Three months into the 1985–6 season, the Football League would lose the financial support of the biggest sponsors in British sporting history, the camera and business equipment manufacturers, Canon UK. Around the same time, John Courage, with whom Steve Davis has an endorsement contract worth £1 million over a period of five years, would announce that they intended to discontinue their sponsorship of the England football team.

If there were people inside snooker who still didn't believe that sponsors were prepared to cut and run at the first hint of scandal, they couldn't have two more convincing examples than these. Which is why, when the morning papers were delivered to the North Staffs and the Stakis Grand in Stoke less than twenty-four hours into the Goya tournament, a collective groan engulfed both hotels.

'Tony was a turn-on in ladies' undies!' The 'exclusive', signed by Suzy Harrison, a former promotions-girl who had lived with Tony Knowles for two years ('It was lust at first sight when she met snooker stud Tony') started on page one of the *Sun* and continued across a further two pages inside. That Knowles allegedly enjoyed wearing stockings, suspenders and 'ladies undies' in 'bedroom romps' was the gist of this saga, which the *Sun* managed to spin out over a total of three days.

On the second day, however, a press conference was called by Knowles and his hastily assembled team of advisers. At this 'the handsome heart-throb of the green baize' owned up to having once appeared in a negligee and suspenders 'at a "vicars and tarts" style fancy-dress party', as the tabloids the following morning all duly reported. 'KNICKERS!' bellowed the *Sun*. 'KNICKERS!' howled the *Star*. 'Knowles puts on a brave Y-front', chortled the *Mail*. 'It's sad that people seem to be more interested in my private life than my snooker,' Knowles was heard to say plaintively, but by then the noise of typewriters was already deafening.

Although the 'revelations' of his former girlfriend were to prove devastating on a personal level for Knowles, they carried far less serious implications for the sport in general than the

scandal which had broken five months earlier and whose rami-
fications were still being felt.

'I Shopped Snooker Stars On Drugs!' the front page of the
Daily Star had shrieked on the second day of the 1985 World
Championship. The paper quoted the South African player,
Silvino Francisco, as alleging that, in the final of the Dulux Open
five weeks earlier, his opponent, Kirk Stevens, had been 'as high
as a kite, out of his mind on dope'.

A month later, in June 1985, the WPBSA had fined Silvino
an unprecedented £6,000 and two world ranking points 'for
bringing the game into disrepute'. Just two weeks after this
ruling had been handed down, however, the *Star* splashed another page one 'sensation', this time signed by Kirk Stevens
himself. In a long article, Stevens 'confessed' to his 'hopeless
mental and physical addiction' to cocaine, on which he guessed
he had spent £250,000 over the previous six years.

'When he lived with us for six months we daren't let him out
of our sight,' a WPBSA board member told the *Star*. 'He was a
mental and physical wreck. He would stay in bed for a week,
unable to move. Pushers were turning up at tournaments looking
for him and he couldn't see anything wrong in it.'

Avril Virgo, the wife of the vice-chairman of the WPBSA,
told the paper that both she and her husband had tried to keep
Stevens 'clean' of drugs when he stayed with them for a period
near the end of 1984. And yet the WPBSA themselves had
persistently denied that there was a drug problem in snooker.
They also denied that there was any connection between the
introduction of drug tests at the world championships in 1985
(and at all major tournaments subsequently) and the incident at
the Dulux between Stevens and Francisco.

On the final morning of the Goya Matchroom tournament in
Stoke, Stevens appeared before his fellow-professionals (plus
Barry Hearn and one or two other non-players) on the WPBSA
board. The meeting took place in a private room at the Stakis
Grand and, by ten o'clock, an upper foyer at the hotel had been
staked out by what *Snooker Scene* calls 'the jackals of the tabloid
press' and Ian Botham has come to recognise as 'the thirty-quid-
suit boys with the Brylcreem'.

In fact, most of the reporters assigned to cover the Kirk
Stevens 'junkie drama' were brightly, even snappily, turned out

in the sort of predominantly pastel, smart-casual wear favoured by continental tour guides and game-show hosts. This could have had something to do with it being a Sunday. 'He drives a Ferrari,' one of the snooker scribes said wonderingly of the *Mirror* man, whose oatmeal-coloured hair and moustache colour-co-ordinated with his suit.

Although several of them had turned up to witness the proceedings, the specialist snooker writers were, in this instance, non-combatants. Their editors didn't expect them to file copy on what was, strictly speaking, outside their brief, and there was no fraternisation – not in public at least – between them and the foot-in-the-door boys from their own papers. Both groups eyed each other with curiosity, and a certain hostility, from opposite ends of a foyer which was really no more than a rather grim, underlit piece of corridor. The newshounds had camped down together outside the room where the meeting was taking place and, although it could have been a trick of the light, their faces all seemed curiously red.

There was a whirr of motor-shutters every time the double-doors opened or a chambermaid came out of one of the other rooms carrying a pile of wet towels and crumpled bedlinen. The sound they made was like a flock of large-winged birds flying low overhead. At length, Kirk Stevens himself emerged, small, stocky, head down, shuffling, only his nose visible through the thick brown hair curtaining off his face. The motor-shutters revved up into high-pitched whinnies. 'Let him be,' a WPBSA official said. 'He only wants to go for a beer.' If they co-operated and laid off him now, it was suggested, Stevens would be wheeled out later.

Kirk Stevens's mother died in a fire at their home in Canada caused by arson when he was a teenager. A sister almost died from drug-abuse. At the age of fifteen he went on the road, fending for himself and hustling in pool halls all over North America. In 1980, aged 21, he became the then youngest-ever world professional championship semi-finalist. In the 1984–5 season he earned £68,356 in prize money and, in the close season, had been paid something in the region of £25,000 by the *Daily Star* for his exclusive story. Now, just two weeks into the new season, and four weeks out of a detoxification centre close to his father's home in Toronto, he admitted that he was having serious money problems.

Standing in the centre of a packed press room at Trentham Gardens, with people perched on the window ledge and standing on desk-tops in an effort to get a better view of him, he looked like a cornered animal: his voice was shaky, his hands trembled, his eyes remained fixed to a point six inches in front of his pearly grey plastic shoes. The WPBSA had announced that it had accepted Stevens' assurances to them that he had never used drugs during a WPBSA tournament, his earlier admissions that he was 'helplessly addicted to cocaine' notwithstanding. They did not intend to take any further action against him. 'I'm just really pleased they gave me another chance,' Stevens said, trying to dredge up a smile but failing. 'I'm just really pleased I can go on with snooker again.'

As he spoke, a television monitor immediately behind his head showed the Grand Hall filling up for the third and last session of the Goya Matchroom final between Jimmy White and Cliff Thorburn: the cameras zoomed in on bare knees and played teasingly over ankles and breasts as the cameramen got their eye in for what promised to be a marathon afternoon session. It was a clunking reminder that, somewhere beyond the sideshows and distractions, a game was about to take place in a precise, ordered and orderly world free of all ambiguity.

'They hit the red and it vanishes into a pocket,' J. B. Priestley wrote half a century ago, when billiards, rather than snooker, was all the rage. 'They have not to convince themselves that they have hit it and that it has probably gone into a pocket, as we have to do in our affairs. What can I do? What can you do? We think this, we imagine that, and we are never sure. These great cuemen are as sure as human beings can be . . . What they can do, they can do, beyond any possible shadow of doubt.'

Having eliminated Steve Davis, Jimmy White had gone on to beat Neal Foulds in the semi-finals of the Goya. But few of those standing around the press room nodding wisely as Kirk Stevens poured out his repentance would have been surprised if it had been Jimmy White who had been standing there with his head bowed instead. At twenty-three, White is the most naturally gifted snooker player in living memory. He's also an obvious successor in the bad-boy stakes to his mentor, Alex Higgins.

Cliff Thorburn, on the other hand, couldn't be more different. Both at the snooker table and in the conduct of his personal affairs, Thorburn has become a byword for application, circumspection and deliberation.

He started the new season ranked at number-two in the world, five places above Jimmy White. But early in the opening session of their three-session final, White had ripped into a four-frame lead over Cliff Thorburn. By the end of it, after what Thorburn himself was to call 'the finest exhibition of snooker I've ever seen', White was winning 7–0.

In the opening frame of the Saturday evening session White had again sprinted into what seemed an unassailable lead, to leave himself needing only four more frames to win not only the tournament but also his first major title. He was leading by 74 points with only four reds left on the table in the eighth frame, but three fouls opened the way for Thorburn to come through to win on the black. No frame in professional snooker had ever been won from so far behind and it was to prove the turning point of the match. Thorburn had soon pulled back to 4–7 and had gone in trailing only 6–8 overnight.

Naturally, the television people who, only a few hours earlier, had decided that they had a whitewash on their hands, were delighted by Thorburn's fightback, as were the sponsors. When the Sunday of the final session dawned and the sunshine of the previous fortnight had been replaced by stormclouds and sweeping rain, they were even happier: dirty weather is always good news in terms of the ratings.

One man who was particularly relieved was Goya's marketing director, Stuart Chambers, who, for a variety of reasons, had not had a happy tournament. Apart from being told to get lost every time he tried to lure a non-Matchroom player into the Goya room to mingle with his VIPs and competition-winners, attendance at the tournament had fallen a long way short of the early predictions. This had been partly to do with the weather and partly to do with the 'cordon sanitaire' of ring-roads and motorways surrounding Trentham Gardens.

But what it mostly had to do with was the lack of pre-publicity and promotional brouhaha surrounding the competition.

There was hardly a poster in evidence anywhere in Stoke; it was almost impossible to walk into any shop or agency in the city centre and buy a ticket. With the exception of the Davis–White quarter-final, the hall had been, at the most, one-third full. Two afternoons attracted twenty-three paying customers whose uneasy throat-clearings and shufflings not only echoed around the Grand Hall but around the living-rooms of several million viewers.

And that wasn't the end of Stuart Chambers' problems. He was engaged in a running battle flushing visitors out of the sponsor's room and down into the arena; and then, once they were in the arena for the final session, he had difficulty finding places for his VIPs to sit. The last afternoon of the tournament found him with a clipboard and a calculator and a flushed and furrowed expression, poring over his sales-returns for the previous week.

He wasn't the only one in the sponsor's room to whom the match playing itself out on the television in the corner was an apparent irrelevance. The fact that the final didn't involve any of the Matchroom players had liberated many of those who might otherwise have felt obliged to sit still and look interested to wander about and drink and generally have a good time. The only person who seemed transfixed by what has happened on the table – Thorburn was two frames into a five-frame winning sequence – was Tony Meo, who was jackknifed forward in his chair, playing the shots with Jimmy White.

Jimmy and Tony grew up together. They stopped going to the Ernest Bevin Comprehensive in Tooting together to play money matches for stakes put up by Dodgy Bob, the London taxi driver who drove the two schoolboys around the country looking for action and let them doss down in the back of his black cab. The least said about all that, though, the better, as far as Barry Hearn is concerned. Jimmy and Tony have stopped seeing all that much of each other since Tony went to the Matchroom and Barry started grooming him for a better life. Tony has gone through a period of what the sociologists call 'deviance disavowal'. He's a married man now: nice wife, nice house, nice children. That is the Matchroom party-line.

Anybody watching Tony watching Jimmy struggling through the hardest eight frames of snooker he has ever played, however, can see that the two of them are as close as they ever were. Tony is willing balls into pockets every time Jimmy gets near the table and making involuntary little cueing actions with his arm.

And then, with Jimmy two frames down with only three frames to play, somebody strides up to the television set in the corner and the snooker suddenly disappears. It's 'Arc de Triomphe' day in Paris and Barry says he wants to see if the racing's on. He's got a few bobs riding on the result.

Barry had only shown his face at Trentham Gardens for the first time the day before, which was strangely low-profile for him. But now he is here he's firing on all cylinders, jollying up the sponsors, kidding along his players, fraternising with the reptiles, quaffing Courvoisier and basically 'verballing' everybody to death.

There was a time, apparently, when Barry Hearn dressed to match his mouth, but no longer. Nowadays it's plain shirts and safe ties and sober-sided suits. One-up-manship among snooker's top movers-and-groovers is coralled into subtle areas like watches and shoes. Real Rolex or made-in-Hong-Kong ('moodies')? Rare animal skin or plastic? At tournaments Barry always turns up in the chisel-toed alligators with the handlasted uppers and has Robbo park the Cadillac where people have to climb over it to get out of the hotel. These are the sorts of things which, in all the games being played away from the table, eventually separate the men from the boys.

When Cliff Thorburn eventually completes his miracle recovery against Jimmy White and runs out the winner, twelve-frames-to-ten, he is accompanied into the pressroom by a deeply tanned man with a cigar almost as long as the bonnet of the Matchroom Cadillac clenched between his teeth.

Like Barry Hearn, who he is about the same age as, Thorburn's manager, Robert Winsor, is a self-made millionaire. He made his money being the first man to introduce wire baskets and point-of-sale display systems into supermarkets in Britain, and now enjoys all the traditional trappings of success: a Silver Cloud, a sable top-coat, a mansion in Totteridge, a glamorous wife (Grace Kennedy, the cabaret singer). And − it is the sort of conversation-capper money cannot buy − he used to live with Prince Andrew's former girlfriend, Koo Stark. Or, rather, she used to live with him, behind the camera-controlled gates in the spun-sugar house in Totteridge.

There has never been any love lost between the Thorburn and Davis camps, thanks largely to an incident in the semi-final of the 1981 world championships, when what Thorburn considered a breach of etiquette — Davis raised his fist in victory at his supporting 'Romford mafia' before his opponent had formally conceded the frame — almost led to the two players coming to blows. Although his number two position in the world-rankings should have made his selection automatic, Thorburn was always conspicuous by his absence on Barry Hearn's summer tours of the Far East.

And so, when he made a courtesy visit to the Goya room before departing Trentham Gardens — 'Ladies and gentlemen, please welcome your 1985 Goya Matchroom champion, Cliff Thorburn!' — Thorburn was greeted by a wave of British reserve masquerading as warm applause.

Barry Hearn, unaccustomed to playing a supporting role, stayed diplomatically on the sidelines as Thorburn and his manager progressed swiftly through the room. But then in many ways the show was just beginning as far as he was concerned.

Barry's boast is that he never pulls out less than all the stops in his dealings with his client sponsors. He likes to give value, as Stuart Chambers is happy to confirm. 'The guy's got all the ability. He is a manipulator of people. And he does it so superbly well. But the point I like about Barry is that he is not, shall we say, entrepreneurial to the degree where he says, Right, we will go for a quick kill. Barry has very long-term vision in business. He is totally innovative. And we've found our association with him has been nothing other than totally pleasurable. Whatever we have contracted for between us, Barry has exceeded his contract without our asking. It has always been offered, and it has almost always been to our benefit, not to Barry's . . . Well, perhaps only *marginally* to Barry's.'

The extra-value bonus that Barry had lined up for his friends from Goya to round off their first tournament together was a chat-show-cum-knock-about-pantomime starring the world champion, Dennis Taylor, 'and a few friends' from Ireland. The joy of it was, the show was to be filmed on the same set as the competition *with all the 'Goya' banners left in situ* and would go out on the full ITV network over the Christmas period.

There has always been a strain of vaudeville running through snooker. During the war, 'the master cueman', Joe Davis, like Eric 'Boy' Boon, the boxer, and other sportsmen entertainers, toured the halls performing his repertoire of trick-shots in front of a giant tilted mirror. Jack Rea, the Irish Professional Champion for twenty years until the advent of Higgins and Taylor, supplemented his always meagre income with a popular 'patter act'. 'Pot Black', the television snooker series which was started in 1969 primarily to boost the sales of colour sets, remained, throughout the whole of its sixteen-year history, a BBC Light Entertainment production. More recently, Steve Davis has had his own Channel 4 chat-show featuring snooker hints, showbiz anecdotes and budget-priced guests, such as Suzanne Danielle, Bernie Winters and Bobby Davro.

It was this format which was to form the basis of the Dennis Taylor show that they were about to record at Stoke. In his twelve years as an also-ran before finally coming good, Taylor, like Jack Rea before him, had had to develop as a 'personality' simply in order to survive. Rea, in fact, had been Taylor's mentor in his early days. A friendship with the Irish television comedian Frank Carson had improved Dennis's timing and furnished him with jokes; and over the years he had worked up an · act that was amusing and popular and could be relied on to get him return bookings wherever he went.

At Stoke, however, he was obliged to spin what is a good forty-minute act out over three hours in order to give the television people plenty to play with, and he wasn't helped in this by the antics of three professional entertainers who, when they were audible were unintelligible, and when they were intelligible were about as funny as a poke in the eye with a sharp stick.

But Barry Hearn láughed. Out of camera range but only a few feet away from the performers, Barry roared and guffawed until he was red in the face and had to hold his sides to stop them from splitting. There weren't any audience cue-cards but they didn't need them; they had Barry. On the far side of the table the Goya top brass and their partners sat with grins frozen to their faces like grease to a plate.

The small, dapper man standing next to Barry and looking slightly less convulsed was Trevor East, the independent television network's 'Mr Snooker'. It was through East, a long-time friend of Dennis's, that Dennis had come together with Hearn's Matchroom team. 'Eastie' was also the executive producer of 'Pot of Gold', a one-hour documentary about Steve Davis that ITV has shown a fortnight earlier. And 'Pot of Gold' definitely rated in Barry's books as a *good* piece.

'Ohhh!' Barry had beamed after being shown an advance print. 'Ohhh! Are you sure! Stunning. Quite stunning. Watch next Tuesday's documentary', he went round telling people, 'and you will see in a one-hour programme how things can work. You watch. Watch on Tuesday and you'll see exactly what *can* be achieved, with a following wind. It's a fu'in' one-hour commercial, that's what it is. Y'see, they want you so bad, they're prepared to waive the rules.'

'The ratings have just been put out for "Pot of Gold"', Barry had announced earlier in the day, bounding through the sponsor's room while the last frames of the final were still being played. 'Ten million at half past ten on a Tuesday. Rating of twenty. Areyewshaw!'

Now Barry laughed until the tears rolled down his face as Dennis ran around the table trying to catch a man with a glove-puppet of a rat on his right hand. Later Dennis, who had a seven o'clock plane to catch to Belfast the following morning, would slip away from the official reception with a few sandwiches which he was hoping to eat without interruption in the scorers' room.

Before leaving Trentham Gardens he returned to the now deserted arena to pose for a set of promotional pictures with Barry and the other players in the Matchroom team. A gang of gaffers, who had already started dismantling the set, stood around and watched the five men in evening suits smiling for the camera. 'Okay chaps,' Barry said to them. 'Think happy, please. Think money. Think *ban-doos* of money.'

It was 1.20 am on the first Monday of October. When they got back to their hotel they found that a pile of parcels wrapped in Christmas paper, a small table with a holly-pattern tablecloth, a holly pattern napkin and a holly-pattern plate, plus a number of nativity figures, had been arranged in the foyer under a poster advertising Christmas lunches.

3 'Accountability, Creativity, Graft'

As far as the armchair enthusiast is concerned, there are only eight or nine snooker tournaments a year: the ones he sees on television. These feature, by and large, the same touring repertory of players who, by virtue of their being ranked in the top sixteen in the world, have always enjoyed automatic entry into the later, televised stages of the major competitions.

But, starting from the beginning of the new season, the rules had been changed, so that the top sixteen were now obliged to enter the fray one round earlier. In addition, the official rankings, issued every year by the WPBSA, were in future to be based on the results of the previous two seasons, and not the previous three seasons, as had traditionally been the case.

The object of both these changes in the rules was the same: to get a few new faces on the television, spread the pickings around a little more evenly and basically make snooker less of a closed shop. The general feeling was that, to sustain the interest of the public, more plot-lines were needed in future. The game had to be opened up.

It still meant, however, that an unranked outsider had to win two matches to earn the right to face one of the top 32 seeded players, in a final qualifying round; and three matches before he got the chance to show what he could do against one of the established stars on television.

Month after month, year after year in some cases, the lesser known professionals slogged away in side-rooms in clubs and snooker centres all over the country and never made it onto the screen. In some club somewhere, on almost every morning of the eight-month season, a young (or not so young) professional who earned less than the mini-cab driver who had brought him from the station, would be removing his jacket to begin a match the only record of whose existence would be a line of small print in the results pages of *Snooker Scene*.

The morning after the Goya Matchroom tournament finished, the qualifying matches started for the third major event of the season, the Coral UK championship in Preston, then still a month and a half in the future.

Joe O'Boye had been lucky. He had drawn a journeyman ranked 94 in the world, in the first round. And he had been drawn to play him at the Willie Thorne Snooker Centre in Leicester, a club which, in the days before he was barred from entering it, he had come to know well.

O'Boye had won the English Amateur Championship in 1980, and had then had his application for professional status rejected three times in the next three years. He had only been given his 'ticket' when a final rejection was over-ruled during the close season, and was now beginning his first season in the professional ranks.

O'Boye's reputation for being one of the bad-boys had been established during his year as English amateur champion, when he had accompanied Jimmy White to the World Amateur Championships in Tasmania. In a spree which has since become part of the folklore of the post-Higgins era, the two of them went AWOL on arrival in Hobart, blew the whole of their spending allowance in one day at the races, arrived back at the hotel still drunk and were threatened with expulsion from the England team.

The difference was that White had gone on to win the competition in Tasmania, becoming the youngest ever world amateur champion at the age of 18; and, two years later, had become the youngest ever player to appear in the semi-finals of the World Professional Championships at the Crucible.

O'Boye's problem was a weakness for the bottle. Jimmy White was also known to like the odd vodka. But Jimmy could take his drink; Joe couldn't. Which was a considerable handicap in a profession where alcoholic refreshment – usually free, with the sponsor's compliments – was as available as tap water. Joe underwent a personality change as radical as any dreamed up by Hammer under the influence of as few as three or four lagers.

He was one of only three people, Steve Davis used to say, who, in his opinion, changed almost beyond recognition after they had had a drink: the other two were the *Sun*'s ace snooker scribe, Alisdair Ross, and the 'People's Champion', Alex 'Hurricane' Higgins. Barry Hearn was, as ever, brutally frank: a brain transplant, he said, was the only thing that was ever going to change Joe O'Boye.

Waiting for the start of his first-round match in the Coral at the Willie Thorne Snooker Centre, O'Boye stood under a large colour picture of Willie at 'Willie's Bar', nursing a half of lager. He is 25, tall, blond, brittle-thin, with a face that seems to glow in the dark, thanks to a classic case of what is known as nightclub-pallor. In common with almost all the other bad-boy players on the circuit, his natural expression is one which flickers uncertainly between arrogance and diffidence, and most of the time manages to suggest the innocence of the infant pyromaniac. Even without a drink, O'Boye can be off-hand and guarded; his uneasiness in social situations finds physical expression in an ungainly, slightly splay-footed walk.

But despite all the mental baggage which he seemed to be carrying – the death of his youngest brother from cancer a few months earlier was another thing with which he was still trying to come to terms – Joe O'Boye was still regarded by many people as one of the most promising of the crop of new professionals as the 1985–6 season got under way.

'I don't buzz with excitement at the thought of getting into the top sixteen on the world ranking list. But the top three, that's a bit tasty, isn't it?' O'Boye had been quoted as saying in one of the snooker magazines. It was good copy. But it wasn't the sort of thing Joe O'Boye would come up with by himself.

Not the least of his problems was that he had acquired a manager with a manner – and, it would turn out, a track record – which did not reassure those looking for some sign that O'Boye's tearaway days were behind him. The former England goalkeeper, Gordon Banks, was one of the many people who had tried to take him in hand in the past, and failed. Now he was having his way paid for him by a man who introduced himself as 'Mike Duke', but who was better known in the betting shops of central London, and at racetracks around the country, as 'Motor-mouth' or 'Mad Mick'.

Mike Duke's father had to place a small ad in the *Sporting Life* when he needed to get hold of him in a hurry to let him know that his mother was dying. It was the only sure way he knew of getting in touch. 'Duke' – or Bebbery, to give him his proper name – is the sort of person who is constantly on the move. 'The Life' is his bible, a telephone box is his office, and wherever he slept the night before is home.

Duke is 'a manoeuvrer', in the parlance. 'He's a good manoeuvrer,' Joe O'Boye will say, explaining why he got involved. On more than one occasion, however, Mike Duke's manoeuvrings have landed him in trouble with the police. The last time had been in an NCP car park near Piccadilly Circus where he had been running a card school in order to make some money to go to Walthamstow dogs. Now he had registered a company, 'ACG', standing for 'Accountability, Creativity, Graft', whose main area of interest was to be snooker.

'I've just signed up a star,' Duke was telling anybody who would listen in the first weeks of the season, in an effort to hustle up the interest that would hasten the arrival of the pay-day he felt must be just around the corner. There was a man in Leicester this minute, an American, over here on unlimited exes, looking for attractive players – *attractive* players, not Davises, not Thorburns; he wasn't interested in grinders – Duke announced, as O'Boye disappeared upstairs at Willie Thorne's club to start his match. He was staying in the Grand, in a suite, Duke, a small man with Leo Sayer hair, raved on.

O'Boye apparently wasn't Mike Duke's first involvement in snooker. He used to have an involvement with Bob Harris, he said. 'He's been a pro for three or four years. All he needs is one big win on television. And who does he get? Only Patsy Fagan. If he'd won, I had a big clothing deal lined up and everything. But Bob Harris,' Duke said, 'Bob Harris, man, has got a bad head.'

A few weeks earlier, Joe O'Boye had won three qualifying matches to get into the final stages of the Rothmans Grand Prix, the second ranking tournament of the season. Now, as he shuffled in his distinctive, splay-footed way around a big room illuminated only by the shade over the table on which he was playing and the shafts of afternoon sun that were able to sneak past the heavy blackout curtains, he was just twelve days away from his first appearance on television. And who had he got? Only Jimmy White.

On the day that O'Boye played White in the Rothmans at the Hexagon in Reading and live on BBC TV, Mike Duke arranged for a mini-bus to collect a group of Joe's supporters from a wine bar in Chalk Farm in London, which was where Joe was now based. They all wore all the bits favoured by the bad-boy supporters – white towelling socks with Farrah trousers and black Dolcis casuals, bright, repeat-patterned sweaters from 'Next' and gold-loop ear-rings in their left ears. The bus they travelled in was a fug of rich marijuana smoke before it hit the West End.

Mike Duke's efficiency, unfortunately, stopped there. Three hours before he was due to start playing, Joe O'Boye was still pacing the foyer at the Holiday Inn in Bristol, waiting for the car – and the money to pay his bill – that his manager had repeatedly reassured him were on their way. In the end he had to make a dash for the station and arrived at the Hexagon with less than five minutes to spare, and minus his dress-suit. 'Sweet,' Jimmy said, grinning, as Joe arrived breathless to shake hands with him in the corridor, just seconds before they were due on.

Joe got off to a good start, coming back from 37 down in the first frame to make an impressive break of 49 and showing no sign of nerves. It was such a good start, in fact, and promised so much, that Tibbles couldn't bear to sit still in his seat and watch. Instead he stood with a pint in his hand, watching on a television in the foyer, and roaring Joe on. Even though he lost the first frame, Joe won the second on the black and then took the third with a classy clearance of 60.

'He's on blob. His head's so fuckin' right. Look at that face,' Tibbles bubbled as Joe surged into a 4–2 lead with a break of 95. 'I tellya, he's just so fuckin' good, he makes me want to give up.'

Tibbles – 'I what they call manoeuvre these days' – is Joe's practice partner at King's Cross Snooker Centre, where he's become a permanent fixture, hanging on the 'phone near the gents. 'A word in the office,' he'll say to Joe, steering him towards one of the quieter tables in the bar. Tibbles was desperate for Joe to do the business his first time on the telly, and Joe wasn't looking like he was about to let him down.

'He doesn't shit it. He's got the bottle. He's got more bottle than Express dairies,' Tibbles enthused. 'I tellya, he dishes up. He dishes.'

But then suddenly it all went. Needing just one frame to cause a major upset in only his second tournament as a professional, Joe choked. 'He's gonzo,' was the unanimous opinion in the players' room at the Hexagon, where they were watching the match on TV. It was 'the old Michael Caine', they agreed. Nasties in the mental department. The old brain.

'He's saw it there opening up,' Tony Knowles said. 'The winning-tape's in sight and there's a fear of breasting it. I've seen it happen so often. You're scared of breaking through that barrier.'

Jimmy White eventually won 5–4 with an unanswerable 78 break in the final frame. But afterwards he was full of praise for his former drinking-partner. 'If he gets the chance, he's going to do the business,' Jimmy told the press.

'Yeh, yeh, 'course, sure I'll 'ave a sherb wivya, Joe,' Jimmy told Joe in the bar at the Ramadda Inn later. But, aware of the importance of keeping his nose clean these days, Jimmy soon quietly disappeared.

Mike Duke, meanwhile, had missed most of the drama happening on the table, because he had been caught up in a small drama of his own. Ann Yates, who presides over WPBSA press rooms with a discreet but voracious eye, had taken an apparently encoded message for Duke – something about somebody wanting £2,000-worth of 'furry rabbits' – which she had refused to pass on.

Learning of this, Duke had barrelled up to her desk in the press room and started calling her all the names under the sun. She had immediately alerted security and had him turfed out. Later, he had been cornered by the tournament director and had his access passes removed. 'All I'm saying', Duke was still saying many hours later, 'is that if I end up under a train it won't be an accident.' He was still saying it almost a whole week later, when he had re-registered at the hotel under an assumed name.

Watching the White–O'Boye match backstage at Reading with particular interest was the player who Jimmy White later said Joe O'Boye's break-building reminded him of. Willie Thorne is fabled for the number of centuries and maximums he regularly racks up in practice; and it was watching him, first at Osborne's snooker hall in Leicester, later at Thorne's own club in the city, that Joe O'Boye got his early tutoring in the game.

Willie had taken Joe under his wing for a while, but there had been a far from amicable parting of the ways. The fact that Thorne had nominally been one of the three WPBSA board members who turned down O'Boye's third application for professional status had led to a lot of speculation about old scores being settled: in fact Thorne had been watching his best friend, Gary Lineker, playing for Leicester City on the day that he should have been on the committee reviewing O'Boye's case.

Like Joe O'Boye, Willie Thorne had started off as an infant prodigy: he was the youngest player on the circuit when he turned professional in 1975. But it had taken him ten years to win his first major title; which is why he watched with such rapt attention when, just when it seemed he was on the point of putting Jimmy White out of the Rothmans, Joe O'Boye suddenly 'choked', 'bottled out', 'lost his bum', call it what you will. Whatever you call it, it was the sort of incident that had dogged Willie Thorne's own career.

Willie Thorne is notorious for being beaten by players ranked several dozen places below him and, in fact, had been white-washed 5-nil in the pretelevised phase of the Rothmans by Wayne Jones, a former bricklayer, ranked 49. He was in Reading as part of the BBC commentary team, which meant that, for the first time, he was having to make himself sit and do something he hates doing, which is watch his rivals play.

Like other 'touch' players, Thorne is only happy when he is at the centre of the action. He likes to please an audience; he likes to leave them gasping at his potting skills; even when the chips are down and safety, not flamboyance, is what is called for, he likes to put on a show.

'He's used to playing the clubs, breaking the pack from behind and going all-out for 147s,' Tony Knowles says. 'But if you don't let him to the table, he's no good. And that's what it's all about: getting in. It doesn't matter about big breaks. The person who makes four breaks of 25 will beat the player who makes two of 40. But that's Willie's problem: he doesn't think.'

It was a weakness that Willie, in the wake of early round knockouts in both the Rothmans and the Goya, was only just starting to diagnose himself. 'The only reason I've gone into the commentary box', he said, 'is to learn how to play safe. Because I'm one of these people, if I go in and sit and watch a match, I can't watch it. After a frame, I'll be talking to the bloke next to me, about racing, about women, about *anything*.

'Doing commentary, though, meant I had to watch every shot. Now, all of a sudden, when you're watching the likes of Thorburn, and the Davises, having to *watch* the way they play safe, having to *watch* the way they get the white ball round the table, all of a sudden now you're picking up a few things. I mean my break-building's always been good. There's no better break-builder in the game than me. And if I get my safety game right . . .

'Because the standard of snooker this week, let's face it, has been absolutely diabolical. I mean, if I couldn't play better than some of this lot, I'd chuck it. But there you are. I'm in the commentary box watching it and it's making me feel bad. Oh! Are you sure! It's driving me crazy.'

Willie was sitting on the edge of one of the beds in the bedroom of his suite at the Ramadda Inn in Reading; his wife was changing their eight-week-old twin sons' nappies on the bed behind him. Running round trying to organise the wedding before the twins were born is why he thinks he went out in the first round of the last world championships to Patsy Fagan. Then the boys were born just as the season was getting started, which he thinks accounts for his poor showing in the tournaments played so far. Always, his critics suggest, when things have gone wrong in Willie Thorne's career, there have been similar extenuating circumstances.

He has earned himself a reputation for being graceless in defeat because of his reluctance ever to admit that he lost simply because his opponent played too well. This has been particularly true of those occasions when he has 'blown up' in apparently unbeatable situations; situations where victory seemed to be finally staring him in the face.

In American racing parlance, he was a 'morning glory': like grease lightning on dawn gallops, but inexplicably dropping to the back of the field as soon as the heat was on. 'Success phobia' – fear of winning – is a phenomenon that has been identified in many sports. In tennis, Arthur Ashe was for years seen as a classic example of the 'nearly-man'. He would come within an ace of a title, and then his serve would disappear, or it would rain on his glasses, or the wind would upset his delivery. In cricket, the England fast bowler and sometime captain, Bob Willis, repeatedly fell victim to the same syndrome. 'I tended to give up at crucial moments, blaming an injury or the wicket or anything convenient,' Willis has said.

Dennis Taylor, one of Willie Thorne's closest friends in snooker, grew used to being routinely referred to as an 'also-ran' in the years following his defeat in the 1979 world championship final against Terry Griffiths. 'People began to characterise me as the eternal runner-up, as a player who lost "bottle" when the chips were down,' Taylor complained in his autobiography. 'The trouble with that kind of comment is that it gradually saps your confidence. You begin to half-believe it yourself, no matter how hard you tell yourself it isn't true.'

It took the sudden death of his mother, to whom he was particularly close, to release Dennis from what was coming to look like an irreversible downward spiral. Bob Willis turned to hypnotherapy as a way of improving his self-image and determination, and to help him sleep and relax properly.

Hypnotherapy was something which Willie Thorne had also tried, but he found that he couldn't 'go under'. 'He tried to get my positive mental attitude right, the killer-instinct bit. Which I think I got for a spell. But I'd still let my mind wander in the middle of matches and things like that.' Now, in the middle of what had all the makings of being a crisis in his career, he was again trying professional help. His therapist, in fact, was somebody who had approached him, after he had been beaten 5–4 by a rank outsider, Steve Duggan, in the early rounds of the Goya.

'He loves snooker and for some reason likes me,' Willie said. 'So I went to his clinic on Wimpole Street. I'll give anything a whirl. I mean, there's no way I should lose to the Wayne Joneses and the Steve Duggans. It's a joke. I mean, they might be *around* for the next fifteen years, but their names will never break into the top sixteen. Never. .

'The problem I think is my motivation. It's common knowledge that I'm half-looking for an excuse sometimes when I'm playing these players I should beat. I've been so good in practice over the years that I think I can't lose, and I keep on losing. I think my temperament is alright. But my motivation is terrible.

'I mean Davis, if he plays a bad player, and he can beat him six-nil, he'll beat him six-nil. He slaughters them, whoever they are. You've got to play the same all the time, which is something I've not been able to do. And now I know I've got to do it, otherwise I'll be in trouble. Which is where this feller comes in. He's into motivation and things, just to get me hyped up before games. We're going through a series of things in my mind to make sure I don't notice anything else. But I won't say exactly what I do, in case it suddenly works. Because if it works, I'll do the lot of them, you know what I mean?'

Asked once what was the best feeling: backing a winner or having a jump, Willie's immediate answer was having a jump, 'cause you can do the other later. Wherever he plays he is invariably supported by a team of characters from the racecourse, and is rarely happier than when he is mixing with them on their own turf. From time to time his gambling has shown signs of getting out of hand, but it is for other than financial reasons that he is now trying to keep it in check: the charge he gets from betting the horses, and the energies he expends, should all be coming out of, and being put back into, his snooker. Punting has proved useful to him in a number of ways, nevertheless.

'And so', writes another inveterate gambler, the French novelist Françoise Sagan, in her memoirs, 'I decided that, come what may, whatever the blessings or blows of fate, I would meet them always with smiles and graciousness ... it was important to conceal one's emotions.'

It's a lesson which Willie learned for himself from hard experience, and one which he is trying to apply to snooker. 'With having a moustache,' he says, 'it looks like I'm pissed off all the time anyway. Yet I work on trying to *look* like I'm enjoying it. It's all false, like, because you're concentrating so hard. But I want to make the opponent think I'm enjoying it and all that game. Let people think whatever's happening, I'm not too disappointed about it.'

In fact, these days, when he's depressed is the only time he finds himself doing any serious betting. And he had found himself falling into a deeper and deeper depression as the week of the Rothmans unravelled. Not only was he out of the competition and relegated to the back-room commentating. Not only had he seen his old friend Dennis make steady and impressive progress to the final, but the launch of Dennis's book had been timed to coincide with the Rothmans and that week when Dennis wasn't on 'Wogan' or 'Breakfast Time' or 'This Is Your Life', he was riding up to London in the 'Matchroom' Cadillac to do a book signing or be fêted at some reception.

Of course Willie was pleased for Dennis: apart from anything else, he had proved it was possible. But his pleasure in all the success Dennis was having was inevitably tinged with envy. Barry Hearn was being as good as his word and earning money for Dennis by the sackful. Meanwhile, apart from the small de Beers diamond which he wears in his bow-tie and which he got for himself, what did Willie have? Only one Mickey Mouse endorsement for 'Rotasnooker', a boardgame whose manufacturer's budget just about stretched to advertising in the trade monthlies.

What crowned it for Willie was when this little French bloke turned up near the end of the week and presented not only Dennis but all the Matchroom boys with these beautiful seven-grand watches. 'Everybody's got one – Dennis, Davis, all the business,' Willie said, a touch longingly. 'They're lovely watches.'

Denys Pasche is actually Swiss. He is the London-based director of Ebel and is the man who had the foresight to sign Boris Becker to an endorsement contract when it looked as if Becker's first Wimbledon title was still three or four years in the future.

It struck Barry as ludicrous that his players didn't have a watch endorsement already, and he blamed himself. He couldn't believe he'd let it ride for so long. What part of *any* sportsman's anatomy got as much concentrated, sustained exposure on television as a snooker player's wrist? It was a bloomin' billboard. It was a heaven-sent merchandising opportunity. And if Becker could pick up twenty-five grand a year – a *tennis* player who was constantly darting round like a blue-arsed fly, with no opportunities for close-ups, zoom-ins, product identification, nothing . . . Are you sure? Barry was thinking *ban-doos*.

Ebel ('The Architects of Time') are an old-established Swiss firm who, in common with the rest of the Swiss watch manufacturing industry, had been in the doldrums throughout the 'seventies. In the 1980s, however, Ebel had been relaunched by a flamboyant young CEO who had taken a staid, failing family business and booted it uncomprisingly into the modern world. He had achieved this by committing 20 per cent of his company's turnover to promotion, and the area of promotion that Ebel had concentrated on was sport – 'this flexible medium, a synthesis of custom and culture whose immediate and direct language has made it the greatest spectacle of our time'.

In addition to tennis where, besides Becker they had entered into commercial relationships with Vitas Gerulaitis, Bettina Bunge and Yannick Noah, Ebel had also invested heavily in golf (Bernhard Langer, Sandy Lyle, Greg Norman); Formula 1 (Nikki Lauda, John Watson), and athletics (Sebastian Coe, Valerie Briscoe-Hooks) – 'sports that express Ebel's quest for a noble, harmonious and dynamic image, in touch with progress and the future'.

Going for his first meeting with Ebel, Barry Hearn was not unaware of the passage in *What They Don't Teach You at Harvard Business School* where Mark MacCormack, the man who invented sport-as-showbiz, explains how he finally managed to sell André Heiniger, 'the world-wide chairman of Rolex', on sports sponsorship: 'He felt it was a waste of money and equated the sponsoring of time clocks at sporting events with the massmarket watch-makers, the Seikos and Timexes of the world. I knew the only chance I had of changing his mind was to get him there, which I finally managed to do during the Wimbledon fortnight of 1979.

'As we sat in the Royal box, sipping tea and watching the match in progress, I could see him taking everything in: the antiquated elegance of the centre court, the excitement of the match, the beauty and the charm of this very special place. When the match was over, Heiniger turned to me and made a slow, sweeping gesture with his hand. "This", he said, "is Rolex".'

Barry Hearn wasn't anticipating anything quite so apocalyptic. But he was well aware that it was the traditional aspect of snooker – plus, of course, the viewing figures – that he would be plugging in his negotiations with Ebel. He was also aware that in the OECD countries people now owned an average 2.5 watches each and that sales were still rising. What Barry hadn't been banking on, however, was the negotiations taking place against the background of the Kirk Stevens drugs scandal.

The drugs scandal, and the risk of more skeletons tumbling out of cupboards in the future, was why Barry could only tie Ebel to a one-year contract in the first instance, rather than the three-year deal that he had wanted. And Denys Pasche, for Ebel, was adamant: should any hint of scandal attach itself to any of the Matchroom players at any point in the twelve months covered by the first contract, then that contract would become void immediately.

He spelled this out to the four players themselves when he presented them with their watches backstage at Reading. An Ebel watch, he told them, wasn't merely a timekeeper, but a status symbol, a stylish, a *prestigious* piece of jewellery. They had been chosen as the British standard-bearers for Ebel because they were representative of the young men to whom Ebel wished to appeal – 'the clean young executive who has been successful in his professional life and appreciates the good things. We wish to be associated with the successful people in the world. That is really our motto. You are in fact joining a club among the top international sports personalities and from now on will become ambassadors for our philosophy and our brand.'

M. Pasche was offered almost instant reassurance that his trust was not being misplaced: within 48 hours of him delivering his pep talk at Reading, two Ebel watches made it into the final of the Rothmans Grand Prix.

It was a producer's dream: a re-run of the Davis–Taylor World Championship final of just six months before which had provided one of the most memorable moments in recent sporting history and smashed all viewing records in the process – the highest ever British television audience for a sporting event; the highest BBC2 audience ever recorded, and the highest ever after-midnight television audience in Britain.

18.5 million people had stayed up until the early hours of Monday, April 29 to watch the conclusion of a match which had engaged the emotions of even the most rabidly non-sporting viewer and made neutrality impossible. You were for Davis or you were for Taylor; there was no in-between.

The merits and de-merits of both players were plain. Davis was dedicated, calculating, humourless, passionless, every inch the modern-day corporate sportsman. Taylor was easy-going, wise-cracking, family-loving, modest, the little man battling his way into the big-time. The Robot versus the Joker.

It was a polarisation which Barry Hearn, a forceful advocate of the 'Coronation Street with balls' theory of snooker, had gone on assiduously promoting, and never more so than during the week of the Rothmans.

As an antidote to all the column-inches and screentime Dennis was getting as a result of his book being published, Barry had booked Steve to do one of his rare appearances on 'Good Morning Britain', ITV's breakfast programme. Even though it came a mere three weeks after 'Pot of Gold', the one-hour documentary on his life and times which the whole ITV network had carried, this merited the cover of *TV Times* and a two-part profile of 'the travelling man of the green baize game', plus a readers' 'Win Steve Davis for the night' competition.

An additional element of drama in the Davis–Taylor rematch derived from the fact that it was taking place in the arena where Dennis had broken his thirteen-year duck exactly twelve months earlier, just three weeks after the death of his mother. Now what everybody wanted to know was whether Dennis had it in him to stand up to the emotional strain of this anniversary; and also whether the workload he had taken on as a Matchroom celebrity was already starting to take its toll. The answer to these questions seemed to be 'no' and 'yes' respectively when, at the end of the first session of the Rothmans final, Dennis had gone five frames adrift.

There was a time, in the twelve months leading up to, and the six months following, his first world championship title in 1981, when Steve Davis seemed all but unbeatable. He was, as they say, 'playing unconscious', and there wasn't a player in the world who, walking out to face Davis, genuinely believed he could beat him. Psychologically, he had captured the high ground, and everything about the way he played and the way he comported himself – the coolness, the blankness, the efficiency, the hauteur, all the elements that were to crystallise into the Steve Davis myth – said that he knew it. He was, as Barry Hearn incessantly told him he had to be, 'the guvnor'.

'It had got to the stage where he believed he could do anything. He *was* more or less doing anything,' Terry Griffiths has said of that period. 'Good players were saying: We can't beat this one because he's way out there. It had just gone out of proportion. He knew that nobody could beat him. He knew it, you see. His confidence was so high.'

Sooner or later it had to end, and it did. Returning to the Crucible to defend his title in 1982, Davis was beaten 10–1 in the first round by Tony Knowles. This was a setback, but it wasn't the turning point. Davis, as everybody knew, was exhausted from a relentless programme of till-ringing engagements which had reputedly earned him £600,000 in his year as champion; and there are still those in the Davis camp who maintain that this defeat doesn't count: Tony Knowles has never 'really' beaten him.

What was to turn out to be the most significant defeat of Davis's career came eighteen months later. After taking a magisterial seven-frames-to-nil lead against Alex Higgins in the final of the 1983 Coral UK championship, Davis suddenly, unbelievably, faltered. Higgins won seven of the next eight frames and, smelling blood, went on to complete one of the most amazing recoveries snooker had ever seen, running out the winner 16–15.

It was the first time Davis had ever been beaten from being so far in front, and the consequences would be both fundamental and long-term. The 'certainty' that Priestley had talked about – 'These great cuemen are as sure as human beings can be' – could no longer be taken for granted; the bedrock of Davis's performance, his belief in his own invincibility, was impaired. He was now, in Terry Griffiths's words, 'nearer the rest'.

One of the reasons Davis's 1985 final against Dennis Taylor lived on in the memories of those who had seen it was that Taylor, always the outsider, had had to claw his way back from a disastrous beginning which saw him trailing Davis by eight-frames-to-nil – 'humiliated beyond anything a nice man should be asked to suffer', as Hugh MacIlvanney wrote at the time in the *Observer*.

When Taylor eventually rallied and achieved what, twenty-four hours earlier, had seemed the impossible, most commentators traced the seeds of Davis's defeat back to his earlier defeat by Higgins. Taylor himself, however, sensed that the real key was to be found in a previous humiliation he had suffered at Steve Davis's hands. In 1981 he had been whitewashed 9–nil by Davis in the final of the Jameson International. Taylor had then had to go out and put on forty minutes of trick-shots and patter while Davis sat in his corner watching, so that the paying customers wouldn't feel they had been cheated.

'I realise now, after all that has happened since – especially against Steve – that evenings like that may have served a deeper purpose that only emerged under the severest pressure in the Crucible,' Dennis wrote later in his book.

'Deep down, Steve knew my character couldn't be beaten and submerged, no matter how well he played or how often he came out ahead on the scoreboard. There's a part of me that never admits defeat. He knew I'd have something to spare, enough to make a joke when he was all coiled up inside, and – who knows? – perhaps that knowledge was just enough to haunt him when it really mattered.'

The most – some would say the only – memorable words Steve Davis has ever uttered were uttered to an interviewer from *Woman* magazine: 'If I had to choose between sex and snooker, I'd choose snooker. Snooker is my justification, my fulfilment.' It was implicit in everything Dennis Taylor said and did that he had come to exactly the opposite conclusion: his personal fulfilment was in his family; snooker was just a way of earning a living.

Brian Walden, the Labour MP-turned-television interviewer, read enormous significance into the fact that, despite his wealth and success, Steve Davis could probably lay claim to being the least loved sportsman in Britain. 'Steve Davis is wholly disciplined, utterly determined to win. Though he has flamboyant elements in his character, he suppresses them in the interests of a successful performance,' Walden wrote in the *London Standard*. '[He] behaves as the British must behave if they are to maintain any position in the world. Order, method, discipline, plus a stern control of eccentricity, is the passport to triumph in the modern world ... [But] the marvellously proficient Davis is clapped with some reluctance. Does this not prove what an essentially frivolous people we are?'

Steve Davis and Barry Hearn have always made a point of

saying how little audience hostility bothers them. In fact they have gone further: they have always claimed to revel in the antipathy that Davis provokes, interpreting it as an indicator of their success. This is especially true of predominantly bad-boy audiences.

The one thing they have always owned up to hating, however, is losing, arguing that if Steve Davis is not a winner, then he is nothing. And the fact was that, in the twelve months leading up to the Rothmans, Davis had been losing rather more consistently than at any other time in his career. It was almost a year since his last major victory – the Coral UK, in November 1984 – and, as the papers hadn't been slow to point out on the morning that his final against Dennis Taylor started, the pressure was mounting.

Barry Hearn's position in the past was that Steve didn't have to win everything, so long as he was generally there or thereabouts: he was already established for all time as 'a legend'. But at the end of the current season Barry was planning to float Matchroom as a public company on the Unlisted Securities Market, and use the estimated £10 million capital that that would bring in to open up North America for snooker. And so there was satisfaction and quiet confidence – not to mention relief – in the Davis camp when, at the halfway point of the Rothmans final, Steve was six-frames-to-one up on Dennis, only four frames away from victory.

'The Davis camp', in the context of major finals, invariably means, in addition to Barry Hearn, Steve's father, Bill Davis, Robbo and Ron, the drivers, and assorted other aides and gofers whose time-proven loyalty and 'schtumness' have earned them honorary membership of the Romford 'Mafia'. These include the former Queen's Park Rangers footballer, Mark Lazarus, and his son, Nicky, himself a budding snooker player. The only female member is Susan Hearn, Barry Hearn's wife, a sleekly handsome woman (she is still smarting from once being described, many years ago, as 'almost beautiful') who seems to tolerate rather than enjoy the many hours she has to stand around in dressing room areas and hospitality suites looking dutiful.

In her uptown sheath-dresses, ankle-bracelets and broad pearl chokers she looks like the Duchess of Gloucester on a never-ending tour of the Tarriff Application and Energy Economics section of the South Midlands and Chiltern District Electricity Council, and in fact prefers talking dog-breeding and donkey sanctuaries to talking snooker.

'C'mon cocker!' When Barry shouts things like that, Susan tends to wince and shoot him sharp looks. But Barry goes on shouting things like that anyway. 'C'mon cocker!' he shouts at one of the half a dozen screens in the expensively appointed hospitality-room at the Rothmans. Decorated in chevrons of grey, blue and white, it is like sitting inside an L-shaped cigarette packet complete with video facility and hostess service.

Although he manages three other players in addition to Steve Davis, one of whom happens to be playing Steve at the minute, Barry has never made any secret of the fact that he regards Steve as a bit special. Before he took on the others, he made it clear that, so long as it was anybody other than Steve Davis they were playing, he would kill for them. But if it was Steve, then of course it was Steve he would be shouting for. No question.

Terry Griffiths, in common with Dennis Taylor and Tony Meo, accepted this unreservedly. 'Barry brought Steve up. They'd grown up together in the snooker world. And if you expect to go in there and be number one, you've got another think coming. Barry said straight away, he said: "Look, if you play Davis, I'll always want him to win." And I said, "Well I should bloody hope so. You've been with him for years."

'They are very, very close. They're as close as two men can be who aren't blood, really. And I think it's nice. There's nothing wrong in it.'

The core of Dennis's support in the wings at Reading was his friend, Trevor East, the ITV producer. And as Sunday wore on and afternoon became evening, 'Eastie' found himself in the unexpected position of having more and more to shout about. By the mid-point of the evening session, all the signs seemed to be that history was about to repeat itself.

The number of close-finishes, featuring players who had fought their way back apparently from the dead – the last had been just three weeks earlier, when Cliff Thorburn had pulled back seven frames on Jimmy White to beat him in the final of the Goya (later described as 'a comeback in the Lazarus mould') – had inevitably given rise to widespread suspicion that matches were being 'fixed'.

And the cynics weren't confined to Britain's lounge bars and living-rooms. There was at least one in the press room. 'Professional wrestling on green baize, if you get my meaning,' Joe Lancaster had said as Thorburn consolidated his comeback. 'There's a banquet booked for tomorrow night, the chairman's arriving, and there's nothing on. Can you see it? There's got to be some manipulating.'

Joe Lancaster is one half of the northern news agency, Lancaster and Crowther, which not only sounds like a music hall double-act but is treated like one when Joe is on his feet and talking what the other reporters on the circuit obviously feel to be nonsense. There was no evidence, for instance, to suggest that the White—Thorburn match had been anything other than straight-forward. Nevertheless, as Dennis Taylor begins racking up the frames against Steve Davis to go from 6–1 down to just two frames behind at 7–5, it is the sort of thing they are hearing down the line from their own Fleet Street offices. 'That was the chief sub,' one of the regulars says as he hangs up. 'Pissed as a puddin'.'

Their best comeback, as always, is the face of Steve. Always pale, his face has taken on a translucent fish-bellyness as he is kept in his seat, helpless to stop Taylor taking his sixth frame in a row. The determination and panic seem to roil around just below the surface, competing for precedence, like oil on water or the spirit in a whisky tumbler held up against the light.

He picks up a glass from the small table containing the Rothmans ice-bucket and Rothmans ashtray and, cocking his little finger, brings it to his lips. He purses his lips into an exaggerated cupid-bow, the unrippled surface of the perfectly clear water flashing briefly in the TV lights. He returns the glass to the table, from where he now collects a white towel with 'Matchroom' written across it. He rubs the palm of, first, his left hand, then his right, then rubs in the spaces between his long, palely freckled fingers as attentively as a mother drying a small child.

Fixing the cue firmly between his open knees, he places the towel exactly at that point on the cue-tip where the cue-chalk ends, and wipes evenly in a single downward sweep. Rolling the cue slowly in his fingers, he repeats, and repeats once again. He places his right foot on his left knee and wedges the cue carefully in the crook that is formed. He flicks the crease of his trousers over his instep so that it is in line with his shoe. He picks a piece of invisible lint off his trousers and breathes it away.

He takes his short fringe between his thumb and forefinger and adjusts it an invisible fraction so that it dips in a perfect arc above his eyebrows. He picks up the glass from the small table containing the Rothmans ice-bucket and Rothmans ashtray and, cocking his little finger, brings it to his lips. He fixes his cue between his open knees and, like a teacher ticking a register, chalks it with short, strong, even strokes. He places his right foot on his left knee and wedges the cue carefully in the crook that is formed. He grits his teeth, sets his jaw and begins breathing deeply in a sort of snarl, as if he is about to begin lifting a very heavy weight.

'I think his mind's gone,' Willie Thorne says, passing somebody in a corridor. 'He's chalking his cue twenty times before every shot.'

'No, he's gone,' Barry Hearn shouts into a telephone on Ann Yates's desk just inside the press room, in an effort to make himself heard above the noise. 'He's gone completely. Nothing. He can't pot a ball. Dennis is just going eight–seven up . . . No, I'm not upset. I'm awright. But it's gonna be a long night . . . You know where to find the key.'

It is approaching midnight when Davis eventually stops the rot and wins a frame to bring him even with Dennis Taylor, eight-frames-all. Davis wins the next to leave himself needing one for the match, but Taylor takes the eighteenth to leave them even again.

In the balcony of the Hexagon, four children are slumped asleep on each other like fallen dominoes as Taylor breaks off in the final frame. They snap awake and loll about groggily in the hubbub that greets the emcee's announcement that Steve Davis is the Rothmans champion of 1985. It is 2.14 am.

Conspicuous in the crush of people outside the press room afterwards is a small man with a walking stick and a quiff like Laurence Harvey's in *Expresso Bongo*, which he is attending to with a comb. Donald Trelford is the editor of the *Observer*, the author of a book on snooker and Dennis Taylor's 'ghost'.

'So it's a good day for Romford, Dennis, one way or another,' Dennis is asked at his press conference.

'Where's Romford?' Dennis says.

In the banqueting suite in another part of the complex, at the Ramadda, the ice swan that is the centrepiece of the buffet has started to melt. Water is dripping from the end of its beak. It is 3.30am, the middle of the night, but the official reception begins as scheduled, with langoustines, profiteroles, and champagne.

Steve Davis, however, asks for steak sandwiches and a lager and, £50,000 richer, is soon sitting off in a corner, the reluctant focus of attention for a half-circle of beaming 'Rothmans girls'. He has a flight to catch in five hours to Toronto, so he won't bother going to bed.

At Reading station, the first editions of Monday's papers were already being unloaded. The late finish had been the cause of a great deal of bellyaching among the reptiles, who had all missed their deadlines. But that morning's 'Girl Talk' page in the *Star* was devoted to a first-person analysis of the wild and wacky world 'where beer and fags meet glossy soap-style living'.

The author of this piece had arrived in Reading wearing a satin 'Madonna' blouse and black lace stockings, some days earlier, and made a bee-line for Tony Knowles. 'I'm not *interviewing* you,' she'd reassured Knowles as she cuddled up confidentially beside him. 'I do a column. No, not gossip. Comment. Like, you know those people who write about battered babies. Well, that *sort* of thing.'

'Eyeing up the balls he's like a tom cat, sleek and eager to paw the opposition out of the way,' is her verdict on 'Tantalising Tony' now. 'After the match, he rips off his diamanté-studded bow-tie just like Steve Carrington at the beginning of the Dynasty titles. He even showed me the special cue stick with the extension he uses for long shots.'

'I warned her she better not say anything bad about this tournament,' a BBC man said when the papers arrived at the Ramadda, where the party was still in progress. 'I mentioned a sports mag to Michael Grade the other week and we might just be looking for a big, blonde, busty twenty-five-year-old.'

4 A peculiar nature

Snooker is a winter game. The mid-point of the season is Christmas, and for the four months either side of Christmas the administrators, the officials and the players – mostly alone, occasionally with a manager or driver in tow – do the rounds of the far-flung towns and cities they would have no cause to visit if it wasn't for the fact that their living took them there.

That many of these places are by the sea is simply a consequence of the seasonal nature of snooker: seaside towns in winter can accommodate snooker people in the kind of numbers and at the kind of prices they find attractive. But the fact is that snooker and depopulated holiday resorts are peculiarly suited. In spite of – or perhaps because of – the fascination it holds for the public, the snooker world is essentially a hermetic world: small, closely-knit, inward-looking and closed to strangers. The empty streets and rain-lashed promenades of seaside towns in the dead of winter, the customerless cafés and lonely bingo-callers, are an appropriate setting for a sport, and a sporting community, which exists within, but separate from, the real world. Whose popularity, in fact, depends on its effectiveness at keeping the real world at bay.

In out-of-season seaside resorts the sense of isolation and dislocation is particularly acute: dull and unlit illuminations strung like junk necklaces between shops whose only reason for existence is holidaymakers and the summer; Christmas decorations still sparkling glumly, with Easter only a matter of weeks away.

In November, all roads for the professionals led to Preston, home of the third big tournament of the season, the Coral UK. But at the same time, only fifteen miles away, the amateurs were celebrating their ruling body's centenary World Championships, in Blackpool-by-the-Sea.

'They had all gone, the fiddlers, fortune-tellers, pierrots, cheap-jacks, waiters and sellers of peppermint and pineapple rock ... Nobody was cooking or enjoying or touting for those Nice Hot Dinners. There was, in short, nothing hot left ... Only the weather was awake, and that was tremendously alive. The sea roared in the deep dusk and sent sheets of spray over the glistening wet railings and seats ...', J. B. Priestley wrote of another November in Blackpool, half a century ago.

It is no accident that Priestley was as affectionately disposed towards what he called 'our first great entertainment caterer to the sixpenny crowd – the Mecca of a vulgar but alert and virile democracy' as he was towards the more sedate world of billiards and snooker. They were among the things he valued – 'the sound of a football', 'gin and tonic', 'waking to the smell of bacon etc.', 'manly talk' were a few of the others – for their timeless and traditional qualities, for the sense of continuity they represented and, perhaps most important of all, for their inherent Englishness. Most of what Priestley had to say about Blackpool is as true today as when he wrote it. And his description of the visit he made in 1932 to Thurston's, the billiards 'Mecca' in Leicester Square, would strike a sympathetic chord in many of today's mass television audience.

'He had an ecclesiastical dignity and gravity of manner,' Priestley wrote of the referee. 'He handed over the rest or the half-butt like one serving at an altar. To see him place the red on the spot was to realise at once the greatness of the occasion. Best of all was to watch him removing, with his white-gloved hands, specks of dust or films of moisture from a ball. The voice in which he called out the scores was the most impersonal I have ever heard. It was a voice that belonged to solemn ritual, and it did as much as the four walls and the thickly curtained windows to withdraw us from ordinary life ... After a few minutes the world of daylight and buses and three o'clock winners receded, faded, vanished. I felt as if we were all sitting at ease somewhere at the bottom of the Pacific.'

Making his approach to the Tower Ballroom, the setting for

the B&SCC centenary World Amateur Championships in 1985, Priestley would no doubt have encountered many things to incur his displeasure. The children yodelling on the ends of ropes, for instance, in 'Jungle Jim's', or the way shabby hardboard flamingoes had obliterated the beautiful engraved flamingoes on the Victorian tiled panels. But, once inside, the old-world courtiers and the atmosphere of calm, the officials in their Brylcreem and heavily-threaded badges and pressed blazers, the bottles of Lime Cordial and Lemon Barley Water standing to attention on the starched linen tablecloths on the players' tables, would all have persuaded him that nothing had changed in fifty years, and that the clock had stood still.

Blackpool Tower is no stranger to snooker tournaments. Championship finals were staged there both before and immediately after the dark days of the 1960s and early 1970s, when snooker became all but extinct as a competitive sport. But matches were played in the Tower Circus in those days, not the Ballroom. It was the idea of playing in the Ballroom, however, with its sprung floor (locked for the occasion) and frescoed ceiling, its echoes of Henry Hall and Victor Sylvester, which had decided David Barron to make the trip 'home' in order to represent Zimbabwe in the world amateurs.

Barron was one of 45 players from 24 countries who had assembled in Blackpool in November at the invitation of the one hundred-year-old Billiards and Snooker Control Council. But his reason for being there was not only to compete at snooker. A former Preston, Chorley and District amateur snooker champion, he was hoping to find some reminders of his former life in Lancashire, and to tie up the remaining loose ends of that life.

Just to get to the table for his matches, Doctor Barron – 'I'm a contented, retired, middle-aged dentist from Zimbabwe,' he would tell people – had to pass a plaque dedicated to the memory of Reginald Dixon, MBE, known as 'Mr Blackpool' for his forty-years' service at the Tower's world-famous Wurlitzer organ. 'Every time I walk into that matchroom,' Dr Barron said, 'I expect to hear Reginald Dixon start up. It's bloody weird.' And in the many hours he would spend in his seat while nine out of his eleven opponents systematically buried him, he had plenty of time to reflect on his youthful adventures in the dimly lit balconies in the Tower ballroom.

'Shit, the performances I've seen in the Gods in that place,' Dr Barron reminisced to two drinking companions one night in the 'Good Tyme' bar at the Tower, interrupting himself only to ask the barman if he wouldn't mind turning the 'jungle music' down. In the years when he was studying to be a dentist in Liverpool, Dr Barron said he went dancing at the Tower three nights a week. The trick, he said, was to pay half a dollar to get into the early session, then hide in the balcony until the second session got under way — unless, that is, you happened to strike lucky and pick up a mill girl, in which case you would slip back to her digs with her and forfeit your two-and-six. He remembered the more high-spirited of his contemporaries urinating from the balcony, and fistfights which were fought according to the rules — 'it wasn't boots in and big damage like these thugos today'.

Dr Barron, a veteran of 'what you people over here call "the liberation war"' which turned white-ruled Rhodesia into black-ruled Zimbabwe, had a chance to recapture some of the irresponsibility of youth in the middle of his second week in Blackpool. After the B&SCC's annual general meeting on the Wednesday, which he attended in his capacity as chairman of the Zimbabwe Amateur Snooker Association, he was one of a party who ended up at a club somewhere in the town at three o'clock in the morning. Invited to remove a stripper's 'scanties' for her, he had his hair covered in talcum powder as he leaned forward, and then slapped to send up a big talcum cloud. Alex Thomson, the reigning Zimbabwe champion, had already fled at the sight of two heavily oiled breasts heading towards him, fearful of them ruining his suit.

In addition to the tortoiseshell spectacles hanging around his neck on a cord, Dr Barron was immediately identifiable for the tan Hush Puppies he chose to wear with his dress-suit for the duration of the tournament. He felt it was a reassuring sign that formal dress was required for every match played in Blackpool, even the ones which started at nine o'clock in the morning. It was proof that *somebody* was trying to uphold the standards which he had seen drop alarmingly since his departure for Rhodesia more than twenty years before. He had taken the opportunity to go to a football match one Saturday, to see the hooliganism that was the talk of the farmers' clubs back home in

Mutare, for himself at first hand. He hadn't seen any, but that didn't mean it didn't exist. 'The very fact that you've got to fit out the police horses with plastic eyeshields means the whole country's far too bloody liberal,' he declared.

The last place he had expected to come face-to-face with a case-hardened British hooligan was across a snooker table under the glowing amber crystal in the Tower ballroom. But that's what had happened when he walked out to play the third match in his group. David Barron versus the young player known to his friends as 'Giro' because of the speed with which he cashed his unemployment cheques in order to stake his next money match, was as glaring an example of the clash of cultures as the *Snooker Scene* diarist had noted between Steve Davis and his coolie opponent in Canton. The fact that he chalked up one of his two victories in the tournament against a player who, on paper at least, should have taken him apart, to Dr Barron was further proof of Giro's contempt. 'His attitude was a bit poor,' Barron said diplomatically afterwards. 'He seemed to me a bit nonchalant.'

Like Joe O'Boye, with whom he has more than a passing acquaintance, 'Giro' Jon Wright had been turned down for membership of the World Professional Billiards and Snooker Association at least once. A change in the selection procedure a few months earlier, however, with the emphasis shifted from reputation to results, had seen him breeze through into the professional ranks. At the time of the World Amateurs in Blackpool, Giro was just half a season away from what he had no doubt, for him, was going to be the big-time. 'Hey Trace, will you marry me?' he called out to one of the barmaids one night, as he stood naked from the waist down, changing his trousers at the 'Number 10' bar. 'I'm going to be rich in eighteen months.'

In the old days, membership of the professional players' association had been in the gift of one man. For thirty years, both before and after the War, Joe Davis ruled snooker with what has been described as 'a papal hand'. By virtue of his multiple role as presiding genius-cum-legislator-cum-administrator-cum-entrepreneur, Joe Davis was in a position to decide which players were going to be admitted into the professional ranks, and which weren't. Davis's abiding preoccupation was to keep the game clean and above reproach. Any player with a history of playing money matches, for instance, or who was in any other way considered undesirable, didn't stand a chance. As far as Joe Davis was concerned, he was out.

This meant that talented but 'colourful' young players like Patsy Houlihan and Dickie Laws were relegated to the sidelines for the whole of their professional lives. Snooker, in the meantime, starved of the players who might have sustained the interest of an increasingly distracted public, gradually wasted and died. The world professional championship wasn't contested between the years 1957–64, because there wasn't enough support to make it worthwhile. When it was revived, it remained the property of the same small handful of dignified, prosperous and ageing men. It took Alex Higgins's raid on the world title in 1972 to effect the sea change which saw snooker finally staggering like a hibernating rabbit into the bright lights of the second half of the twentieth-century.

Even then, though, players continued to be accepted or rejected for membership of the WPBSA on the say-so of a panel of established professionals who all had their own positions to protect. It had taken the Association until 1985 to devise a system of selection which was not vulnerable to, at best, misinterpretation and, at worse, manipulation.

Under the new system, aspiring amateurs would now play each other in a series of 'ticket' tournaments; the eight players who came out on top would then play the bottom eight professionals and, if they won, would replace them as members of the WPBSA. As the top points earner in the first round of professional ticket tournaments, 'Giro' John Wright had easily secured the place that just a few months earlier had been denied him. For the time being, however, he was still an amateur and therefore qualified to be in the three-man team representing England at Blackpool.

Giro, in fact, although still only 23, had been a full-time snooker player for years. In the three months leading up to Blackpool, he had collected a handful of £1,000 and £1,500 prizes at pro–am tournaments in various parts of the country. He had then invested substantial parts of these betting on himself in money matches in clubs in and around his native Hackney. Just playing for the glory, as he was at Blackpool, didn't give him the same 'buzz' as playing for money; he had anyway already reached the semi-finals of the world amateurs the year before in Dublin.

He therefore didn't have much incentive to turn out for his match against an Icelander who name he couldn't pronounce at nine o'clock in the morning, and so he didn't. A second non-appearance, after failing to return from watching his friend Joe O'Boye competing in the Coral UK championship over in Preston, would result in Giro's expulsion from the England team and an official complaint about his behaviour being forwarded to the WPBSA.

He had been surprised, on arriving in Blackpool, to find that his reputation had preceded him to the other side of the world. A member of the New Zealand team, at that time a complete stranger, had come up to him at the eve-of-tournament cocktail party and asked if he wanted 'some blow'. Now, at two o'clock on a Thursday morning in the middle of November, Giro, who had just been forcibly ejected from the discotheque in the bowels of the Imperial Hotel, was being invited by a member of the Egyptian team to go up to his room and smoke dope. The Iceland team, meanwhile, were on course for another all-nighter, the excuse this time being the victory of Miss Iceland in the Miss World competition, which they had watched that night on TV.

'You're playing first thing tomorrow morning?' the Iceland captain asked Jon Wright.

'What are you?' Giro asked him back, good humouredly. 'A detective?'

'Hey, come over 'ere, doc,' one of Giro's companions shouted as Dr Barron stepped out of the revolving doors into the foyer, his glasses still bouncing on his chest. The speaker was a man known as 'Jelly Baby' because of his shape, clearly visible underneath the shirt he was wearing, which had come unbuttoned to the waist, and his size. Jelly Baby is a pool player who was all set up with a road show consisting of a car, a manager and a couple of go-go girls until the usual – drink, drugs etcetera – got in the way. Now he was sleeping on Giro's floor. It was while he had been in Jelly Baby's company some months earlier that Joe O'Boye had had his cue stolen in another seaside hotel. Dr Barron chose to ignore the little man with the white belly trying to attract his attention and headed straight for the lift.

Dr Barron, in the final reckoning, finished eleventh in his group of eleven players. But he was returning to the Railway Club in Mutare, in Zimbabwe, fired with a new resolve. 'I'm going back this time,' he said, 'and I'm going to iron our table like a bastard. I'm going to iron it until you get those extra little ergs of energy we're not used to that we've been getting here. Until it's true as a bloody nut.'

*

Steve Davis signed his first professional contract with Barry Hearn in Blackpool. In fact, it is the only written contract they have ever had, and it was signed against a lamp-post on the seafront one night in 1978.

Two years later, Davis used Blackpool as his base when he defeated Tony Meo, Terry Griffiths and Alex Higgins on his way to winning the first major title of his career. Every day for the two weeks of the Coral UK championship he made the short trip from Preston to Blackpool to practise on the tables in the town's Commonwealth Club.

The snooker coach at the Commonwealth Club in those days was a local fishmonger whose advice Davis had first sought some years earlier and who, with the passage of time, had been elevated to the position of his 'guru'.

Anybody less guru-like than Frank Callan, however, it is difficult to imagine. Dour, cantankerous, impatient and blunt, he is every southerner's idea of what a man-of-the-north above a certain age is like. 'I'm a peculiar nature,' Frank Callan likes to say of himself; and it is a nature that in the past has led to a series of head-on collisions with the snooker establishment, whom he regards with barely disguised contempt.

Callan is a snooker technician; his skill lies in spotting faults in a player's technique and correcting them quickly. 'I can't change a plug at home. I'm no good with anything mechanical,' he says. 'But I like sports. I like taking things to pieces and putting them together again, are you with me? I like to look into things. I don't stop at the surface.'

After studying the game and coaching it in his spare time for many years, he had gone on the official WPBSA coaching course at Lilleshall – 'the joke factory', as he calls it, 'they're all comedians' — and been failed for refusing to toe the party line.

Now he stands outside the official set-up, lobbing hand-grenades and waving two fingers whenever he gets the chance. Frank Callan does it his way, and anybody who doesn't like his way is welcome to go elsewhere. He unburdened himself of one of his most promising pupils after discovering, to his horror, that her mother was 'a communist'.

The B&SCC, the amateur body, were another part of the snooker establishment that Frank had fallen foul of and so, although it was on his doorstep, he never went near the Tower Ballroom in the weeks that the B&SCC-organised championships were being held there. Instead, he got into his car every morning and drove the fifteen miles to Preston where, just as the World Amateurs reached a climax in Blackpool, the opening rounds of the 1985 Coral UK Championships were being played.

On the first Saturday, Steve Davis was due to meet Tony Meo in the 'Coral'. And Friday night found Frank — who had had a difference of opinion with the management of the Commonwealth Club in Blackpool — brooding over a mug of coffee in the corner of the bar at his new base, the Royale in Preston, waiting for Steve's arrival.

When Steve finally did arrive, he didn't stand on ceremony. 'D'you want a game or not?' he said to Frank, and brushed past Cheel and Nula, the two broadbacked Rottweilers who patrol the Royale, without waiting for an answer. His other commitments had kept him away from the table for a day and a half, and he was anxious to get in some practice.

Thursday night, twenty-four hours earlier, he had been in Coventry doing a Courage night. Friday lunchtime, he had appeared on 'Pebble Mill At One' at the BBC in Birmingham and, back in Preston, he had just talked his way through every shot of the 68-minute deciding frame of his 1985 world championship final against Dennis, for showing on television over the Christmas period.

Although more than six months had elapsed, it was the first time Davis had been able to bring himself to watch the match that he was growing weary of hearing described as the best game of snooker ever seen. It was the last thing he wanted to rake over halfway through another important competition. He was looking drained when, shadowed by his 'minder', Robbo, he walked into the Royale Suite at about 8.30.

Dressed in a plain sweater, jeans and trainers, Davis slipped onto the table that had been reserved for him in the corner of the eight-table room and started his practice without attracting anybody's attention. Davis and Frank Callan know each other well enough to be able to communicate without speaking; in the three hours they played together at the Royale, getting Steve right for his following day's match with Meo, not more than half a dozen fractured sentences passed between them. Callan broke off, Davis built a break, Callan extemporised until Davis was in a position to start break-building once more, Davis racked up the balls and was ready to start again within seconds of the previous frame being finished.

Even when they broke for tea and sandwiches, these were consumed in silence: Davis concentrated on a pocket game of snooker, tiny balls suspended in liquid, which he balanced on his knee. All he did say was that he had a cold and that anybody who wanted to was welcome to pass that 'scoop' onto the *Star*. 'They'd probably get three pages out of it, judging by Ray,' he said. For the previous two days the *Star* had run front-page headlines – 'EXPOSED: MY CHEATING HUSBAND – Snooker star's nights of passion with a redhead' – on the breakdown of Ray Reardon's marriage.

After Barry Hearn and his father, nobody is closer to Steve Davis than Frank Callan. Unlike the 'cueists' – the Whites, Stevenses and Higginses, who rely on instinct and intuition – Davis is not a natural snooker player. For Davis, success depends on technique. And the technical aspects of his game – his stance, his grip, his bridge-building and his cueing action – need constant overhauling and retuning. When he isn't playing well it often takes an outsider to tell him what he's doing wrong, and Frank Callan is the only outsider whose opinion Steve Davis respects.

They met for the first time at the end of the 1970s, in the days just before Davis turned professional. He was about to take part in a competition at the Commonwealth Club in Blackpool and, not knowing which table he would be drawn to play on, had sought out Frank Callan as somebody who was familiar with the tables: producing a notebook, he had asked him to enumerate the special qualities – big pockets, small pockets, fast nap, slow nap, dead cushions etcetera – of each table, and had conscientiously written it all down.

Such thoroughness and attention to detail were the kind of things Callan had despaired of ever seeing in the new generation of players and he was profoundly impressed. The fact that it had taken considerable effort of will on Davis's part for him to do it, impressed him even more. Steve Davis was almost painfully shy and introverted at that stage, but he was 'wide'. It was a combination of qualities – particularly when applied to snooker – that Callan admired.

After he beat Bill Werbenuik in the final of the 1983 Lada Classic, Steve showed Frank the torn-off piece of cigarette packet with the Callan dictum scribbled on it that he had kept sneaking glances at whenever he got the chance. 'Get your eye on the FUCKING object ball' Davis had written. He claimed it had won him the match, and treated Frank to a dinner afterwards – Chinese, the sort of stuff he'd never eaten.

It was part of 'the drill' that Steve had agreed to accept, in common with all the other players who turn to Frank Callan for advice. It is this drill, Frank thinks, which explains why Steve Davis is a three-times world champion and Jimmy White, for instance, is not. 'There's five things you need to be a champion. Number one is: talent. So, okay, Jimmy's got more natural talent than Steve has, so Jimmy's in the lead there. Number two: bottle. That means Jimmy's still in the lead. Number three – dedication. Okay, so now we see Steve start to draw level. Number four is: method. Steve is a methodical player. He knows his drill, which we've gone over and over in practice. So now we see Steve start to shoot in front. Number five: application. Now Steve is well away. Jimmy never plans his shots. He never thinks. Steve is always planning; always thinking. The sixth thing you need, it goes without saying, is luck. I mean, you can walk down one side of the street and have an accident, or walk down the other and get rich. Are you with me? Not that I want to get rich. I'd make a bad millionaire. I don't want to live in a mansion. I don't want to go on a cruise.'

Frank had given up his fish business a year earlier. Now all his energies went into the players that came to him for coaching. Most of the time he felt he was banging his head against a brick wall, but the job did have its compensations. 'When he's doing it right, it's like hearing classical music, which I know nothing about, I should add,' he said about watching Steve when he was playing at the top of his game. He closed his eyes for a second and pretended he was playing the violin, bowing across thin air. 'It's a mystery. I don't know where it comes from.'

As far as Frank is concerned, there's only one thing that stops him and Steve making the sweetest music together, and that's the constant presence of the man always accredited with making Steve Davis the player he is, Bill Davis, Steve's father. History, in the form of two autobiographies, several documentaries, and countless newspaper and magazine articles, has recorded that it was Bill Davis who, by encouraging him to play snooker, first, at home with wooden beads and, later, on a full-size table at Plumstead Common Workingmen's Club, where he was a member, instilled into his son both his love of the game and the skills with which to play it.

Prematurely retired from his job as a storeman, Bill Davis has become part of the backstage furniture on the circuit, affable, unchanging, as comfortable as the woollen cardigans he wears. He rarely ventures into the arena but watches every shot of every match that Steve plays on one of the monitors, a pint of lager at his elbow and a large cigar working backwards and forwards over his lips, keeping time with the cue sawing across the screen.

A week or so before the Coral tournament started, Terry Griffiths got in touch with Frank Callan and asked him for his help. He said he was desperate for somebody to take a look at his game. After beating Silvino Francisco in the Coral, Terry went on television and publicly thanked Frank for helping him pull his shots together. In all the years of their association, it was something Steve had never done. The name Frank Callan never crossed his lips in interviews; it never came up at the press conferences after matches, although Frank was often hovering in the background; Stalin-like, he had been written out of all the official Davis histories, as if he was somehow an un-person. 'Why does he never mention you?' Frank's wife's bridge friends, who all liked Steve, were always wanting to know.

'Frank is not my coach. My father's my coach,' is Steve's own answer to this question. 'Nothing against Frank, because he's one of my best friends. It sounds big-headed, but we know so much more than anybody else about the game, that we talk on a level that very few people do. Usually you start talking to some-body that you think should know about snooker, and you can see you're losing them. That doesn't happen with Frank.

'But having said that, my father's my coach. He's been my coach all my life. He's the person that spends a great deal of time with me doing all the basic stuff. And when anybody sug-gests that he isn't, I just . . .' Like an organ prodded with an electrode, or a child protecting itself against a beating, he balls his shoulders and shrinks in on himself. 'Obviously Frank wants to get recognition for how good he is, because everybody does. But I'm in the position where I don't want to take away all the hard work that my father and I have done, and don't want to alienate my father from anybody. So I'm like . . . I'm in a diffi-cult situation. I'm in-between.'

The uneasy truce between Steve's father and his most trusted adviser had occasionally degenerated into all-out warfare in the past. As the Coral moved into its final stages, war looked like breaking out all over again.

5 'Losers make their own arrangements'

November was a busy month. The first week of the Coral UK overlapped with the finals of the World Amateur Championships in Blackpool. The second week of the Coral coincided with the second ticket tournament of the season, at Butlin's, Barry Island.

For a number of those competing for their professional ticket at Barry, it merely meant swapping the waves and howling winds of the Lancashire coast for the waves and driving rain of South Glamorgan. One minute they were in the four-star comfort of the Imperial Hotel, Blackpool; the next they were feeding fifty-pence pieces into the meter and filling hot-water bottles in an effort to fend off the cold that swept in under the doors and through the threadbare curtains of the chalets at Barry.

'It's on the edge of a cliff . . . I said, it's on the edge of a cliff!' The only public telephone in the whole of the camp which was still in working order was in the security hut by the main gate. It was necessary to shout because of the noise of the television that the man who issued exit permits was constantly watching, and because of the boiling, belching sea. Nothing at Butlin's, Barry Island seemed to be working in late November. But even at the height of the season, with everything shipshape and Bristol-fashion rather than sad and peeling, it didn't look as if Barry Island would be much of a fun place.

It was an old camp, built in the years immediately following the War, an unkempt, gerry-built, sprawling, dispiriting kind of place. Tower Hamlets-sur-mer. Toxteth-by-the-sea. Accommodation was in low-rise tenements with flooded landings, and weather-warped, candy-coloured doors. With steep cliffs on one side and high, barbed-wire-topped fences on the other three, there was little chance of unauthorised persons gaining entry. In fact, and hardly surprisingly given the conditions, traffic was very much the other way. As soon as they had been elminated from the tournament, the tendency was for players to sling their keys into the concrete hangar marked 'Reception', and make an immediate escape.

Those remaining hung around the games hall, whether they were competing or just killing time between matches, because it was the only refuge from the cold. It was a huge area, as wide and as high as one level of a multi-storey car park, and about as inviting. It was heated by roaring electric braziers the size of crematoria, and kept to almost human proportions by sets of heavy black-out drapes. Behind one set was a bowling alley and a television; behind another was a television and a video featuring non-stop Sylvester Stallone and Chuck Norris, or a small stage featuring musical cabaret, depending on the time of day.

The only sign of real activity occurred at 1.00 and again at 5.30 when there was a stampede for the stairs leading down to the canteen. There, local girls with chilblained legs and plastic hairnets dispensed bread and marge, brown sauce in plastic sachets, and gluey soup and lumpy custard from big aluminium jugs. Twenty-year-old Christmas decorations had been strung up in a attempt to take the chill off the slabs of icy Formica.

What with all the hanging about and the cold, food loomed large at Barry. The tournament officials sat under a red and white awning in a small kiosk with the words 'Sno Balls' and 'Candy Floss' floating in fluffy clouds above their heads. Between meals, when they weren't sipping glasses of Pils and puffing their way through packets of Silk Cut, the young hopefuls were tipping helpings of sweet-and-sour sauce onto the plastic platters of deep-fried chicken nuggets sitting in their laps.

The mysterious thing was that, with the exception of the 17-year-old who had won the previous ranking tournament at Pontin's, Prestatyn three weeks earlier, a dumpling-faced youth who was shadowed everywhere by his equally pale and podgy, Jaguar-driving manager, none of them was fat. They were all, in fact, eaten away by nervous energy the way that old tombstones are often eaten away by the wind.

The predominant fashion, set mainly by the competitors from South London areas such as Ilford, Chelmsford, Mitcham, Canning Town and Barking, was for ice-blue jeans and counterfeit copies of Fila, Lacoste, Tachini and other 'designer' sports shirts. These were the boys who made up the bad-boy academy that sat in permanent all-day-and-all-night session in the 'leisure area' closest to the bar. Walking through here was like walking through North End Road market or Oxford Street on a summer Saturday. It was impossible not to get accosted by somebody trying to sell leather jackets, jewellery or cheap perfume. ''Ere, pal, 'ow's about this for a nice jumper ... We got some nice Lacoste jerkins comin' in tamorra.'

Anybody who didn't talk like Terry in 'Minder' and walk as if they were on a boat out at sea was regarded as a legitimate target for the card-sharks and spielers. 'I've got forty-quid that says she's wearing tights not suspenders ... Okay then I'll do you a tenner ...'

But the main source of speculation was the outcome of matches being played 175 miles away in the Coral at Preston and behind mists and fizzing snowstorms on the televisions at Barry. There was special interest on the Wednesday when one of their own, a player who had twice had his application for professional status rejected and was appearing on television for the first time, faced Steve Davis in a quarter-final match. But after nearly winning the first frame and actually winning the second, he eventually went down 9–1.

Most people had given the appearance of not watching and of not really caring much about what happened. But there was a sense of disappointment hanging around for a while once the result was known. It was as close as most of them had yet come – and as close as many of them were going to get – to the big-time.

Steve Davis was earning more than many of the middle-rank professionals long before he was accepted for membership of the WPBSA. The top one hundred amateurs still earn as much in prize-money as the bottom forty professionals, and they do it without the additional pressure of knowing that they *have* to win in order to meet the HP payments on the Honda and the video.

But there are still thousands of, mostly young, players whose

ALEX HIGGINS
'I've been waiting for Higgins to be destroyed for years.
But the fact is: people *like* watching the process.
This is what I think is one of the biggest things in our game.'

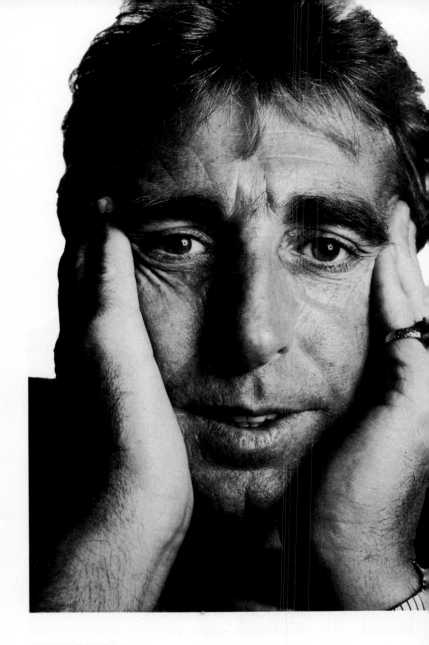

TERRY GRIFFITHS
'I've changed a great deal over the years. And, being truthful,
I don't like the kind of person I've turned into.'

BARRY HEARN (top) STEVE DAVIS (bottom)
'They've grown up together in the snooker world.
They're as close as two men can be who aren't blood, really.'

TONY KNOWLES
'He needs help, obviously. His head needs completely clearing of a lot of things he's got in it.'

JIMMY WHITE/TONY MEO
'Oh, we done things together, we could put each other away for a long time.'

CLIFF THORBURN/ROBERT WINSOR
'When he first visited Britain in the early 'seventies, Thorburn still sported
the Afro haircut that was a legacy of the same North American drug culture
which was later to produce Kirk Stevens.'

JOE JOHNSON
'The thing that was becoming clear about Johnson was that he had
no interest in pumping himself up and turning big-time.'

DENNIS TAYLOR
'The inconceivable happened: Davis lost his title to an equally well-groomed
but undeniably small, round, ruddy and bespectacled person.'

STEPHEN HENDRY
'It's a big, bad world we live in and it can be dynamite, what with the drugs and drinks scares. You can't be too careful,' believed 'Super Bairn's' manager.

performances at club and local league level are just good enough to persuade them that they have the ability to take on and beat the best. Reading about Steve Davis's Scottish forests and silver Porsches, his Mayfair properties and his Essex 'castle', it obviously strikes them as a better option than working — assuming, that is, that there's work to be found, which there often isn't.

Most of the best young amateurs find sponsorship from local businessmen or the owners of local snooker centres who contract to give them travelling expenses plus unlimited free table-time in return for a percentage of any future success. The competition to secure one of the 128 professional 'tickets' issued by the WPBSA is fierce, and the pressures of having to constantly 'perform', intense.

Some of those competing at Barry Island had come near the top in the previous year's series of ticket tournaments, but not in the top eight. The strain of having to start all over again a whole year later told in their faces, which gave the appearance of being both puffy and drawn. One boy in particular, who had come within one place of getting his ticket, made Terry Griffiths look like Benny Hill. When he wasn't playing he was drawn to the television and the play at Preston as irresistibly as a moth to a flame.

One of the most popular players at Barry was one of the oldest and also one of the most relaxed. This was only partly because he had come second out of a field of more than three hundred at the first ticket tournament at Prestatyn and, because of that, had virtually guaranteed himself a place among the professionals for the 1987–8 season. 'All he's got to do from now on to qualify is turn up and knock the balls about,' one of Tony's friends said enviously.

Tony was 26, married, with a new baby, and had had a close-up look at success from the inside. For three years he had worked as barman and table-boy for Barry Hearn at the Matchroom, the super-deluxe, members-only club which Barry had fitted out with acres of pink velour and miles of flashing disco strip-light in a large space above his business headquarters off Romford High Street.

Although he had had a table put into the big new house in the country which he shared with his parents and his younger brother, it was at the Matchroom that Steve Davis still preferred to practise. Whenever his diary allowed it, that was where you would find him. Now, wherever he went on the circuit, Tony met people who wanted to know, was it true what they'd heard, that Davis liked to practise without any balls on the table? That he practised just walking round the table before he did anything else? They'd watched his instruction video, and he'd given nothing away in that.

Without giving too much away himself, Tony would tell them that, in his opinion, they'd had the sloping mirrors put up between the walls and the ceiling in the Matchroom because Steve — or 'The nugget' or 'Golden bollocks' as he is better known at Romford — likes to watch himself. He has always said his confidence comes from his cueing action. His rhythm comes from how he's moving and the way he walks into a shot, and that's why he likes to be surrounded by mirrors when he practises, because that way he can always look up and see himself.

A big advantage that Tony's relative maturity had given him was that he hadn't gone straight from school into fulltime snooker, like most of the others. He had worked for quite a long time as a kitchen porter and he hadn't disliked it. Working at the Matchroom had also given him an insight into the other side of what it was like being famous. In 1984, Steve Davis signed what was then the most lucrative individual contract in sports sponsorship in Britain, as a result of which Courage breweries 'owned' him for forty nights a year.

On some of these nights Courage would bring a couple of dozen of their best customers down to the Matchroom and Steve would be there to drink with them, be photographed with them, give them a demonstration of trick-shots and tell them a few jokes to send them merrily on their way: 'Looks like Christmas is coming early this year. Knowlsey's put his stockings up in the dressing-room already ... Have you 'eard? Jimmy White's bringing out a book — The ABD of Snooker.' It was at times like these that Tony, who still wears an ear-ring in his left ear, was relieved that he was only working behind the bar.

He had only left the Matchroom a few weeks earlier. He needed a sponsor who was prepared to pay his way and give him free table-time if he was going to make any significant progress, and he realised he was too small time for Barry Hearn. Barry always kept him too busy doing the reordering, brushing and ironing the tables, taking bets at the bar, working out the odds. He had moved two bus rides away to Barking Snooker Centre, whose owner had made his first million manufacturing aerosol nozzles and containers and was happy to back him just for the buzz.

Tony had two rituals at Barry Island. For a couple of hours before he played he stood in the amusement arcade whose coloured lights blinked through the mist just beyond the perimeter fence at Butlin's and made a boy on a bicycle repeatedly dodge little old ladies, skate-boarders and on-coming traffic in 'The Paper Boy Team', his favourite video game. 'Steve used to play the machines when he was an amateur,' Tony said. In the morning, he'd go down to the security hut and phone his wife, Delia, at their council flat in Bush Green, just outside Romford, to give her his latest scores.

One night he paid one of the other boys seven pounds for a bottle of 'Eau de Plaisir' that had a large '£30' sticker on it, but Deel wasn't pleased the next morning when he gave her his daily accounting of where his money had gone. There were only three weeks to Christmas and he thought it might be his last chance to get her a present, he protested, although he agreed she'd told him she wanted 'Anais Anais'.

Tony had had 'a bit of a shout up' with the management at Pontins about mildew dripping from the ceiling onto the baby's bed. But Delia still intended to come down to Barry anyway if he was lucky enough to get through to the final. He beat Frank Callan's star pupil from Preston to qualify for the last sixteen, but then crashed out 4–2 in the next round.

'We have a saying here: Winners win. Losers make their own arrangements,' somebody at Barry had said. Tony was back in time to see the final of the Coral on his own television at home.

One of the few of the older generation at Barry who hadn't been wearing an official tie and a dress-blazer was a man dressed in the flat cap, muffler and layered sweater outfit of the old-school London cabbie. Bob Davis – Dodgy Bob or Taxi Bob as he is variously known – has been a cab driver for thirty years. In his spare time, though, he has always run a string of promising young snooker players, much in the same way that other people keep a string of greyhounds down at Walthamstow dogs. His current pair, a small, whippy coloured boy and a wound-up, whey-faced youth in the standard South London bad-boy mould, were both strongly fancied for the future and consequently had been entered, for the experience, at Barry.

Taxi Bob was known to have a good eye. He was the man after all who had 'discovered' Jimmy White as a twelve-and-a-half-year-old and set him on the road to fame and fortune. And he had a recent article from *You* magazine carefully folded in his inside pocket to prove it. It was all there: how he had walked into Zan's in Tooting and watched mesmerised as this scruffy, buck-toothed little kid knocked off century breaks in less time than it took to drive from Clapham Common to the Junction.

Taxi Bob had been convinced there and then that Jimmy was a genius. And there was more. Jimmy had a friend who, at the comparatively advanced age of fifteen, was, if anything, even better. For the next two or three years, Jimmy, Taxi Bob and Tony Meo were a team. They travelled the country in the back of Taxi's black cab, playing money matches for stakes that Taxi had got together: he took 75 per cent of the winnings; the boys shared the rest.

'Villains and thieves' are who Jimmy has said were his constant companions in those days. 'It was nothing for somebody to rush in an' dump a load of hot watches under a table.' Needless to say, as snooker gained a reputation for being wholesome and legit and good, all-round family entertainment, the pressure grew for Jimmy and Tony to go respectable. They signed with a club-owner called Henry West and Taxi Bob saw his style of living change dramatically. He wasn't living in a big house any more. Now, he said, his grey stubble illuminated by the glow from the screen in the darkened TV room at Barry, he was living on his own in a bed-sit.

'Them days, ten years ago, there was nothing you could do. The professionals was a closed shop. To play in the amateurs you had to be over nineteen. To play in the under-nineteens you had to be over-sixteen. So where does that leave Jimmy and Tony? I'll tellya. They was becoming billiard hall bums.

'When the rules changed, I was the one what they had to thank for that. I banged away at the authorities for years on their behalf until it happened. An' what d'you get for your trouble? A kick in the bollocks. We had an unwritten contract, but a lot of good it's done me. He was the best player in the world when I had him, Tony Meo. But he needs special treatment, which I give it to 'im every day he was with me in my cab. I could turn him back into the best player in the world tomorrow if I wanted, by why should I? I see no reason I should help Tony Meo. What's Tony Meo ever done for me?'

As with Terry Griffiths, everybody said there had been a hoodoo on Tony Meo ever since he went to the Matchroom. He hadn't beaten Steve Davis once in the years that they'd shared the same manager, and when he knocked Tony out of the Coral, that had made it ten wins in a row for Steve.

Steve had also beaten Jimmy White in the semi-finals and had made it through to his fifth Coral UK final in six years. That, however, was in spite of, rather than because of his father, as far as Frank Callan was concerned. The final was the best of 31 frames, played over two days, and Steve had ended the first day 6–8 down to Willie Thorne. Sunday morning found him and Frank Callan and his father in the Royale Suite in Preston, preparing for the third session, then just an hour and a half away.

Bill Davis sat wedged in the corner nearest the table, legs crossed, impassive, smoke curling from his cigar. Frank was partnering Steve as usual. In an unpleasantness the night before, however, Bill had let Frank know in no uncertain terms that he intended to play with Steve. Frank usually opens the balls up and misses deliberately to give Steve the run of the table. But twenty-four hours earlier, in the last practice session before the start of the final, Frank, with Bill as a captive audience, had found himself going for his shots, and had ended up making a break of 63.

Bill Davis had said nothing at the time, not wanting to upset Steve just as he was about to go out and play the second most important fixture of the whole snooker calendar. But back at the hotel after the day's play was over, he had told Frank not to bother turning up at the Royale the next day. 'Who've I come to watch?' Bill said. 'You don't give him enough table.' Frank had sought Barry Hearn's intervention, and Barry had told him to turn up for practice at the usual time.

'Bill's very dogmatic, that's his trouble,' Frank Callan would later say. 'There's no room for other people's opinions with Bill. Once he's said something, that's it. He will not retract. And Steve has picked that up to some extent from him.'

It wasn't the first time that the two older men had crossed swords. Two years earlier in Preston, on the traumatic occasion when Alex Higgins came from seven frames behind in the final to beat Steve in the last frame, Bill and Frank had again collided head-on. That time it was over how important a factor pressure was in big matches. Bill had said he thought there was no such thing as pressure, and Frank hadn't been able to believe that, coming from somebody who had had to give up darts because he'd started 'fudging': every time he went up to throw, the dart just stayed in his hand. 'Your problem is you've never been in the pit,' Frank told Bill.

The atmosphere between the three of them was strained when they left for the Guildhall to resume the Thorne match. At the Guildhall, it was Barry Hearn's turn to do his bit.

Standing in the dark in the wings as the emcee informed a packed house that they were about to go 'live to the nation', Davis stared dead ahead into the bright lights bathing the table while, looking like a boxing manager in his fighter's corner, Hearn jabbered animatedly into his left ear. When his name was announced, Hearn propelled him forward with a 'Gwornmasan!' and an encouraging double-tap on the rear. Davis went into an immediate 50-point lead in the afternoon's first frame and led by 56 in the second, but lost both. Six frames behind at one point, he ended the session trailing Willie Thorne 8–13, with Thorne needing only three more frames to complete the most important victory of his career. Frank Callan was so agitated he couldn't keep still.

'I can see what's wrong but I daren't tell him. I *daren't*,' Frank said. 'He's got enough on his plate with this lot, are you with me? But he's invited me down to the house over Christmas to try an' get him sorted out.'

'Songs of Praise' was just finishing in the tournament organiser's room, within earshot of where the players were waiting to go out to play. Willie Thorne left his lucky Lucozade on a table

and sauntered over to watch the opening credits of the programme that he and the many members of his family who had
travelled over from Leicester had every reason to believe was
about to mark the greatest achievement of his long career. Steve
Davis needed eight of the ten frames remaining and had never
previously won from so far behind. Willie, who had outplayed
Davis in a way that nobody had since Tony Knowles beat him
10–1 in 1982, only needed three. The therapy, still a secret, was
apparently working.

The first frame of the evening looked a formality. Thorne
was 59 in front when he went for a blue of what was later to be
called 'extreme simplicity', and missed. It was a miss whose significance the experts would chew over tirelessly in the weeks and
months to come but, at the time, Thorne couldn't have believed
it was going to cost him the title. Davis, however, who was well
aware of Willie's history of snatching defeat from the jaws of
victory through 'bottling', immediately sensed his chance. He
powered his way back to 11–13 and, as Willie sat rubbing his
eyes in disbelief and incomprehension, levelled the match at
thirteen-all.

Thorne took the twenty-seventh frame with a 96 break to go
back into the lead. But when Davis came back with breaks of 43
and 86 in the next it was clear that it was all over. When it was,
sections of the crowd stood up and booed. 'After playing so well
and competing so hard for a fortnight, Thorne had reverted to
the bad habit of his early career of underestimating the qualities
of heart and mind which need to be allied to technique when
the going is rough or temporarily disappointing,' Clive Everton
summed up afterwards in *Snooker Scene*.

The scene in the press room afterwards was pandemonium.
'What can I say, lads?' Willie said as he slumped behind a heap
of small, softly whirring tape machines. He said he hadn't looked
at the-blue-of-extreme-simplicity and deserved to get beat after
that.

Steve and Barry had both been crying. Their eyes were red
and their cheeks tear-streaked and raw. The Coral trophy was
the first thing they had ever won together, five years earlier.
Now it was as if they had gone through another manhood ritual,
and survived; Steve clearly believed some new milestone had
been reached. He waxed philosophical. 'Somebody once told

me that if you try and hustle in snooker – in other words, if you play worse than you can – the balls never forgive you. And the balls didn't forgive Willie tonight. I was hanging onto the cliff edge there for a long while, but a comeback like that somehow makes you feel more like a man.'

As usual, Frank stood on the sidelines while Steve posed for group shots with the trophy and his father, and Barry and Susan Hearn. Spotting him, though, Steve waved Frank over. 'You've got a stake in this, Frank,' he said.

He remained in an expansive mood at the party afterwards where, unusually, he was joined by a girlfriend, a slight figure in a fluffy white Angora sweater and fluffy white-blonde hair. Even more unusually, he stripped to the waist to take part in a cabaret which involved a blindfolded local Kung Fu expert chopping a cucumber in half on his chest. Susan Hearn said she had never seen Steve do anything like that before in her life. She was flabbergasted. Her expression said she hoped she never saw him do it again.

The imminence of Christmas meant that Coral's parties were always particularly spirited affairs. This year, however, marked the end of their eight-year association with snooker; they could no longer afford the prize money the WPBSA were asking, but they were going out with a bang.

Barry Hearn had been responsible for having the Coral UK declared an open ranking tournament two years earlier by the simple expedient of threatening to withdraw his players unless it was. But now business and politicking were forgotten as he led a chain of revellers out of the disco into the foyer and around and around the bar. This conga wasn't a spontaneous phenomenon, however. Barry, as he is the first to admit, is a conservative person, and the conga, having become an institution by the simple fact of happening two years in succession, was something he now expected to happen every year. It was heralded by a blast of 'You'll Never Walk Alone' over the speakers and by Robbo going round spreading the word.

Not everybody joined in. The shadows held a number of notable abstainers. But, for the time being at least, the abstainers had to yield the floor to the majority who were happy to dance to Barry's tune. Over the chairs and tables they went, along the velvet benches past the pool tables and the hot-food cabinets and the 'Please wait here to be seated' sign, following a man whose head was back and chest was out and whose face was suffused with a sense of achievement and well-being; a man clearing everything in his way.

FEBRUARY, 1972

Steve Davis is fourteen. Jimmy White is nine. Terry Griffiths is a postman in Llanelli. Dennis Taylor is driving a television rental van in Blackburn. Alex Higgins is 22, a professional snooker player and is about to change the face of snooker overnight. Some will welcome this as a good thing; many others will try to resist the change.

With his friend Bernard, a headwaiter from Oswaldtwistle, Alex is staying in an attic room at The Pebbles. The Pebbles is a boarding house on a busy road in the Selly Park area of Birmingham. There is a fish and chip shop next door, and a pub – the Selly Park Tavern – on the corner. Both will see a lot of Alex and Bernard. Directly opposite is the British Legion club where Alex is playing John Spencer, the 1971 world snooker champion, twice a day for six days in a bid to become the youngest ever holder of the title.

Spencer, when he turned professional in 1967, had been one of only two or three new recruits to the professional ranks since the end of the War. At 36, he is in the same careful, uncontentious mould as his elders. Alex, on the other hand, with his kipper-coloured fingers, his early morning clubbing and his late morning hairs-of-the-dog, appears delinquent. He is a product of the Jampot, the billiard hall in the Donegal Road area of Belfast, where he grew up on Mars bars, Coke, and Players Extra. He's raw, abrasive, and contemptuous of authority of any kind. He believes he's the best player who has ever played the game and, unbelievably in a world where restraint and discretion have long been bywords, keeps going round saying that he is.

'Fred Davis, Rex Williams, people like that, they seemed old before but . . .' Alex tosses one half-smoked cigarette onto the carpet and lights another. 'Listen, nobody's as fast as me, nobody's as attractive as me to watch. I'm the Cassius Clay of snooker. Snooker needs somebody like me, somebody *young*, somebody to get in there an' pull the crowds. That's what it's all about bay-beh!' Bay-beh!

The trouble is, there's nobody to listen. There are no television cameras at Selly Park British Legion and, with the exception of the editor of *Snooker Scene*, no representatives of the sporting press. Alex and Spencer are two of no more than half a dozen players who can make a living from snooker. Every morning Alex scans the papers for a mention, and every morning there's nothing. Fleet Street doesn't want to know.

'I'm moving out of my digs on Thursday', Alex says at the beginning of the week, 'into a hotel. Well, you can't have a proper celebration in digs, can you? I've got the champagne already and it's going to get drunk. Win or lose, it'll get drunk. But if I win I expect half of it'll get wasted.' And he empties an imaginary bottle over his head.

Across the Pershore Road in the attic room at The Pebbles, a bottle of Asti Spumante stands by itself on the top of a wardrobe between two unmade beds. Alex's socks, a couple of inches above the ankle, are coming into holes.

By the end of Wednesday, the halfway stage of the final, Alex and John Spencer are level at eighteen-frames-all. The snooker establishment appears increasingly apprehensive. There are rumbles.

'He hits the bottle some, you know.'

'I tell you what'll be his downfall – girls. They can twist him round their little fingers.'

'You see that little feller, that cocky wee bastard there, if he keeps going on the way he is, he'll be finished in three years. He'll burn himself out.'

'Sitting playing cards, gambling for money right in front of people. What way is that for a professional to behave? No class. And he'll always be the same.'

And all the time there is the nagging question: What if he were to win? 'What if you win, Alex?'

'I'll win alright. I've got no doubts, none at all. I'm a fiend for this game, it's an instinct, a natural gift. I'm . . . I'm phenomenal.' The Hurricane bounces out of the studios of Radio Birmingham, into a fine drizzle, ducking and skipping and rolling his shoulders like a prize-fighter, feeling good and putting himself on. 'This is the Higgins shuffle. Look out for Higgy's hammer . . . I wanna win! I wanna make history!'

At the beginning of the week he had walked up to Aston Villa's star forward, Asa Hartford, in an Indian restaurant and introduced himself. Hartford hadn't even known his name, but it didn't matter; Alex told him he soon would.

Like almost every other workingmen's club and social club in the country, Selly Park British Legion looks as if it was designed with one hand and a pin from a club-fittings catalogue and built in two weeks from the bar pumps outwards. It is not an ideal venue for the world snooker championship, especially since each session, afternoon and evening, Monday to Saturday, is packed to overflowing.

Every intermission there is the inevitable scramble to – as the emcee puts it – 'do the necessary'. Because there is only five minutes to do the necessary in, and room in the Gents for only three, they relieve themselves in washbasins and cans and up against trees and cars outside. Minutes later, they are back with their pints in the gloom, hundreds of men hunched forward on hundreds of chairs stacked on beer crates, which have been brought in as a makeshift form of tiered seating. Boilersuits, haversacks, kit-bags and overalls form a hillock in the corner of the bar. There are very few women present.

The total prize money is £800, with £480 going to the winner. The top professionals can expect to play two hundred exhibition engagements a year, and the status of champion will add £10 or more to each fee. Overall, a year's income for the world champion should come to between £10,000 and £12,000. Characteristically, Alex has started to talk about growing his hair down to his shoulders and attracting the kind of following that would boost his earnings to as much as £20,000.

'I reckon', he says, 'that if I won the world championship this year I'd be worth twenty-thousand – for exhibitions, bookings, perks, all that sort of thing . . . be worth about twenty thou', I should imagine.' More raised eyebrows.

But at 21-frames-all at the end of Thursday afternoon, the seventh session, Alex is in with a real chance. Thursday night virtually settles it. On Thursday night, he wins all six frames and proves what he has been saying for days now, that he is some sort of phenomenon. The referee is out of breath, sweating and wheezing. He almost shoots balls out from between the referee's white-gloved fingers. He throws himself onto the table like a boy on a toboggan or a surfer. He jams his knee in a pocket or stands like a mongrel at a lamp-post and waves his bony bottom at the world.

It is a demonstration of snooker which, in its insolence, its exuberance, its confidence and its sense of danger, few of those present have ever seen before. In the following morning's papers, however, there is still not a single mention. Head down, Alex plays at his breakfast spaghetti with his fork, round and round, picking without eating. 'It'll come,' he says. 'It'll come.'

Friday finishes with him needing only five more frames to win the championship and he celebrates by staying out at La Dolce Vita in Birmingham with Bernard until nearly four. He loses £45 at blackjack and chemmy and they have to borrow the money for a taxi home.

On Saturday afternoon Spencer pulls back to within two frames while his wife, in her real suede and towering grey rococo curls, files away the good-luck telegrams in her handbag. Alex has received two and, with them in the same post, a letter from a girl back home in Belfast accusing him of being the father of her baby. The letter is in his trouser pocket as he plays, once again effortlessly drawing away from Spencer. At the end of the afternoon he needs only two more frames to become the youngest-ever world champion and the only player to win the championship at his first attempt.

Within fifteen minutes of resuming play that night, and with very little ceremony, he has done it. The trophy is presented by one of the old-stagers, a former champion who, in common with many of those present, does his best to put a brave face on what he suspects could turn out to be a catastrophe.

With his 'manager' – a club-fittings rep from Oswaldtwistle – his ex-managers, his friends and their wives, Alex walks out of

Selly Park British Legion, headed for a party at the hotel that he has booked into earlier in the day, ready to begin the first day of the rest of his life. At the scene of his triumph, seats have been overturned and the floor is puddled with beer and littered with broken bottles.

He will celebrate his title by travelling to Australia, where he will be thrown out of one club for rubbishing a senior player and out of an hotel for demolishing his room. He will move on to India, where he will be escorted onto a return flight less than twenty-four hours after arriving, for getting drunk, stripping off and sticking his hand up an old man's dhoti.

For Jimmy White, Kirk Stevens, Joe O'Boye, Giro and the countless thousands of others who hadn't seen themselves in Fred Davis's swivelling spectacles or his contemporaries' small-businessman's approach to both snooker and to life, the 'People's Champion' had demonstrated that there was another way. Bad-boy rampant. He was going to be a hard act to follow.

6 *A certain amount of class*

When you're with people you never met before, for about the first fifteen minutes they're impressed that you're even there, that you're actually breathing the same air they're breathing. It's like you have a glow and they're tickled pink about the light. But after a while you see them looking at you ... They're waiting for you to *say* something. And not just anything, something *outtasight*! They're waiting for you to be a *character*. They're waiting for a little hot-shot *personality* to go with the hot-shot athlete they see on the ball field.

If you happen to be somebody who believes in self-control and you don't believe in saying something if you don't have anything worth saying — well, the hell with you! I can't tell you how many times I've met people and afterward I know they've gone away saying 'Well, he's nothing but a piece of furniture!' That goes double with the sportswriters ... They start writing that you're 'soft-spoken', 'unassuming', 'reserved', 'remote', 'aloof', you're 'a man of quiet dignity', you 'let the bat do the talking' — and what this really is, it's a code. What they're really saying is, 'Hey chief! This guy's dull! a deadbeat! a washout! poor copy! nerve gas! He'll put you to sleep!'

Tom Wolfe, 'The Commercial'

'Excitable youngsters' are who Barry thinks identify with the Alexes and Jimmies – 'all that untamed . . . the violence and frustrations of youth an' all the usual cobblers.' The grans like Steve. 'It's comfortable,' as Barry says. 'It's nice, it's controlled, it doesn't frighten anybody. You can turn it off.'

At the Cooper's Arms, a recently renovated Courage pub in Northampton at which Steve is about to perform the official reopening ceremony, it's the grans in their party chiffon who crowd the table in the corner where he will be signing their pictures and receiving their peppermint-flavoured pecks on the cheek, long before he arrives. Their granddaughters, meanwhile, decked out in backless dresses, fingerless gloves and ropes of pearls, their hair teased into identical wind-blown fashions, compete for space at the bar in the hope of catching his eye.

In fact, Sue, the PR-person for Courage, says that these girls, in their high street versions of the popular Madonna look, stand more chance with Steve than the glamorous 'model-types' that you see out and about with the other sportsmen-superstars at Stringfellows and Tramp.

Sue says she's discovered that there's three Steves. There's the tournament Steve; there's the working Steve; and there's the normal Steve. She says it's taken her six years to get to know the last one.

He was always shy. He had been turning up at the Lucania, the flagship of Barry's twenty-strong billiard hall chain in Romford, for a year before he said a dickie-bird. He came and went, always hiding behind his screen of red hair. He has acquired a patina of sociability and ease over the years, but can still come across as aloof and supercilious when caught off-guard.

Some time ago the British pop star, Phil Collins, found himself staying in the same hotel in Glasgow as Steve. 'So I went over with a piece of paper and asked for an autograph – I didn't say who I was or anything,' Collins later told an interviewer from a magazine. 'Anyway, he didn't even glance at me, just sent me off to get a pen, and then signed his name still without looking at me. And that was it . . . that is my memory of him. So when I meet people in similar situations I want them to go away with a good memory of me, because that's the only time (we're) going to meet . . . Life just seems so much easier for everyone if they can leave with a *nice* feeling.'

'Oh no, I'm gutted,' was Steve's reaction when he was told about his non-encounter with the singer from 'Genesis', a group whose records he happens to like. Even this, though, was a semi-programmed response. In much of what he says when he is being formally 'informal' or professionably approachable, like tonight – 'the working Steve' – experienced Davis-watchers hear unmistakable echoes of Robbo.

Steve has admitted that he was 'pretty lacking in the worldly-wise department' when he arrived at Romford: 'I was getting the mickey taken out of me something chronic.' More than anybody, more even than Barry, it was Robbo, a former storeman at Texaco in Dagenham docks, now employed by Barry as a tidier-upper-cum-bookie's-runner-cum-minder, who toughened him up.

Robbo is famous on the circuit for two things: for having the second most famous hairstyle after Terry Griffiths – an elaborate, lacquered, burnt-sienna production that looks like two onion bhajis sitting side by side on a plate. And for having the loudest voice in the legendary 'Romford roar'. 'Gworn-ma-san!', the cry that has punctuated every final that Steve Davis has ever contested, has become a catchphrase that Robbo scribbles alongside the name 'Robbo Brazier' in the fans' autograph books these days.

Robbo is Steve's regular driver. And inevitably, because they spend so much time in each other's company, quite a lot of Robbo rubs off. 'Awrigh'?' Steve will say. Or, 'Yeh, we've had it off.' *Oh no, I'm gutted.* Even Dennis has picked up 'Are you sure?' 'Are-yew-shaw?' 'Are-yew-*really*-shaw?' But then it has been said so often in the first few weeks of the season that it has begun to sound like a mantra, humming along corridors and through dressing rooms and bars, identifying those-in-the-know.

'If you want them to play special, they've got to *feel* special. A player should get used to a certain amount of class in his life.' This has been Barry's philosophy from day one. It is epitomised in the 30-foot Cadillac – the 'lucky motor' fitted with colour TV, quadraphonic stereo, refrigerator and dark tinted windows in which Steve burns up the miles watching back-to-back episodes of 'Beverly Hills Cop' – and which has become known in snooker circles as 'Robbo's rumping machine'.

This week, however, 'the limo' is in for a refit and overhaul and they make a low-key arrival at the Cooper's Arms in Northampton in Sue's, the PR person's, little red saloon. 'This awrigh'?' Steve says as he climbs out of the car, indicating the Courage cockerel logo in the bottom left-hand corner of his tie. His shirt is starched and freshly ironed. There's a high gloss on his conservatively styled crocodile shoes. He looks immaculate, as he invariably does.

'Oh I don't like it when he's trying to be trendy,' Steve's girlfriend had complained in Preston at the Coral party, when he tried on somebody's wide-shouldered linen jacket, just as a laugh. 'I think he looks like a tramp.'

'Right from the start', Steve writes in his autobiography, 'Barry and I agreed that courtesy, politeness, smart presentation and always being on time for an appointment would help me make it to the top. . . . I cut my hair and had it styled. I went out and bought my first dress-suit. I began to take more interest in my appearance because I realised a good image is an important part of the act.'

In Hong Kong, he had stood out among the Camus executives in their continental-cut slubbed silk and satin reveres in his no-frills, saggy-bottomed, almost obdurately old-fashioned evening suit. 'The classiest type of wear', he believes, 'is traditional, because it always keeps coming back.' The red, 'fifties-style fleck on the black suit he is wearing this evening is as far – it's actually quite a lot further – as Steve usually goes.

(Tony Meo, his partner in the Hofmeister World Doubles, which are being played in Northampton, will turn out in an identical suit for their match the following day. They are 'Sam specials', run up in a few hours by Sam-the-tailor in Nathan Road, in Kowloon, and Meo, who prides himself on cutting a bit of a dash, will be less than thrilled at the duplication: it does nothing for his 'Italion stallion' image to be seen out in the same suit as super-square Davis.)

The interior of the Cooper's Arms has been 'Spanish plastered' – cowpats of plaster painted white – and this provides Steve with his first joke. 'It'll look nice when it's finished,' he says into the microphone that has been handed to him behind the bar. 'Nicest Christmas cake I've seen for a long time.'

'He's a funny boy. Very dry,' Robbo says. He's standing, 'clocking the action', at the rear of the large crowd. 'People don't realise.' Robbo's got on one of his deep-vented dude-suits and a narrow red-and-white spotted tie. His arms are folded across his chest and wedged beneath them is Steve's crash-proof metal cue-case, something he guards with his life.

It is a point of honour among the bad-boy players not to be too protective of their cues. 'I've left me sun-glasses,' Jimmy White will phone up and tell the housekeeper, twenty-four hours after checking out of a hotel. 'Oh yeh, an' can you hang on to me cue?' Joe O'Boye had his cue stolen; Alex Higgins had his favourite, the one with which he won the world title in 1972, trodden on by a hotel porter and smashed.

Steve Davis forbids anybody outside his immediate circle to touch his cue, and rarely lets it out of his sight. If he is interrupted for any reason during an exhibition, he immediately slips the cue back into its case and, folding his Matchroom towel into a wedge precisely, almost ritualistically, tamps it securely in place.

He is not given to expansive gestures of any kind. The Cadillac, for instance, is much more Barry's style than his. He had spent the previous summer, as usual, at a family hotel in Dawlish, with his parents, Barry, Susan and their two children, and other members of the Romford 'family'; the rest of the time he'd spent cataloguing his record collection at home.

For a big man, his movements are deft and controlled: he butters a piece of bread the way he chalks his cue, with delicate, economic twitches of the wrist. It is a reticence which extends to every area of his life. He has learned how to work a roomful of strangers pleasantly and efficiently and developed a useful line in repartee. He gives value; he performs. But when the meter's off, he steps being Steve 'Interesting' Davis and instantly goes back to being simply Steve Davis again.

'It's almost as if the shy type of reserved introvert that he always was, he still is other than when he's performing,' Barry says. 'Which means he hasn't really changed at all. What he's actually done is just developed an extra gear: Okay, I'm being interviewed, or I'm on TV. I will now be "Interesting" Davis. I will talk and my eyes will be very much alive and there'll be a bit of colour in my cheeks. And as soon as that's finished I can go and be myself again. Whooooo! This might be the longest acting role the world's ever seen.'

When the call came from Conservative Central Office towards the end of the 1983 general election campaign, seeking Barry's permission for Steve to make a platform appearance at a youth rally which the prime minister was addressing at Wembley, Barry's answer was an automatic and unqualified 'yes'. The things Margaret Thatcher believes in are very much the things he believes in himself. No nationalised industry, total private enter- prise, low taxes, minimum government control, a basic welfare safety net for those in dire need – a return, in other words, to the self-help Victorian values which Mrs Thatcher has always espoused. That's the kind of society Barry would like to see his children growing up in. A society, in fact, not unlike Hong Kong, the free-market, free-enterprise capital of the world.

'I personally think they're on our side,' he told Steve; and a few days later Steve found himself running down the ramp onto the stage at Wembley, just behind Jimmy Tarbuck and Bob Monkhouse, and just ahead of Kenny Everett and Alan Minter. Afterwards, he would come to view it as one of the few strategic blunders in their careful planning of his career: it was alienating people for the sake of alienating them; it was giving people the chance to have a pop at you for no tangible return. It's not the kind of thing he would ever do again.

But, having said that, he doesn't regard it as a total waste of time. 'It was quite an experience,' he says, 'sitting up close to Margaret Thatcher and *watching* her perform. And that's some- thing I wanted to watch, because she's in performance the same as everybody else is. I learned a lot from that.'

Too much, the critics who believe that 'Steve Davis' is merely the creature of Barry Hearn, would say. 'Watching Margaret Thatcher speak now in this trained way, half-acting – what is she doing? She's not reading a speech, she's not acting, she's doing something in between. I part company with someone like that – they have stepped onto a different channel of reality for me.' The novelist Martin Amis's analysis of what her constant appearances on television have done to the prime minister is one which, on a less exalted level, is constantly being applied to the world's most televised snooker star.

The suspicion that everything that comes out of Steve Davis's mouth has passed through Barry Hearn's synapses first is one which can be traced back to the early days of their partnership when nothing — not the socks he wore, not which side of his head he parted his hair on, not the way he walked into a room — was left to chance. Even preparing for an interview with the Romford *Observer*, everything was rehearsed and, if possible, scripted in advance.

While not denying that all this was true maybe even five years ago, Steve — TV quizz-master, chat-show host, cabaret artiste, much sought-after interviewee — is understandably anxious to make the point that, these days, he is all his own work. They are complementary talents, is how he sees it. Equal partners in a business they have built up from scratch. They each have their own special talents and they are prepared to exploit them to the full.

'I see him on the phone doing business deals, not *manipulating* people, but doing what a businessman does: working with people as a salesman. I see him there and I think: Well, the bloke's the business. He's exceptional,' Steve says about Barry.

'It's got to the point now where he's telling *me* what to say. He's come on so much in the last few years it's unbelievable. I watch him at the exhibitions and the sporting-cabaret things we're into these days, and he's unrecognisable. He's hilarious. Brilliant. Oh, he's Joan Rivers,' Barry says about Steve.

There is nobody who knows him who doubts that Barry Hearn would have been successful whatever path he chose to follow in life. 'Barry's a driver,' Terry Griffiths says. 'Barry *drives* himself and looks for ideas all the time. He was the same when he was a chartered accountant. He was a tremendous success. Barry's the type of person who would have been good at any type of job.'

Even at the beginning, his approach to snooker was never starry-eyed. He had a game-plan and the game-plan depended on Steve becoming champion of the world. 'We're on a mission from God,' Barry used to say in those days, quoting one of the American comedian, John Belushi's, most famous lines. When Steve did eventually become world champion in 1981, at the age of 23, that was it then. The floodgates opened. They were in business.

The British public's introduction to Barry came seconds after Steve took his first world title in Sheffield: a burly figure, tie flapping, eyes streaming, both fists pumping, appeared at the righthand side of the screen and launched itself at the new champion. 'I saw Barry charging towards me, teeth clenched, fist clenched,' Steve recorded in his autobiography. 'He hit me like a tank, grabbing me hard around the shoulders, and almost knocking me to the ground.'

'One of the worst sights I've ever seen in snooker is when Steve won the title,' John Spencer said a number of years later. 'Within seconds Hearn was at the table. He was like an animal. Steve's unrecognisable now as the person I knew even a couple of years ago.'

'All they want to do is make money. They don't want to enjoy their life or see anything,' Ray Reardon, another player who reached his peak too soon to cash in on snooker's boom years, says of the new breed of professional which the Hearn–Davis alliance ushered in. 'If going round chemist shops autographing boxes of aftershave is what you want to do, then fine. You should sign with Barry Hearn. But I'm glad I did it when I did, before they turned the game from a game into a business. I wouldn't like to do it now. There's no fun in it now. It's too ruthless. It's a different phase of the game today. It's all money. But you can't stop, can you? You can't pick up where you left off something, and go back to something that was nice. Life isn't like that. Nothing goes backwards now. You've got to go forward. Onward! . . . Onward!'

It was hard to understand and all I knew was that you had to run, run, run, without knowing why you were running, but on you went through fields you didn't understand and into woods that made you feel afraid, over hills without knowing you'd been up and down, and shooting across streams that would have cut the heart out of you had you fallen into them. And the winning post was no end to it, even though crowds might be cheering you in, because on you had to go before you got your breath back, and the only time you stopped really was when you tripped over a tree trunk and broke your neck or fell into a disused well and stayed dead in the darkness forever.

Alan Sillitoe, The Loneliness of the Long
Distance Runner

'You can't stop. This is the drag, in a way. You can't say: okay, that's done. Because you're absolutely left with it. I mean, I started off years ago talking about the money in the game to let everybody know that we were gonna be dear. To upgrade the image. And it was done on purpose. I was always talkin' about money so that people knew, when they come on, that it was expensive. *Because* it was expensive, you upgrade the sport. Then you're saddled with it *forever*.'

Originally, Barry Hearn had never had any intention of getting involved in snooker. He was the finance director of a fashion design consultants – a firm which sold information about what was new in the rag trade – and managing director of a couple of textile companies when, in 1974, he acted on a tip from a friend at Thomson McLintock, the City accountants who had once been his bosses. He sunk £500,000 in what turned out to be a chain of twenty billiard halls of the old walk-up, spit-and-sawdust variety but which to him were just a straight-forward piece of property speculation.

He had never been in a billiard hall in his life until he bought the Lucania chain. But, after several years in the fashion trade, where he had never quite felt at home, he found himself immediately seduced by the atmosphere. 'I loved the snooker world, the aggressive male thing of it,' he says. 'Because I'm a real traditional working-class lad. I believe in men in one role, women in another.'

The problem was that, even as late as the mid-1970s, the public still associated snooker with no-goods and no-hopers; they associated it with the sort of semi-criminal underworld where fly-by-night promoters disappeared with the takings (this happened at the 1976 world championships), and even worse. When most people thought of billiard halls, they thought of somewhere like The Regal in Eric Street in the East End of

London, the notorious hall owned throughout the 1950s by Ronald and Reginald Kray, and described by John Pearson in *The Profession of Violence*.

'Many of their friends were criminals, mostly thieves, and they started to play host to a fair slice of the up-and-coming criminals of the East End. Most thieves require a well-run base if they can find it, somewhere they can relax, talk freely, pick up the latest gossip and know they are safe. For them the billiard hall was perfect . . .

'Thieves could leave the tools of their trade on the premises; in an emergency the twins might even look after a thief's takings for him . . . Before long the billiard hall was offering local criminals a genuine service. It was all carefully organised. There were lock-up cubicles under the seats for the thieves' tools; stolen goods could be left round the back of the hall . . . The billiard hall was a good receiving ground for criminal information, a word from a fence, a tip-off from a taxi-driver, a telephone call from a barman.'

When Barry decided to go into snooker seriously, which he did when he signed his one and only management contract with Steve in 1978, he knew that his first task was to take a rag to the old public perception of snooker and wipe it clean. 'Oh but definitely. The moment we went in we said, Right, the game has got to have an absolutely cleaner-than-clean image. Whiter-than-white.' It is a tribute to his marketing abilities that he achieved what to many people appeared the impossible in a period of a little over five years. In many ways, the story of snooker in the television age is the story of 'the Matchroom Professionals'.

Turning up a player as dedicated, intelligent and, above all, as scandal-free as Steve was, was the ace-in-the-hole. 'In many ways, if you'd had to manufacture a player', as Barry says, 'you'd have manufactured Davis.'

Bill and Jean Davis, a storeman and an infant school teacher from south London, provided the raw material. Barry stripped it down, kept the good bits and, with the aid of spares from his own workshops, embarked upon the delicate task of image and personality reconstruction. The handshake – shaking hands with Steve in those days was like strangling a lettuce, Barry would say – was one of the first things to go.

'He used to have a very weak handshake. And I used to say, Now, when you shake someone's hand, you give it to 'em and you give 'em it straight in the eyes and let 'em know you're gonna be the guvnor. 'Cause he used to always look away. And then he would work himself on his facial expressions, making sure that he looked dead so the opponent would never know when he was in trouble or under pressure. He does it even now, making *sure* there's no emotion in his face, avoiding any conflict with concentration.'

The long hair and the 'Caravan' and 'Soft Machine' T-shirts of course went, replaced by the bible-black that has become the Davis hallmark. Realising the importance of showmanship, and in the interests of becoming more 'outward' as a person, he put together a little routine of trick-shots and some linking material. The old Maxi that Barry had given him was replaced by a Rover 3500 and that, in turn, eventually gave way to a Porsche and the company Cadillac.

The most important step, however, was learning to develop an attitude, and Steve's model in this department was the player who had dominated the game in the 'seventies much in the way that he was going to dominate it in the coming decade. The first time he saw Ray Reardon play was at Pontins, Prestatyn in 1975, and he sat all day watching him, trying to analyse what it was that put him a cut above the rest, unchallenged as the best player in the world.

There was one technical thing Reardon did, pausing at the end of his back-swing before hitting the ball, which was eventually incorporated into the Steve Davis style. But it was something far less tangible that he absorbed as a result of all the hours he spent watching Reardon in action: his attitude of ineffable superiority − disdain, almost − at the table. Ray Reardon behaved as if he thought he was special. And Steve − with a little encouragement from Barry − decided that was how he was going to behave from now on.

His sense of specialness was constantly reinforced by the unasked-for refinements and improvements which Barry was always introducing into his life and his routine. Hotels were booked ahead and schedules confirmed weeks in advance; somebody was always on hand to carry his bags, order his food, deal with fan mail, intercept calls. The opposition, meanwhile, with nobody between them and the daily grind, were left to take care of all these things themselves. It had the desired effect, as Dennis confirms.

'He puts space between himself and everybody else. If you're not careful, you find that you're slightly intimidated by the remote glare that comes from his chair. Joe Davis apparently affected people the same way: his opponents were made to feel inferior before they'd even played their first shot.'

'The idea,' Barry says, 'is to be promoted a little bit above; a little bit disdainful. Like, always, when the other feller beats you, you say: "Well, I'm very pleased for him. I think he deserves it." Give 'em all that ... all that patronising bullshit, I suppose.'

After a while, Steve's separateness extended into his off-table life; his social contact with the other players withered from minimal to nil. He appeared, played, and disappeared, never to resurface until his next match, further proof, if further proof were needed, of what the Press were to call his 'Borg-like dedication'.

In 1979, after playing him in Canada, then Bombay and feeling that they had developed some rapport, Cliff Thorburn remembers telling Steve that he was going to do well in the game and to enjoy himself, not take it too seriously, have a good time. It was their last conversation together. After that, the curtain came down.

'He learned as he went along and is now very, very professional at what he does. But I think, if he was honest about it,' Terry Griffiths says, 'he used to be terrified. He used to be hopeless speaking. Oh, he used to be terrible if he had to go up and give a speech. Steve has always been terrified of *all* of it really, apart from the snooker.'

Terry feels he is probably closer to Steve than any of the other players, but he still doesn't claim to know him at all. He has made friendly overtures in the past, but Steve has always been at pains to keep him at arm's length. He offers a kind of explanation as to why this is in the official published version of his life:

'Perhaps it has something to do with a conversation we had shortly after both of us turned professional. We had just finished a match at Louth when Terry asked me whether I thought he attacked too much . . . I was surprised he asked my opinion, and it is something I would never do myself. I don't believe professionals should go around asking other professionals to comment on the way they play.'

Not long afterwards, Terry would again betray what was interpreted as his naïveté in Romford. Steve had just whitewashed him 9–0 in the semi-final of the 1980 Coral UK and Terry got on the phone to Barry to tell him he thought he should put the boy's price up. He was going to be a name in the game, and Barry should put his fee up a lot. Barry told him he already had.

After disposing of Terry, Steve faced Alex Higgins in the final of the 1980 Coral. It was to be the first important title of his career, and the clear-headed way in which he approached this milestone indicated how far in front of his rivals he already was, in terms of preparedness and sophistication. At 15–6 up and needing just one more frame for victory against Higgins, Steve left the hall to meet Barry in his dressing room, as arranged, for a last-minute run-through of the speech they had worked up for the occasion.

'I didn't like doing it. But it was important,' Steve now says, six years on. 'Your first winner's speech is the most important one in lots of ways. Because you want to be successful at *that*. Because it's part of being a professional. And I had the opportunity to give a nice speech. To make sure that you thank the right people and don't let an opportunity go *to* thank the right people, the people who had supported you in the past, and could also open new doors for fresh contacts in the future. It's part of it. It's part of the whole game.'

Earlier in the year, in the spring of 1980, Steve had again beaten Terry, then the holder, in the second round of the world championships in Sheffield. After being 7–nil in the lead at one point, he had ended the first day 10–6 in front. Before resuming the match the following morning, he sought out Barry in the hotel.

'Barry,' Steve said to him, 'tell me I won't be a mug if I lose this one.'

'Don't be stupid,' Barry said.

'That's not good enough,' Steve insisted. 'You have to say the actual words.'

'Barry looked at me, puzzled,' he later confessed, 'but I was deadly serious. I realised I had reached the most important point in my playing life, and I needed just the slightest reassurance from a friend. Looking me straight in the eye, Barry said, "Steve, you won't be a mug if you blow it." That was good enough for me. I said "Fine", and we went off to the Crucible.'

Willie Thorne, among others, is convinced that Steve, at some time, has undergone positive motivation therapy or some other kind of motivational training. 'If you look at him when he's sitting in his chair, you can see it,' Willie says. 'He's all hyped up. He's never going to tell anybody, whatever it is, but he *definitely* does something.' Steve says it's nonsense; all he has ever needed in the mental department is Barry.

'I have somebody who's not qualified as a psychiatrist but probably could be one, and that's Barry. Wherever you go, I think all you need is somebody you can confide in. Some people might have to look to a professional confidant, or whatever, because they don't have anybody. But I'm lucky. When I need reassurance I've got Barry. It gives you confidence if somebody who is very strong, who doesn't suffer weaklings – which Barry doesn't: not just in the physical sense, but in every sense – is on your side. If somebody like that's on your side, then you think: Well, I can't be a weakling. It's a big boost.'

In Northampton for the Hofmeister Doubles, Steve is ensconced in the high schlock of the Bavarian Suite at the Moat House, a modern high-rise hotel in the town centre.

Barry, at that moment, was in the process of finalising a 'Matchroom' men's leisurewear contract with the manufacturers French Connection, and a shoe contract with Pirelli. For the time being, however, Steve is wearing the Lonsdale T-shirt and non-designer jeans and trainers that he lives in whenever he's not competing. In Stoke, earlier in the year, he had been refused entry to the Ray Reardon Snooker Centre because he wanted to practise in jeans. In the end he had shrugged his shoulders and gone elsewhere.

On the dining-table there is an, as yet unopened, crate of the sponsor's product. On his left wrist is the watch which M. Pasche of Ebel had presented him with six weeks earlier. For such a firm believer in ritual and superstition, and in the importance of finessing and fine-tuning, it had been a major step to introduce such a potentially powerful new talisman into his life. Every time he placed his bridge hand on the table a foreign landscape loomed before him; the weight and balance were different, his self-image had to undergo a minor, but crucial, readjustment. However, he hadn't baulked; challenges of this kind were part of being a Matchroom Professional. Part of the game.

'There's a subtle difference between me saying, "Oh, look, I've gone out and bought meself a watch here", and somebody saying: "We're doing a watch contract, and as a manager I say you're wearing one". You accept it in a completely different way.

'I'm a bit of a *worker*, right? But I don't want to be me own boss. That's not what I'm strong at. So it's nice to work *for* somebody. In some ways, I work for me father, in being the machine that we work on to get the technique right. But then I also work for Barry as a sort of . . . being used as an item to be shipped out. You're a *product*. I know you're a human being as well. But when you're being sold, you're a product. And I get a lot of enjoyment watching me being . . . marketed.

'It's part of the *game* of being a professional. You can opt out by not doing anything. That's getting out of the game. Or you can try to become the complete professional. You can try and play the game to the best of your ability. And when I say "the game", I mean the whole game of progressing in a sport and progressing in life.

'I mean, I was pleased that we did the Ebel contract. I thought it was triffic. It was something we should've done as soon as possible. Not that I've got great views that way. But it was long overdue for the image that snooker had, and I was only too pleased to boost the image of snooker. It's taken over for the working classes from boxing as a way of becoming successful through your own ability without having the brains. It's attainable. It's something that's up there to be grasped. And having a classy watch is something . . . "aspirational".'

One of Steve's periodic rifts with Frank Callan had happened after Frank started coaching John Parrot, the young Liverpool player who was being widely tipped as 'the new Steve Davis'. Parrot, however, was so far failing to fulfil his promise, and Frank had quickly diagnosed the reason: a 'serious' girlfriend. Frank's remedy for Parrot's lack of form was therefore equally simple: the girlfriend would have to go.

Steve's much bruited preference for snooker over sex — 'A battle on the baize gives him a bigger buzz than bed!' — is one which he is constantly being called on to defend. But it's one which seems to intrigue his fellow players as much as it does the fans of 'Coronation Street with balls'.

'There must be something wrong with anybody who can put snooker in front of sex,' Willie Thorne says. 'You've got to have some sort of private life. I mean, you've got to *live* as well. But there you are, I take my hat off to him. He's a great ambassador for the game and a brilliant player. Maybe when he's thirty-five or something he'll pack in and then have his good time. But at thirty-five some of your best years have gone. If I had to be like him, I wouldn't play. I think he's sacrificed too much.'

'They've always said that your personality will always come out on the snooker table,' Terry says. 'And I think that's true of Steve Davis especially. He's aggressive on the snooker table, and his whole life comes out there, you know. It has been said that that's where his life begins. Obviously it's been good for him. But I can't honestly say if people just finish work and dedicate themselves to snooker and shut themselves off from life, they'll be sucessful. Those are not the ingredients for success. The thing I think Steve's missed out on, which I always tell him so, is married life, you know, and children, which I think everybody should experience.'

Normality — being 'normal' — is something that, appearances to the contrary, Steve claims he has never hungered after.

'You've got to be a little bit abnormal. Unnormal. You've got to be *different* to be very good at something. Because most people don't commit themselves to anything that strongly. And to ask if it's worth it, the answer's got to be "yes", because it's such a *good* way of learning about yourself. You do get a great feeling out of being able to control yourself during a match. *Disciplining* yourself. That's something I just enjoy.

'So the reason I sacrifice a family an' all the rest of it is because it doesn't really mean that much to me. I don't need it. I wouldn't want a wife. The only way I can do it is how I do it. And I'm having it off. I'm having a great laugh.'

Once, when he was a boy and still playing on a Woolworth's table in his family's small kitchen, he sent a ball crashing through the window. It only happened because he was messing about. His mother had the man next door replace the pane before his father got home from work. But when he found out what had happened, his father confiscated the table and shut it away in a cupboard. If he wasn't going to play properly, he told him, it was better he didn't play at all. That is still Bill Davis's attitude in a nutshell.

He is a perfectionist. Under the homely cardigans he is a stickler for hard work and dedication, an implacable disciplinarian. 'Even my dad couldn't find fault with me that day,' Steve wrote of his 9–nil whitewash of Terry Griffiths in the 1980 Coral UK semi-final. 'And this, surely, was the greatest compliment of them all.' From being a child, Steve's father had insisted that he strive for perfection all the time in everything that he did.

'It's what the game's all about,' Bill still says. 'Perfection. Every time your opponent breaks off, there's potentially 147 up. Even if he snookers you on the first ball, it's still possible for you to get the one-four-seven. That's what I've always hammered into Steve and that's why he always wants to be the best. That's what he's in the game for. He always wants to win. He's been taught that's the way. None of the rest of them are prepared to work at it the way he works at it. They just haven't got the application. The dedication. The *discipline*.

'People talk about what he's missing. I look back from here and I think: What are all these things he's missing? You look back now and you wonder what all the rush was for. I don't think he's missing so much. He's got the money. He's got all his life.'

Bill is a Puritan at heart, and Steve has inherited that from him. The guilt he feels if he is out enjoying himself when he knows he should be practising, he has found is too high a price to pay for temporary pleasure. He hears about the Whites and Knowleses out discoing every night during a tournament and knows he couldn't live with himself if it was him. Without the self-denial, he believes he doesn't *deserve* to win. Compared to winning, the money is incidental. 'Money,' Steve says, 'is a game Barry and I play together.' Winning – being the guvnor – is what it's all about.

'There's a film called *Whose Life Is It Anyway* with Richard

Dreyfus in. And a woman comes up to him and says, "Even though you're crippled, like, why do you want to take your own life?" Which is what he wants to do in the film. "There's so much you can do. You can teach people to be sculptors" — because he was a sculptor — "Or you can write a book about it." And he says: "You don't understand. That's not what I got out of it. What I got out of it was the *doing* of it." And I related to that *so* much. There was like tears in my eyes. It was such a great way of putting it over.

'I mean, I don't know what the prize money is for this tournament. And don't care. Because the winning of it — and not just the winning of it, the doing of it — is the thrill. That's where the thrill is. And that hasn't changed for me.'

The thrill, however, is relative. It is more thrilling with the television cameras there than without them. At the Hofmeister the cameras were there one minute, and then the next minute they weren't.

Steve has said that he doesn't feel he's really playing snooker unless there's cameras. 'It's not the fan adulation, it's the thought of the TV staring in, so close, knowing everything. You are naked, more naked than in other sports. I know full well I don't get the same feeling in a match that doesn't have TV coverage.'

A technicians' strike robbed the weekend ITV audience of a doubles final that, perhaps owing to the very fact that it wasn't being broadcast, offered unparalleled tedium. 'Steve's bored out his skull,' Robbo said. 'I thought he was going to fall asleep there tonight.' None of this was detectable, however, on Steve's face, as he pressed on, putting on a show for the capacity 'live' audience.

The picture which appeared in some of the papers the next morning and in the following month's snooker magazines also suggested that the Hofmeister World Doubles final — Hofmeister are owned by Courage, who are Steve's biggest sponsor — had, far from sputtering to a halt, reached a nail-biting conclusion. After potting the final pink to make his team the winners by twelve-frames-to-five, Tony Meo collapsed flat on his back on the floor. It made a good shot, and the photographers present took this as their cue to move in.

The more cynically minded detected the hand of Barry Hearn in this piece of 'business'. He denied it, as he would deny that Steve's early disappearance from 'Pot Black', a few days later, had anything to do with it keeping him from more remunerative engagements in the last few days' run-up to Christmas.

Just before Christmas, Barry, Steve and the other Matchroom players appeared on Channel 4 News talking about the proposed flotation of Matchroom as a public company. The projected profits for Matchroom for 1985 were £$\frac{3}{4}$-million. They hoped that the 25 per cent of the company that they were selling would raise £10 million. The flotation was a prelude, the commentary explained, to the game being exported worldwide, but particularly to North America.

'The ultimate aim of snooker players, particularly the Matchroom team, is to crack America,' Steve said. 'The Americans must look at this and think, if it can go public, and it can be successful, there must be something more to this game than we see through our eyes.'

'I wonder how many people would've liked to have been involved in the tennis or the golf earnings of ten years ago,' Barry added. 'And really that's what snooker's going to be.'

It was a *good* piece. It was also the latest shot in a propaganda battle which, up to that point, had been kept relatively discreet and lowkey. In the coming months, however, as the race to establish toeholds in the foreign markets that were coming to be seen as the key to snooker's future, accelerated, it was a battle which was to be fought in increasingly public places.

7 Entouraging with Jimmy

'He may not have been an utter social boor, but he was something less than tactful, something less than gracious, something very much less than sensitive ... He was not humble in his change of fortune. He knew that he was the biggest name in [his sport], and whatever his skill brought him, he not only accepted but demanded.' This description, of the 1920s American baseball legend, Babe Ruth, could be applied to a dozen sporting heros of the modern era. But perhaps none is more deserving of it than Alex Higgins.

The ten years following the Hurricane's capture of the 1972 world championship title had been ten years of wall-to-wall tantrums, scandals, walk-outs and brawls, resulting in reprimands and fines, and more reprimands, fines and big black headlines.

He had remained far and away the biggest box-office draw on the circuit, but he had never recovered the title he lost in 1973. Just four months away from the 1982 championships, a sports magazine reported that Higgins was 'lying in a private clinic in Lancashire, incapable of holding down food, moaning that his talent had been thrown down the drain and that he had been exploited, talking of crying himself to sleep in lonely hotel rooms and of the consolation of vodka'. At the same time, he disparaged Steve Davis for sipping water during matches. 'He'll be haunted by me till I'm carried out in a little brown box,' the Hurricane said.

By April 1982 and the world championships even his most fanatical followers had despaired of him. 'He has been harried from defeat to defeat, from one humiliation to another,' the papers reported. It was entirely in character, therefore that, as the climax to a four-hour final-session psychodrama, he should go out and beat Ray Reardon for the title.

'How he won it, God only knows,' one of Alex's many former managers marvelled later. 'During sessions he was sat there reading the Bible. He was sucking a crucifix. I couldn't believe it. Bloody rabbits' feet everywhere.'

Of course it was only a matter of time before he was once again making the more usual Higgins headlines. 'It would appear to be Alex Higgins's fate in life,' one sportswriter commented, 'to attract flying dirt.' When it wasn't sex it was drink; and when it wasn't drink it was violence. In the classic Higgins scenario, you got all three. 'Alex Higgins's hands tightened round his wife's neck. He was drunk, naked, hysterical with anger. Once again his wife had refused to have sex with him,' was a typical first paragraph of a typical set of Higgins-the-wild-man-of-snooker allegations.

The paradox was that his talent depended on the very impulses which constantly threatened to destroy it. It was one which, fourteen years after he first stepped into the limelight, he was still trying to wrestle to the ground.

The first Alex sensation of the season had happened when the season was just two days old. It was the latest episode in the break-up of a marriage which had kept the popular dailies supplied with circulation-boosters for years. This time it involved a television being hurled through the window of the tempestuous superstar's '£250,000 Cheshire mansion', nicknamed Hurricane Hall, a ride to the local police station in handcuffs, and an au pair.

That was September. In October it was death threats – 'a deranged killer has marked snooker wild man Hurricane Higgins for assassination' reported the *News of the World*. In December, a '*Sunsport* exclusive' quoted 'an old mate' of Alex's saying that, while he may have a temper 'as fast as his potting style, when it comes to a fight the Hurricane is all hot air'. But these were just the usual pot-shots, to be filed alongside the peeing-in-plantpots and the sex-pest-Higgins-and-the-beauty-queens stories. It was only at the beginning of the New Year that the papers started going for him with a vengeance. And, as usual, Alex had brought it on himself.

On January 5 he appeared for his first match in the Mercantile Credit Classic at Warrington sporting an enormous black eye. 'WHO POTTED ALEX?' the *Mirror* demanded in a front-page headline the following morning. It was something that the viewers who jammed the switchboard at London Weekend Television also wanted to know. 'I was riding a racehorse called Dreadnought this morning and it suddenly threw me. I was kicked in the face,' Alex assured the nation, when his match had been completed (and won). A week earlier he had been bound over to keep the peace for a year.

'YOU LIAR!' the *Sun* boomed on January 7. The truth about the shiner, the paper revealed, was that he was 'potted' by another player, Paul Medati, during a private match for money in the back room of Medati's Stockport club.

Alex was eliminated in the next round of the Mercantile and in a fit of pique afterwards threatened to 'blow the game apart to the highest bidder'. The *Mirror* reported that he had asked them for £300,000. After that 'the People's Chump' was considered fair game for 'sexsational' stories by the *Mirror* and all their rivals.

On January 19, under the front-page headlines 'HURRICANE IN COCAINE SENSATION', the *News of the World* broke the story of the '£1,000-a-week habit of snooker star Alex' and his recent 'dope-and-booze binge in a posh Costa del Sol resort'. During the binge, the *News of the World* reported, 'he snorted *seven* fixes of the jet-set drug "coke" in an hour.'

'SUICIDE BID BY ALEX: Higgins doped, drunk and near to death' was the headline on the front of the following morning's *Daily Star*. For a whole week the *Star* would give a blow-by-blow account of the collapse of the Higgins marriage. Tuesday: 'The man's a pig and ten times so in drink . . . he sickens me', by his father-in-law. Wednesday: 'How he blackmails wife Lynn', by his mother-in-law. Thursday: 'SAVE ALEX: Don't bring him home in a box says his mother'. Friday: 'Lynn's sex war on Alex', by his eldest sister.

It was now no-holds-barred. 'I WAS HURRICANE'S COCAINE PUSHER' was the lead story two days later in the *Sunday People*.

Manchester-based 'cocaine king', 'Smokey Joe' Thickett, revealed how Higgins: 'CELEBRATED his second world championship victory by getting high on cocaine in a toilet. SNIFFED cocaine frequently through rolled-up £10 notes. PHONED up with orders to provide 'fixes' at parties and nightclubs. SENT couriers and girlfriends to pick up supplies. DECEIVED his desperate wife, Lynn.'

The *Sunday People* story ran on January 26, the first day of the Benson and Hedges tournament at Wembley. The following morning the seven players who had won the world championship in the previous ten years assembled backstage at the Wembley Conference Centre to be photographed for the cover of *Radio Times*. Alex had made an effort: he was wearing a multi-coloured shirt with a white wing-collar and a red satin bow-tie; he had had fresh blond streaks put in his thinning hair and it was neatly combed. But he looked nervous and drawn. The black eye had faded, but his pupils were inflamed and there were sores clustered in the corners of his mouth.

He looked stretched to breaking point. He has developed a concatenation of nervous tics and mannerisms over the years and, as he put down his drink to take his place in front of the camera with the other players, they seemed to start up all at once, jerking his arms and shoulders and scrambling his features, as if somebody had their finger on the fast-forward button.

'I've been waiting for Higgins to be destroyed for years. He's looking worse and worse,' Barry Hearn had said just before Christmas. 'There's nothing on him. Sores all over his face ... But the fact is: people *like* watching the process. This is what I think is one of the biggest things in our game.'

Barry was standing by, supervising the session and waiting to accompany Steve, Terry and Dennis to a personal appearance for Riley's at the Toy Fair in Olympia. Cliff Thorborn, the 1980 champion, had a car waiting to take him to a lunch engagement in the City.

Thorburn is now the most debonair of all the players. When he first visited Britain from Canada in the early 'seventies, however, he still sported the 'Afro' haircut that was a legacy of the same North American drug culture which was later to produce Kirk Stevens. No trace of this earlier Cliff Thorburn is detectable in the urbane, elegantly dressed family man who now chokes up accepting gifts of babies' booties from fans on television and advertises automatic washing machines in the women's weeklies.

An image overhaul. Some good PR. That was what Alex Higgins desperately needed. And, as the season got into gear for the run-up to the world championships, just three months in the future, there was at least one high-powered public relations person in London who was convinced that, given the chance, he could get Alex, if not exactly into Mothercare ads, then at least out of the scandal-sheets and into the glossies.

Even after the savaging he had taken in the press in the previous few weeks, Greg ('I'm regarded pretty much as a trendy whizz-kid hotshot and I mix in glitterati-type circles') was pretty certain he could do a job for Alex.

'I'm a pretty omnipotent PR. Basically, what I say goes,' Greg said. 'And for him to come on board my ship for a time, he'd have to accept my ropes. His past certainly doesn't scare me at all. Far from it. The crass publicity that occurs with somebody like Alex usually catapults them into the public eye anyway, so they shouldn't be that ungrateful for it. It's only yesterday's newspapers, and you hardly keep the *Sun* on your bookshelf. I'd want to do a communications audit before I firmly committed. But as of this minute I'd love to get involved with Alex. Absolutely. I would regard it as an excellent challenge.'

At the time of speaking, in late January, Greg was in fact just a matter of weeks away from the most challenging assignment of his career. For the time being, he was cutting his teeth on Alex's friend and doubles partner and the player who was increasingly coming to be seen as his natural successor as the 'People's Champion'.

After five years as a professional, in the course of which he had been the youngest-ever world professional semi-finalist at the age of nineteen and the youngest-ever finalist, two years later, Jimmy White had just won his first Open title, the 1986 Mercantile Credit in Warrington. To mark his coming-of-age, Greg had been brought in to make Jimmy suitable for human consumption.

This meant having Jimmy photographed in some trendy gear

in a trendy Chelsea studio, which was what was in the diary for this afternoon. But first, Greg, who was 'entouraging with Jimmy everywhere at the moment, media-wise', was lunching Jimmy in a glitterati-type King's Road trattoria. Greg was immaculate in a Brooks Brothers shirt, a Ralph Lauren tie, linen suit and tassle-loafers. Jimmy was wearing a bilious yellow shirt he could have slept in the night before and was bleary-eyed, blotchy-skinned and unshaven. The waiters hovered round him as if he was royalty.

Twelve months earlier, Jimmy had had to move out of the tournament hotel in Warrington for leaving his room 'looking like a pig-sty' and refusing to settle his bill. It had also been discovered (as a result of Jimmy ordering four egg-and-bacon breakfasts in his suite one afternoon) that three of his pals had moved in and were sleeping on his floor. In 1981 he had been arrested during the Brixton riots with his girlfriend (now his wife), but later acquitted. It was now part of Greg's job to stop these kinds of things happening and to minimise the media fall-out from them when they did.

With the Benson and Hedges Masters, in which he was the runner-up, following hard on the heels of his Mercantile victory, Jimmy had won just under £80,000 in the four weeks since Christmas. His eventual winnings for the season would total £161,575. Gate-receipts at all the major tournaments showed that he was taking over from the Hurricane as the biggest crowd-puller in the country.

'He has everything the people could wish for,' *The Times*' correspondent wrote the morning after Cliff Thornburn beat him in the Benson and Hedges final. 'A great crashing adventurousness with the balls, staggering skills, awesome power . . . He makes snooker seem a gay, chivalrous thing, one in which a young man could happily toss his life away with a smile: if Harry Hotspur had been a snooker player, he would have been like Jimmy White of Tooting.'

Harry who? Jimmy never reads the posh papers with all the writin'. It's no secret that Jimmy didn't read much of anything until recently because he couldn't. 'I wouldn't say I'm an expert writer neither,' he says. 'Either. But I don't need to work on it, know what I mean? The things I need to do writing-wise I can do.'

Jimmy didn't see much of school after about the age of eleven. With his pal, 'The Spic' – Tony 'The Spic' Meo – he was too busy hustling. The first time he won any money, he took it home and ironed it, but that soon wore off. It didn't take him long to discover that blowing it – on cards, horses, booze, the dogs, anything – was more fun.

He had 'suss', he was street-wise, before 'the street' was a desirable place to be from. When he was thirteen, he went to his father at work one day and asked if he could borrow three pound. His father said he didn't have three pound to give him but he could have thirty bob. By the end of the day he had turned the thirty bob into £1000 playing money matches and, that night, at Streatham Conservative Club, he took on one of the top amateurs for a £1000 stake and won. He went home and showered his father with notes as he lay in bed.

A string of managers each tried in their turn to knock the rough edges off him and make him more presentable. He was finally persuaded into a bow-tie and a dress-suit from Burtons when he was sixteen. 'A bleedin' waste of time,' the manager from those days later said. 'As soon as your back was turned the tie would be off and the jacket chucked under a table somewhere.'

Another manager, further down the line, had his teeth capped and his hair 'poofed up', as Jimmy put it, and had him photographed through a Vaseline-smudged lense by the Queen's cousin. All any of this proved was what had always been glaringly obvious: you can take Jimmy out of the street, as the old saying goes, but you can't take the street out of Jimmy.

Everything about him – the 'tasty' gear, the delinquent shuffle and the wide-boy lingo; the cigarette clamped between thumb and first finger and cupped behind the back – signals a rough-and-ready upbringing as part of a large family on a tougher-than-tough council estate in south London.

His strength is that he acknowledges this and feels no compunction to apologise. Neither does he feel he's done anything particularly clever. He might have a house in 'the stockbroker belt' in Wimbledon and be looking to buy another, bigger house, in the country, even further away from his old haunts. But 'deviance denial' as far as he is concerned will never mean trying to be something he knows he isn't.

All he's trying to be these days is a bit more consistent. He's always been able to win matches; what he's trying to do now is win tournaments and keep in the big money. That means knowing how and when to play safe, instead of always giving audiences what he knows they've come to see, which is a demonstration of wham-bam, leave-'em-laughing, superhuman snooker.

He's always been unreliable, off as well as on the table. Even after he married Maureen, two years after their daughter Lauren was born, he'd still disappear for days on end. Once he got on a plane for Dublin carrying nothing but his dress-suit. He was supposed to play an exhibition and be home the next day but ended up staying six weeks.

These days, wherever he goes, his father, two of whose previous jobs, scene-shifting at the old Tooting Granada and managing a drinking club in south London, might seem the perfect training, travels everywhere with him. Even with his father in tow, though, Jimmy, three weeks earlier, had managed to mislay his cue during the Mercantile Credit tournament in Warrington (the cue was in one pub, he was in another); later he was made to forfeit a frame when he arrived late for the second session of the final.

None of this, though, had done anything to harm his popularity with either the public or his fellow players who, after the Mercantile, his first big win, were queuing up to express their delight and admiration. Calling his own fouls when nobody else had noticed them, as he had in Warrington, was just one of the reasons that made it the most popular victory since Dennis's elevation to world champion.

'The sadness', Barry Hearn had to go and say, 'is that we need the Higginses and the Whites, these flamboyant, natural players – a phrase which I think is hilarious: "natural ability" means you miss – we need them to keep the game fresh and alive and exciting. But from a commercial point of view, nobody needs them at all. It would be a disaster to have them front any campaign. No multi-national would touch them. Which means they can only ever get their incomes from tournaments and live-show exhibitions, which is a dwindling market. The game's changed now.'

The game now was all about image projection and audience

targetting. It was all about glitterati-type King's Road trattoria and media professionals like Greg who had spent the last few days explaining to Jimmy what an interview was and why it was worth his while bothering. 'The difference between Joan Collins and you is she's been retaining a better public relations man.' There's where Greg stood in a nut-shell. 'You can't make someone what they're not, unless they're a real shrewd person.' That was another of Greg's fundamental beliefs.

Unlike Tony Knowles, who Greg had also recently taken on ('Mentally he's still anchored in Bolton. Nothing wrong with Bolton, but . . .') he's got Jimmy numbered as a pretty shrewd person. He flashed him 'Keep off!' warnings with his eyes whenever drunk-and-disorderly or drugs, or anything else that Greg considered to have a negative vibe surfaced in the conversation. And Jimmy is learning not to volunteer snippets about his colourful past, such as the time him and Meo systematically took a rich Arab to the cleaners over a two month period at Ron Gross's snooker centre in Neasden.

'He sorta taught me an' Tony. He taught us quite a lot about life. He was a professional, y'know', Jimmy said, talking about his first manager. 'We still go into clubs now to play exhibitions and they say, "Listen, we sent off to your manager for a deposit for a table, what's going on?" He lives in Spain now. He . . .' But Greg started a-hem-ing as if he was choking on his frutta di mare at this point and Jimmy never reached the end of his story.

'I'm merely catalysing just a little further evolution of Jimmy,' Greg said when Jimmy excused himself to make a telephone call. 'So, he has a bit of a past, *some* of which has been publicised. But the sheer seedy side of it . . . I do not want Jimmy to be projected in any way as being seedy. And he isn't seedy. Jimmy's past isn't relevant to where he currently is at – or, maybe even more so, to where he is going in terms of commercial value. He's really very, very switched on. And he's reached the stage where he wants to be switched on publicly.'

The studio where the picture session was to take place was in a converted flour mill on the river at Chelsea. The photographer was a young woman in pixie-boots called Antonia who appeared to move in the same social circles as Greg. 'I was always invited to the right parties at the right time with the right people and I function very well there,' Greg had said earlier, accounting for his success.

Greg and Antonia said 'Hiiii!' and 'Great!' and 'Brilliant!' and kissed each other on the cheek and then on the other cheek and held each other at arm's length. Jimmy shook hands with Antonia and said 'Sweet', which is what he often says instead of 'thank-you' and 'hello'. He looked puzzled when Melanie, one of Antonia's assistants asked him 'How do you take it?' But when he realised she meant tea he said, nah, thanks all the same love, he'd stick to lager.

Antonia explained that she was between studios but that her new studio – 'black venetian blinds everywhere – it's going to be brilliant' – was nearly finished. 'D'you know he's booked through to next September?' Antonia said when it emerged that Jimmy's last publicity pictures had been shot by Lord Lichfield. 'They're all such star-fuckers.'

As well as Antonia and her two assistants, there was a photographer from one of the colour supplements who was photographing Antonia photographing Jimmy, and his teenage daughter and a woman journalist and Angela, who had come to poof Jimmy's hair up, and they all squeezed into the tiny dressing-room at Unit-11 while Jimmy hopped about on one leg trying to change his trousers.

The clothes were from somebody called Van Gils but they were being loaned on a purely informal basis; it wasn't an endorsement per se. There was no commercial tie-in at this stage because Greg wanted Jimmy to be free should C & A or Burtons or one of the majors come forward with a deal. 'Jimmy's a very real person. He has a very real wife and a very real daughter, so I'm not projecting him as some kind of screen hunk. But Jimmy can do fashion work; he's a good-looking guy. He can do regular profiles for feature work, and Jimmy and his family are ideal feature interest material for a whole host of women's magazines. So we'll develop a passage of usage for him, particularly where it's been under-exposed. Van Gils are basically no hassle. That's the joy.'

A Talking Heads cassette was now playing at medium volume and Jimmy was standing on the end of a roll of rag-rolled backing paper in a grey, slubbed-silk suit which was several sizes too big for him. The jacket hung off his shoulders; the trousers cascaded around his ankles. The only point where it made any significant contact with his body at all was at the waist-band.

Basically Jimmy is the standard bad-boy build of nine-to-nine-and-a-half stone of concave sinew and gristle, kept that way by a regular daily intake of vodka, lager and Bensons. But, being just a few weeks after Christmas and him being rather partial to a jolly-up, he was about a stone heavier than he normally is, and most of it seemed to have settled around his middle.

'You might think he's a superfit athlete, but he's not,' Roly, Antonia's male assistant, said. 'We'll have to do something with that beer-gut.'

As far back as the Goya in September, when he had lost after being seven frames in front to Cliff Thorburn in the final, Jimmy had said that he was going to make an effort to knock himself into shape. 'I think I ought to get a bit more fitter, y'know, for the stamina.' Over lunch he had repeated his good intentions. His mate Colin, who runs an office cleaning firm in Wandsworth, had been on at him for months to do some training.

'In life anyway you've got to be half in shape. See, I smoke like a ... I smoke like thirty-to-forty cigs a day when I'm playin'. But I've just got to get fit for the world championships comin'. Because it's two weeks of non-stop play. So this weekend I'm going to buy some stuff an' have a few hours Sunday. I've got all the weights an' everything indoors. I bought them all and never touched them. A bike an' one of them pull-up things. I've never been near 'em.'

They put some sticking tape at the back of the jacket Jimmy was wearing and a bull-clip at the back of the trousers, but they pulled the material in all the wrong places. For a quarter of an hour, Melanie and Roly busied themselves sticking and unsticking and clipping and unclipping him, while Jimmy chewed on a cigarette and swigged from a can of Heineken. Finally, the suit hung to Antonia's satisfaction.

'Okay,' Antonia announced, 'let's do a reading. When you're ready ...'

'I don't think we can have that collar like that.' Greg had noticed an unsightly kink in Jimmy's shirt collar. Greg's own shirt was now open at the neck. He wasn't wearing his Ralph Lauren tie any longer. Jimmy was wearing it for the picture.

'Do we have any double-sided tape, anybody?' They tried

double-sided tape on the collar but it was still kinky. Greg decided that what they needed was a steam-iron. Antonia thought stiff card might do the trick. 'Should we attach some card to it?' she asked Greg, but Greg wasn't listening. 'Has anybody seen about the ironing-board?' Greg was shouting down a deserted corridor.

Meanwhile, there was still the problem of what Jimmy would be wearing on his feet for the long-shot. 'We need something really cute for close-ups, but also something really cool and trendy in long-shot,' Greg had told Antonia. Jimmy's own shoes, a pair of battered brown Oxfords, had immediately been deemed unsuitable. All the male feet in the studio were being auditioned when the solution – a pair of almond-toed blue casuals with brass-tipped tassles – strode in through the door.

The young man in them was wearing his hair in an 'Ian Botham' – long and full in the back with no sideboards – and carrying a titanium briefcase with a replica American Express gold-card tagged to the handle. He was wearing a heavy, diamond-studded, maybe-a-Hong-Kong-Rolex and a navy blue Georgio Armani blouson jacket. He'd been given the Armani jacket by Jimmy. Well, he'd paid Jimmy £150 for it.

Howard Kruger of the Kruger Organization, 'a multi-interest entertainment group', was Jimmy's new ... Jimmy himself wasn't quite clear what. 'Oh he's me new, er, agent . . . er, marketing, inn'e?'

Howard – 'Aitch' – had been brought in by Jimmy's manager to take care of all the things like personal appearances, promotions and endorsements that his manager, a successful property developer, was too busy to get involved with himself. 'Aitch', in turn, had hired Greg to handle all the Press and PR side of things. 'Aitch' and Greg go back a long way. They grew up together in Brighton. And when, five months earlier, Aitch's friend, Tony Knowles, found himself in hot water over the 'Tony wears ladies undies for sex romps' story, Aitch had immediately put Greg on the job.

Aitch had met Knowles – 'TK' – on holiday in Tenerife. Greg met him for the first time in Stoke-on-Trent shortly before the press conference which he organised to kill the 'undies' story, and quickly realised that Knowles didn't have 'that street-wise thing'. Greg's advice to Knowles had been to admit that he had worn ladies stockings 'to some reasonably hideous party somewhere north of the Watford Gap'. Through following this advice, Greg believed, he had killed the story stone-dead.

That had been both Aitch's and Greg's introduction to snooker and, although they found some of the behind-the-scenes characters both 'archaic' and 'bloody-minded', they had apparently liked the rest of what they saw. Aitch had agreed to become TK's manager, Greg had been retained as his publicist, and now they were looking to expand. Aitch stepped out of his shoes and handed them to Jimmy, who he thought was looking ace.

'He's never been anywhere near clothes like this. Of this quality,' Aitch said, which wasn't strictly true. Exactly twelve months earlier, just before he changed managers, Jimmy had landed himself in trouble with both the BBC and the game's administrators for turning out for a match in the Benson and Hedges with a big Tommy Nutter logo under the waistcoat pocket. The BBC had refused to show the match unless the name of Nutter, a flamboyant young Savile Row tailor, was taped over.

To Barry Hearn, it was a classic example of the sort of Mickey Mouse management that made the management game a no-contest. 'It was done the wrong way,' Barry said when the dust had settled. 'Silly stuff. I mean, Tommy Nutter is a great tailor. But Tommy Nutter isn't volume. They were taking on trouble for nothin'.

'To wear a Tommy Nutter suit means five to six hundred pounds. So how many people, even if they recognise the name, will go out and buy one? Answer: virtually none. Point: why do it? If there was more, Tommy Nutter himself would be *paying* you fortunes to do it, rather than just saying 'Here's half a dozen free suits.' Waste of time. Coupled with the fact that you're taking on aggravation. There's nothing wrong with having aggravation, one, if you can win, and, two, if you can earn. You gotta play the odds. You got to be talking about a lot of money.

'As it happens, because of the sticky tape, because of the banning, which is a *better* ploy, you got more advertising than you could ever have got in a million years. I mean, if you'd've stuck Tesco Home'n'wear on, or Marks and Spencer – *real* volume – the mentions, the Press over the next two or three days, would . . . have . . . been . . . worth . . . a . . . *fortune*.

'But it's a short-term gimmicky thing. What is the better way to do it is to slowly–slowly perhaps do discussions with the BBC and ITV over a couple of years, during which time we've got every major multi–national wanting to put a little thing here and a discreet logo there for lotsa money like the tennis players.

'The other thing, of course, is that you've got to work in such a way that you don't put pressure on the players. This is why it's good with us, where it's a team thing. We all discuss things and nothing's done to embarrass anyone. We like to earn, but we don't wanna make ourselves look ridiculous. We wanna be in the business for twenty years, not a coupla years. I mean, I saw Jimmy White's face when he put that suit on, the stripey one. Jesuschrist! Are you sure!'

Since Tony Meo signed with Barry Hearn in the early 'eighties, there has been a barely–contained hostility between the Hearn and the White camps. 'Barry who?' Jimmy's pals will say whenever Hearn's name is mentioned. 'Never mention that name round here.'

Back in the restaurant, with Greg hanging on his every utterance, Jimmy had minded his tongue. 'I often get Meo's minders come up and say, "Come where the money is" an' all that business. This is a coupla years ago. An I always say, "If I come where the money is, there's no–one to beat your little firm then, is there?"'

But now Greg and Howard Kruger had gone haring along the King's Road to find him a new shirt and tie to wear with the problem whistle, and Jimmy was less reticent. 'They've got no class anyway, that little firm over there in Romford. They're . . .' – he tried to think of the worst thing he could imagine being called by anybody, while he ripped open another can of lager – 'they're *actors*.'

Ten days earlier in Belgium, during the first WPBSA–organised tournament in Europe, Barry had reiterated the importance of Jimmy and Tony not being seen around together in public. 'He told me he wanted me away from Tony. He didn't mean it nasty or nothin'. He was like half–joking. But I told him: "You'll never be old enough to see it. We go too far back. Oh, we done things together, we could put each other away for a long time. We'll always stay tight."'

He had, in fact, spent that morning with Tony in Brixton. Tony had dropped him off at the restaurant. ''E's into this meditation,' Jimmy said, looking perplexed. 'Gettin' out of himself or some'ing. The people that wear them purple clothes. That bloke, what's 'e called, Buddha? Last night 'e said 'e was in a room with all these people an' 'e was like out of his own body, lookin' down. His eyes were bulgin' the way they do. I said, "What you been doin', basin' coke?"

''E's tried to get me into this meditation but I says, "My head's messed up enough. I don't do dope nor nuthin' these days. I just kip."'

Jimmy gave the thumbs-up to the shirt and tie Greg and Aitch had bought him — 'You're an angel', he said as he rummaged in the carrier-bags — and at last Antonia was ready to shoot. 'Right,' she said. 'Can he pick up his cue? Is it called a cue? I don't know what to call it.' Jimmy said to just call it a stick.

Antonia said she thought he had a pleasant face. Greg agreed It had a lot of character. But he was a bit toothy so it was better if she got him to keep his mouth shut.

'Okay,' Antonia instructed him over the continuing disco throb, when she was satisfied that she had the standard snooker-star pose in the can. 'Now drop the doo-dah.' Happy to oblige as always, Jimmy flicked his stick like a cigarette stub over his shoulder and sent it clattering across the raked concrete floor.

It was Thursday. Howard Kruger said that, by Monday, he expected to be managing another of the two biggest names in the game. 'Barry Hearn knows who I am,' Aitch said. He said he was the first serious challenge to the Hearn monopoly in snooker. He said he felt he had Barry Hearn on the run.

Monday came and went and nothing happened. But very soon afterwards the headlines — 'I'LL TAME ALEX!' — announced that Alex Higgins's career was in new hands. Greg had been granted his ambition: he would show the world it was possible to turn base metal into gold.

8 *Integrated circuits*

Barry Hearn's acquisition of the twenty billiard halls that made up the Lucania chain coincided with the legalisation of one-armed-bandits and other gaming machines. With the exception of the hall above his Romford headquarters, he off-loaded the old Lucania rooms at the end of the 1970s at a personal profit of £2,500,000. He hung on, however, to the fruit-machine end of the business.

He still has a fruit-machine and amusement arcade 'empire' in the East End of London which is kept ticking over for him by a former lightweight from the Jim Wicks/Henry Cooper stable called Freddie King. Barry manages to keep up-to-date with what is happening in the arcades during regular training sessions with his ex-boxer partner in his home-gym.

When he sold the Lucania chain it was to Riley Leisure, the snooker table manufacturers who now represent Matchroom's biggest single source of income outside tournament earnings. The future of Matchroom is inextricably bound up with the future of Riley, which means that Barry is dedicated to helping Riley secure a lion's share of the tables and equipment market. He is a director of Riley Leisure. Steve has a substantial holding in the company. Steve and all the other Matchroom players have cue-endorsement and promotional contracts with Riley Leisure worth £350,000 a year. Naturally, if Barry can score a point for Riley he is going to *do* it, however and whenever he can.

'There's two games going on here: the game on the table, and the game off the table. And I hope my blokes play as hard on as

I try to play off. We work for Riley Leisure and our aim is to *grind* the opposition into the ground. I mean, that's what the game's all about.'

When Barry talks about 'the opposition' in this context he invariably means BCE, which was once shorthand for Bristol Coin Equipment but now stands for Billiard Cues for England. The change in usage is an indicator not only of the ingenuity of BCE's founder and chief executive, David Fisher, but also of his pragmatic approach to business and his willingness to change.

In the same way that Barry Hearn was able to switch from accountancy to fashion; from fashion to property speculation and gaming machines; from property to sports management and snooker-as-showbiz as new opportunities presented themselves, so too has David Fisher demonstrated that he is the kind of 'popular capitalist' entrepreneur on whom Mrs Thatcher has repeatedly insisted the future of the country depends.

He made a fortune in the one-arm-bandit trade with Bristol Coin Equipment and multiplied that several times over through a series of property deals. He got out of property just before the market went bust in the late 1970s and reinvested in coin-operated pool tables. Unable to get hold of any cheap pool cues, he imported a few from Taiwan, first for himself, later for other pool table operators. A visit to a machine trade fair in London in 1979 proved to him how big a gap there was in the market for cheap cues, chalk and other necessaries.

'We took this tiny little booth', David Fisher remembers, 'and in five days we took orders for £250,000 and made everybody give us cash up-front. We come back every night to the Hilton in Park Lane and we had *pocketfuls* of money. We're in the business. We can't get out now. We sold off all our tables and started developing the supply side.'

Before long, he had opened a factory manufacturing his own cues. He took over the company that made Super Crystalate snooker, pool and billiard balls. The obvious next step was to make his own slate-bed tables, from the ground up. Suddenly, Riley Leisure, established 1897, found themselves being pressed for business by Billiard Cues of England, established 1981.

Now, in February, David Fisher had just bought what he claimed was the biggest quarry in Europe, in Portugal, to quarry his own slate. Riley, meanwhile, continued importing slate from

Italy. It was the latest move in a trade war whose ultimate objective was to see Riley driven into the ground. Being a combatant in such a high-risk enterprise kept David Fisher buzzing in a way that made him feel vigorous and glad to be alive. It was one of the reasons he had just turned down a tempting offer for BCE.

'I had two gentlemen from the Lebanon here the other day. They came with their English banker and offered me seven million pounds in cash for the business — *without* the machines and the arcades. And I was terrified that I might say yes. Because, at the end of the day, what am I gonna do? *What* am I gonna do? Get up in the morning and . . . what?'

Like Barry Hearn, his most resourceful rival, who he is more or less the same age as and who he in so many ways resembles, David Fisher was a millionaire before he turned thirty. Again like Barry, he regards the accumulation of wealth as a game, but one which, nevertheless, keeps him at his desk for as much as sixteen hours a day.

'I have a brand-new Rolls Royce in my garage, I have a brand-new BMW which I drive here, I have a home in Monte Carlo, I have a home in Toronto, I fly first-class around the world maybe five or six times a year, I stay in the best suites, I have God-knows-how-many pairs of shoes and tailored suits,' he says. 'I'm not embarrassed to tell you I earn a fortune. What d'you want me to tell you? That I'm ashamed of making money?'

Seven people run the whole of BCE. David Fisher structured the company around the computer, and the computer can tell him how much he is worth every second, day or night, to the nearest penny. 'As of this minute', he said, tapping in the code which brought bundles of acid-green digits crowding onto the screen at his elbow, 'we're one-million, one-hundred-and-sixty-four-thousand, four-hundred-and-seventy-three-pounds and twenty-eight-pence ahead on the last eleven months. That's clear profit. Not even including the arcades. Bottom-line. And I'm accountable to nobody. I could go out and spend it tomorrow. It's all mine.'

The visual display unit on his desk can tell him if any door on any of his machines in any of the ten arcades he still owns in and around Bristol has been opened when it shouldn't have been.

'Every coin in, every coin out, percentage pay-outs, if the cash-box door's opened . . . It's all monitored. All the machines are computerised. It's all integrated circuits. It's standard kit today. And it's *very* profitable. Oh! The money's horendous. The arcades will take . . .' – he punched in another code to bring up another set of figures – 'the projection on the financial year just ending is five-hundred-and-three-thousand-pounds. *Clear*. We have public companies that have *very* heavy money invested in machines today. They're quite legitimate business.'

Like Barry, David Fisher's recreation is business. Striking deals is his favourite pastime; accounts sheets are his favourite reading. Unlike Barry, however, David Fisher isn't drawn to the bright lights. He is rarely, if ever, seen in the bars and hospitality rooms of the circuit, and never on television; he fights shy of interviews and the press. He sees his wife one night a week, on Thursdays. Thursdays are sacred. The rest of the time he is to be found in his office at BCE's smart, modern headquarters, poring over computer print-outs and delving into documents stored away in the darkest corners of the system.

The man who is in many ways the public face of BCE keeps similar hours in another lavishly appointed office in another part of Bristol. Derek Simmons – never known as anything but 'Del' – was brought to Bristol by David Fisher to take up the £25,000-a-year post of manager of BCE Tables. Del Simmons still retains a 24 per cent shareholding in the tables division of BCE but he is now the £65,000-a-year contracts negotiator and chief executive of the World Professional Billiards and Snooker Association. And Del, a clubbable individual, is high-profile in a way that his natural out-goingness and the job both demand. 'He looks like a grizzly bear, talks like a barrow boy and is built like a brick shit-house', as one of Del's many non-admirers says.

With Barry Hearn, Del Simmons is one of three non-playing members on the board of the WPBSA which makes every decision concerning the organisation, administration, financing and policing of professional snooker. Until the appearance on the scene of Howard Kruger, Del – 'a hard man', according to the *Daily Star*, 'who, in his time has crossed swords with the Mafia and been caught up in a vicious gangland war in which he was shot at, firebombed and threatened with murder' – had also been Alex Higgins's manager for the best part of ten years.

At the end of the 1969–70 season, the WPBSA reported a turnover of £23 3s 0d. In the financial year ending 31 December 1985 the WPBSA's turnover was £2,584,902. Many of those who were responsible for running snooker when it was a small-time sport are still responsible for running it now that it has become one of the fastest-growing areas of the booming leisure industry. Between those simple statements of fact are strung a network of allegiances, vested interests and deep-seated rivalries which, even for the wary, can prove to be tripwires, and for the unwary can easily turn into a spider's web.

Del Simmons' involvement with snooker dates back to the Tonic club, a drinking club in Weybridge (always known as 'Toni's after the 'c' dropped off and was never replaced). He retreated to Toni's after his previous business venture, a country club in Essex, failed to get off the ground. The financial backing for the country club had come from the former England football captain, Bobby Moore, and Sean Connery, who Del had first met at a celebrity golf tournament at Wentworth. Del was in the motor trade at the time. Connery ploughed some money into the business and they also set up a finance company together, which Del says was going very, very well.

'Then we got involved in the country-club business which didn't go so well. Part of it was set alight. I was told I'd better get out or else. There was threats made against me. Then one night I was sitting there, no curtains drawn, and a shot-gun was fired through my window. It blew the chandelier off the ceiling. So those sort of things don't particularly enhance you to keep in.'

At Toni's in Weybridge in the mid-1970s, however, he soon fell in with a new set of friends. There were two snooker tables in the club and he was responsible for booking in professional players for exhibitions. 'He was surprised how cheap they were,' Janice Hale later wrote in a profile of 'The sheriff of Snookertown' in *Snooker Scene*. 'It struck him that there was no real organisation. Players handled their own club bookings, got what they could, and competed against one another for a very small market.

'There were three big names at the time. Two of them, Ray Reardon and John Spencer, accepted his suggestion that they form a company, the International Snooker Agency, to handle bookings for leading players. The third, Alex Higgins, became their first client.'

Higgins was soon joined at ISA by Doug Mountjoy, Dennis Taylor, Graham Miles and most of the other leading players of the day who, as long as he succeeded in getting them more-money, were happy to have Del represent them. He showed his mettle as a politician in 1979 when, acting on behalf of the players attached to his agency, he decided 'to thump the WPBSA'. The result was what he regarded as 'a new WPBSA' with Del, as the Association's newly appointed part-time contracts negotiator, installed in a position of some influence.

1979, the year Del chose for his putsch, was also the year that the world championships were given live, day-by-day television coverage for the first time. 'We opened the champagne when we got the first week's viewing figures,' Nick Hunter, the producer in charge of all BBC snooker coverage, has said. 'But we were premature. As the tournament went on, the audience simply kept growing.'

Three years earlier, the organisation of the world championships had been a shambles; the promoter disappeared immediately afterwards and was later seen driving a taxi in Canada. It took a new promoter – Mike Watterson – and a new venue – the Crucible Theatre, Sheffield – to persuade Embassy, the cigarette manufacturers, to stay in as sponsors and the BBC to film the tournament in 1977.

The success of the championship in that and succeeding years enabled Watterson to prosper. He inaugurated, found sponsors for and secured television coverage of almost all the tournaments that are still the staple of the snooker calendar. But Watterson's gold Rolls Royce with Joe Davis's old CUE 1 number-plate, his string of snooker clubs and other evidence of his accumulating wealth, did not endear him to the players who were his bread and butter.

Their dissatisfaction with 'Harry Grabbit', as some had started calling him, crystallised around Del Simmons, who agreed with the players (most of whom were still his clients) that more cash from the tournaments should be finding its way into their, and not Mike Watterson's, pockets.

Pre-1979, the WPBSA had made no attempt to control televised snooker. From the beginning of the 1980s, however, the 'new WPBSA' under Del Simmons resolved that, as the governing body, it would hold all television contracts for professional snooker. The WPBSA set up its own promotions company and the number of Watterson events dwindled. 'It seemed that every time I missed a board meeting,' Watterson later complained, 'I lost a tournament.' By 1986 he had been squeezed out completely. Del Simmons was by then grabbing it on the players' behalf.

Even before 1986, though, there was growing concern that Del wasn't grabbing it quickly, cleverly or efficiently enough. It was Barry Hearn who had brought Goya in as sponsors. It was Barry Hearn who had done all the groundwork in building up a Far East circuit. And it was Barry Hearn, many people believed, who was getting organised to impose himself on the governing body of the sport much in the way Del had seven years earlier.

These rumours were fuelled when, at the beginning of the Dulux tournament in mid-February, Barry announced that Willie Thorne was joining his roster of players, and followed this up shortly afterwards with the signing of one of the most promising of the new professionals, Neal Foulds. This brought the Matchroom strength up to six and few believed that Barry intended to stop there.

Barry had used his powerful position in the past for the general good of the game. He had, for instance, had the Coral UK declared an open tournament and had the prize money in a number of minor tournaments increased by the simple expedient of threatening to withhold his players.

But, given the breadth of his involvement, conflicts of interest were bound to arise. There was the strange case, for example, of the 1985 World Team Championships, at which England, the holders, were allowed to field two teams, 'England A' and 'England B'. The three highest ranking Englishmen at the time of selection were Steve Davis, Tony Knowles and Jimmy White, which would have meant that Tony Meo, the only English player in the Hearn camp apart from Davis, would not have been selected.

Being a board member, as Snooker Scene was not slow to point out, Barry Hearn was in a position to suggest that the trio who had won the title for England – Davis, Knowles and Meo – should defend as holders to allow a 'B' team, to comprise White and the next two highest-ranked English players at the time, Willie Thorne and John Spencer, also to compete. As Thorne and Spencer were WPBSA members, 'England B' came to be referred to in some quarters as the Rest of the Board.

The 'Rest of the World' team at the 1986 team tournament, which was to comprise Sakchai Simngam (Thailand), O. B. Agrawal (India) and Tony Drago (Malta), was also viewed in many quarters as a Barry Hearn production. Neither Sim nor Agrawal was formally contracted to Barry, but both had been helped by him in various ways and were closely identified with his camp: the young Thai player had become Robbo's lodger in Romford, and Agrawal's base was the Matchroom.

As promoter of the Far East summer tour, Barry appeared to have more to gain than most, in an immediate way, from television exposure of players from the Far East. But once again it took *Snooker Scene* to spell out the implications: 'Teams must be *seen* to be selected according to understandable and consistent principles', the magazine emphasised, 'rather than the expediency of factional self-interest.'

To complicate matters further, Del Simmons, in additon to his WPBSA responsibilities, was still Alex Higgins's manager and a major shareholder in the rapidly expanding tables division of BCE. It had been while he was still working part-time as the Association's contracts negotiator that Del had met David Fisher, the thrusting young managing director of Bristol Coin Machine. The introductions had been made by John Spencer, one of Del's partners in the International Snooker Agency, who was helping BCE design and market the first British two-piece cues.

Del's close association with BCE and Barry Hearn's association with Riley, BCE's fiercest market rivals, very quickly threw up the inevitable complications. Which of the two firms, for instance, was going to install the tables at the major competitions and reap the reward of having their name seen repeatedly on television? Del went in pitching for BCE, Barry went in pitching for Riley, and BCE, through offering more money than Riley were prepared to pay at the time — £15,000-a-year for three years — got it.

'Dave Fisher had the foresight to go in and put his money where his mouth was,' Del said later. 'I didn't heartily agree with it, I must admit. But Dave Fisher's a lot more wealthy boy than I am. And I guess that's how he's made his money, because he can see things futuristically, which I possibly can't.'

The internal politics of the WPBSA aside, commercial considerations have always assured that Del and Barry's relationship was combative. They are both pleased to describe themselves as 'men's men': Del was a physical training instructor in the army; Barry entertained thoughts of becoming a boxer. And occasionally at the end of a long and tiring day, in a hotel bar somewhere, Del and Barry can be seen squaring up for a spot of arm-wrestling or single-arm, press-up endurance in their lounge-suits on the floor. Although they come face-to-face with each other far less often, and their rivalry is focused on which of the two of them has the bigger bank balance, the 'needle' between Barry and David Fisher is every bit as acute.

For a long time – for as long, in fact, as snooker remained relatively small beer – the feuds and status tussles remained a purely in-house issue, rarely discussed outside snooker's own 'smoke-filled rooms'. But, as domestic sales of snooker tables and their associated side-products started to level off after the boom years of the early 'eighties, and television coverage of snooker reached saturation point, the race to capture the foreign markets where everybody realised the rich-pickings of the future lay became both intense and increasingly public.

'There's 6,000 million people in the world', Barry liked to say, 'and only 600 million have ever heard of snooker. That means we've got another ninety per cent to go.'

'The potential', David Fisher agreed, 'is *enormous*. We've hardly even started.'

Because they had seen that the way ahead was expansion into foreign markets, BCE had changed their marketing strategy accordingly. Instead of paying out large sums to the players whose signatures were stamped onto his company's cues, which Riley were still committed to doing, David Fisher decided he would get a better return on his money by rechannelling it into tournament sponsorship.

In November, as well as providing the tables for the World Amateur Championships in Blackpool, BCE had sponsored the tournament to the tune of £30,000. More controversially, however, they had also sponsored two new, overseas competitions: the Canadian Masters in Toronto, in October, and the Belgian Classic at Ostend Casino two and a half months later. Barry wasn't alone in thinking that Del had let BCE get both tournaments too cheaply.

'On a commercial, commonsense basis, the first involvement was a ludicrously small amount of money,' Barry would say some time later. 'I found it difficult to believe, for example, that we couldn't get a *Belgian* sponsor with eight hours of Belgian TV, as opposed to BCE. For me, as a commercial animal, if I go into a country — which I do fairly successfully — I go in with *local* sponsors. And I can't believe we didn't. I think it was diabolical. And that's an understatement.

'Now, if that has established the event, and next year we go in and capitalise in Belgium with major sponsorship, then we *forget* the first year. It doesn't happen again, is what I mean. It happens once, because you are arguing that this opens the door. And you are arguing sponsors don't exist, sponsors are conservative, sponsors want to wait and see. Okay. We'll swallow that for one year. And we'll wait and see'.

It was in Belgium in January during the week of the BCE Belgian Classic that an incident happened which laid open the trade war between BCE and Riley to public scrutiny for the first time.

In the middle of the tournament, the Matchroom players, who had been the first of the British groups to attack the European market, staged an exhibition at a Riley club in Bruges, only twelve miles away from Ostend. This appeared to be a contravention of the rules of the WPBSA, which state that players may not play exhibitions within fifty miles of a tournament. Just before the start of the Belgian final, Kirk Stevens submitted a written complaint to the WPBSA signed by himself and the three other players who were coming to be associated with Howard Kruger — Tony Knowles, Jimmy White and Alex Higgins.

The incident made headlines in the following day's papers, but Barry Hearn was scathing in his dismissal of what he saw as the latest example of boys trying to play men's games. The fifty-mile rule, it seemed, was only enforceable where the sponsor had specifically requested that it be written into the contract. And in this instance, the sponsor – BCE – hadn't. It gave Barry the greatest of pleasure to make Del Simmons issue a statement withdrawing any criticism of either himself or the Matchroom team.

'I think we go by the letter of the law. We run close to the rails sometimes, but if the rules are there, we abide by the rules,' Barry said when he was back in Romford. 'My players have to work. And if we're in Belgium, and we've got a spare day, we're not gonna laze around, get pissed, play cards and stay up all night. They're not allowed to do that.

'The whole issue anyway was thoroughly questionable, when you think that the people who objected to our 'unprofessional behaviour" was Kirk Stevens, Alex Higgins, Jimmy White and Tony Knowles. It became laughable. I *mean*, the thought of Kirk Stevens and Jimmy White sitting there with the rule book saying, "Here, this is out-of-order . . . I think this breaks Rule 17c, don't you Jim?" "Oh absolutely, Kirk." It's just beyond belief. Incredible. They like to have a little go at success, don't they? Everybody does. But that is a *bad* case of boys playing a man's game. And if they're gonna do that sort of thing, they really gotta learn better. Or try harder.'

The BCE Belgian Classic was won by Terry Griffiths. A week later Terry walked out at the end of the first frame of his quarter-final match in the Benson and Hedges Masters at Wembley to file an official complaint about the (BCE) table. 'The standard of snooker was exceptional, considering the pockets and the cushions,' Steve Davis said when *his* quarter-final match was finished.

A fortnight later Terry was highly critical of the BCE table in use at the Welsh professional championship: the top right hand pocket was suspect, the cue-ball was very difficult to hold off the springy cushions and the shaved nap made the use of side unduly hazardous. He berated the table in his victory speech.

The Welsh Championship took place in the middle of February. It was around this time that the doubts and misgivings about Del Simmons in his role as WPBSA contracts negotiator, until then indistinct rumbles, started to receive a public airing. The criticisms focused on Del's lack of success in finding a replacement for Guinness, who had pulled out as sponsors of the

World Team Cup eight months earlier. The 1986 Team Cup tournament was now just four weeks away and, even with sixteen hours BBC television coverage guaranteed, Del was still hawking it round prospective sponsors.

Del's explanation for the difficulties he was experiencing in getting a suitable sponsor to come forward centred on the bashing snooker had taken in the first five months of the season in the national press. Sponsors were nervous now of having their products associated with sex and drugs and whatever else might fall out of the cupboard at any point in the future.

'Infidelity, wife desertion, murmurs of arranged matches, and hints of betting coups have brought further discredit,' the *Sunday Telegraph* had warned in mid-January. 'Coral Racing did not renew their UK Championship sponsors contract last November ... Undoubtedly other sponsors are waiting in the marketplace, but not for long. The get-rich-quick attitude of the governing body, bad management and players' back-street behaviour, is killing the game.'

Del reckoned he'd worked a miracle by getting Dulux, at whose inaugural tournament the whole Stevens-Francisco drugs scandal had blown up, to pick up their option for 1986.

His way out of the hole he found himself in over the World Team Cup was to offer the tournament at a special, once-only, knock-down price. Not the £125,000 that Guinness had put up in prize money last year. Not even £100,000, or £75,000. He was only asking £50,000, and he was giving it away for that money. The WPBSA would make up the difference themselves. He exchanged contracts with a new sponsor – Car Care Plan – two weeks before the World Team Cup was due to begin but, in doing so, found that he had only made the hole he was in even deeper.

'The bell begins to toll for ding dong Del' was the headline of a prominent piece in the *Sunday Times* of February 23. The determination of 'the best paid administrator in British sport to run snooker as his personal fiefdom', the paper said, 'may become increasingly untenable ...' 'Today snooker management has taken a far more ambitious and business-like turn than Simmons could ever have envisaged,' it continued, and quoted Barry Hearn on the urgent need for the running of the game to be placed in the hands of 'outside people, specialists with a balanced business approach'.

'Snooker needed someone like Del to make the initial commercial breakthrough,' Barry told the *Sunday Times*. 'But now we are in a secondary stage ... We are a multi-national operation and the next five years are vital. The game has come a long way in the last five years but the *next* five years may be a different story. The warning signs are already there.'

Barry had heard all the stories about sponsors being frightened off by snooker's tarnished image from the horse's mouth. He'd heard them from Del himself, and he frankly didn't buy any of it. 'If you're dealing with a product company – a company that is advertising its *wares* – at the end of the day, mud-wrestling, if it hit the right figures, they would wanna be on,' Barry insisted, a few weeks after the *Sunday Times* story had appeared.

'That's just commonsense. Statement of fact. Embassy, for instance, do not really care about snooker as such. As a sport. Nor do they care about Grand Prix racing. They're up in arms when they get blacked, because all they care about is their name coming over on the box. Which is why they put in the money. Any televised event that's got the hours and hours of coverage of snooker, and the number of people, is good value. Now, alright, some people are not into sponsored sport. But I don't accept that the image of snooker now has fallen to such an extent that people don't want to get in where the *action* is. Because the viewing figures slaughter everything else. Our viewing figures this year are 10 per cent up on last season.

'If you tell me that people turn off snooker when Kirk Stevens comes on because they think he was or is or has been a drug addict, I'll tell you you're crazy. It might be: "Oh that Alex Higgins. Did you read about him in the *News of the World*?" But they don't turn off. Because the colourful characters and what-have-you, even the also-rans, they're all part of the whole scenario.

'At the end of the day, the only thing sponsors wanna see is the numbers. We're all in a numbers world. If you turn round to a sponsor and say, "Oh drugs, women, topless, bottom-less ...", the reaction of a good marketing and advertising man should be: "Tell me what the ratings were." That's the *only* reaction.

'There's lots of reasons sometimes why you don't get sponsors. But, please God, they're *always* there when you need them. If you do it the right way. All these excuses I'm starting to hear about snooker having the wrong image these days, I think people use that as a ready-made. What we in Romford call "a *ready-made*". I'm not interested.'

For his part, Del thought that all this was rich coming from the man who, in his early days as a manager, had regularly phoned him up to ask his advice on what kind of prices he should be asking for his star player. More recently Barry had urged Del to take the £2.3 million the BBC were offering for the world championship contract when Del himself, by holding out, eventually got £4 million.

'I've got a letter on file, where he says bite their hand off at half the price I got from the BBC for the television contract,' Del said late one evening, in his newly refurbished office in Bristol. 'And this is a man who's advocating he can get a lot more money. It's easy after you've done it. It's easy to look back . . .

'I mean, it's a fact that a historian won't get as much money as somebody who can tell you what's happenin' in the future, whether it be in shares or whatever it is. It's like me telling you a racehorse winner after it's won. I'm not advocating gambling, by the way, because I don't think that's any good news at all.

'Do people think then that I should be a promoter like, if you like, Barry Hearn is in the Far East and that I should get fifty-grand, and you as a player should get eight? I'm saying fifty-grand. I don't know what's being got. But is it really such a big deal?

'It's against everything we've tried to put together. We've tried to put together that there's no appearance money in snooker. Now, if Steve Davis, whether he goes out in the first round or the last round, gets a lot more money than, say, Ray Reardon on the Far East tour, it's against the spirit of everything we've tried to build up. It could end up like golf, where Alex Higgins and Jimmy White demand twenty-five-grand to turn up, and your other guy who's down the rankings, he could end up winning the tournament and coming away with the same money or less.'

Del was equally critical of what he considered to be the hopelessly naive notion of having a WPBSA board which, at present, is made up of him, Barry Hearn, an independent

Yorkshire businessman and seven players, wholly comprised of individuals who have no vested interest in the sport. 'Who hasn't got an interest on the board? With possibly one exception, everybody has got a commercial interest. If you're a player and you're number eighteen you want to see at least the top eighteen in the tournament. Rex Williams has got Rex Williams Leisure. So it must help him being chairman of the WPBSA to a degree. You could carry on and on. So now bring in ten guys who've got no interests whatsoever. They're going to know nothing about the game anyway.

'Same as they say: bring in a *professional* man for getting snooker sponsorship. Show me somebody who knows more about snooker sponsorship than me. *I* wanna see 'em. It says here' – he had reached into a pile of magazines behind where he was sitting and fished out a paperback book – 'that there should be more people on the boards of British companies like Del Simmons. Like me. In a *book* that is. An' that was written by the editor of the *Observer*, for chrissakes. It's there in black and white.'

The most stringent and persistent cataloguer of Del's alleged shortcomings as chief executive of the WPBSA had been the monthly magazine, *Snooker Scene* and, in particular, its beady-eyed editor, Clive Everton. As the owner not only of *Snooker Scene* but also of its downmarket sister publication, *Cue World*, as snooker correspondent of the *Sunday Times* and the *Guardian*, proprietor of Everton's News Agency, a professional player and television commentator, Clive Everton was perfectly placed to be both a spanner in the works and a fly permanently stuck in the ointment of the snooker establishment.

Very little gets by Clive Everton and his doughty colleague and former girl-apprentice, Janice Hale. Together they are the Solomon and Bathsheba, the Scylla and Charibdis, the Dempsey and Makepeace of the press room, sniffers out of all scandal and scourge of all inaccuracy and pretension.

Janice, through the medium of her *Snooker Scene* 'Diary' and via the yearbooks of which she is editor, is a fund of both snooker ephemera and invaluable statistical information. Which player achieved a tournament record break in the 1979 Holstein Lager International? Which master-of-ceremonies at which big tournament was formerly an ice hockey referee? Ask Janice. But

Janice also has her sterner side and never hesitates to attack the excesses of what she regards as the gutter press.

'This type of cheap, sensational journalism makes me ashamed of my profession,' she thundered, on the subject of the *Sun*'s front-page Tony Knowles 'knickers' lead. 'There is no excuse for intrusions of this nature into the private life of anyone, least of all a single man whose antics behind closed doors are no-one's business but his own and his sexual partner's ... This is mindless titillation with ruthless disregard for Tony's personal feelings. Just how is he going to feel walking in here on Wednesday to play a match?'

And on press speculation about the breakdown of Ray Reardon's marriage: 'All this would be nasty for any couple and has obviously increased for Ray the kind of stress which can so easily impair the functioning of a professional sportsman.'

Unlike the correspondents of 'the pops', as she calls them, Janice and Clive are rarely seen around the bars and hospitality rooms, and Janice never on her own. Their natural terrain is the moral highground. From here they are able to survey the antics of the other creatures in the snooker jungle and blow the whistle whenever they spot behaviour that seems unbecoming or a boundary that looks in danger of being breached.

From the beginning of the season, Del Simmons and the activities of the World Professional Billiards and Snooker Association had been coming under particularly close scrutiny. An editorial in the March issue of the magazine summarised where *Snooker Scene* stood: 'Snooker found its success by finding a new market – through television ... That was fine until nasty reality started intruding. [It] was too much reality for some to take and what doubled the problem was that the game's elder statesmen – i.e. the governing body – were seen to be unable to cope with what was happening ...

'Neither through formal education nor business experience do they have the background to cope with the ever increasing legal and financial complexities which have begun to dominate the agendas of the WPBSA's monthly meetings ... What snooker desperately needs is someone in authority who is not only authoritative and independent, but, most important of all, trusted enough to be given responsibility for aspects of the game which are, at present, decided upon by the players who mainly constitute the board.'

The *Daily Telegraph* had made much the same point eight months earlier, in an editorial: 'Snooker has made the transition from a small-time sport played in grubby halls to a highly paid, televised, multinational extravaganza in a very few years. To the outside world it seemed to have made the transformation without any of the traumas that afflict the other money-dominated sports. Its stars did not indulge in the pre-pubescent tantrums of many leading tennis players, nor did they follow the example of footballers by abusing their colleagues in newspapers.

'Sadly the reality has not lived up to the image. From the moment of Silvino Francisco's alleged accusation that his rival in the British Open final, Kirk Stevens, was on drugs, snooker's reputation has looked shaky. The ruling body responded by fining Francisco 'for physical and verbal abuse' of Stevens, having earlier introduced drugs' testing at the World Championship. All the tests were negative but this week [June 1985] Stevens announced to the world that he was addicted to cocaine. Whatever the merits of the ruling body's treatment of Francisco, it does seem clear that snooker has a drug problem and has done its best to sweep it under the carpet.'

The Kirk Stevens–Silvino Francisco episode had been allowed to drag on throughout the entire season. The WPBSA's lurching from crisis to crisis had highlighted the weaknesses of a system in which a single body – the WPBSA – functioned as both union and management and, in the case of Francisco, as both judge and jury.

'We wanted to cover it over as much as we could,' Willie Thorne, a WPBSA board member, admitted on television in February. 'We did it the wrong way round.' After taking two world ranking points away from Francisco and fining him £6000, the Association had just announced that the money and points were being returned to Francisco and that his case was to be re-heard by an independent tribunal.

Snooker Scene, however, immediately questioned the independence of a tribunal which was to consist of a former world champion and current ITV commentator who had recently undertaken public relations work on behalf of the WPBSA, and the chairman of Riley Leisure, four of whose contracted players were managed by Barry Hearn, a member of the board which made the decision to act against Francisco in the first place.

As the most senior full-time official of the WPBSA, all these criticisms ended up outside Del's door. All the direct and implied criticisms of the way the Silvino affair had been handled were, in the end, criticisms of him. It was Del who, both the *Sunday Times* and the *Daily Star* alleged, had leaned on Francisco to withdraw his original published statement that, during the 1985 Dulux Open final, Kirk Stevens had been 'as high as a kite on dope'.

Although Silvino had been fined for 'physical and verbal abuse' of his opponent, this charge hadn't been made until after Silvino's (unauthorised) accusations appeared in the *Star*. It was Del, it was being said, who was responsible for Silvino being dropped from the World Team Championship, an additional part of his punishment for being foolish enough to rock the boat.

The WPBSA, Clive Everton concluded, should learn to conduct its affairs with a little less 'defensive paranoia'. They should learn to distinguish between what were legitimate areas of enquiry by the press and what were not, rather than throwing a shroud of secrecy over everything and, that way, always appearing as if they had something to hide. A lack of confidence in how the game administered its own affairs, Everton suggested, was more likely to frighten away sponsors than any number of scandals involving the players.

This was confirmed by Barrie Gill, a former journalist, now chairman of Britain's biggest sports promotion company, CSS. Gill had brought Dulux and Mercantile Credit into snooker, a sport whose clean, across-the-board appeal was attractive to both his clients. 'There are very few games,' he said, 'where granny can actually play her grandson. It is, by its very nature, colourful. It is instantly assimilable by the general public. It is *totally* classless. Starting off from zero, snooker has done an unbelievable job for itself.'

That is the up-side. The down-side, in Gill's experience, is its incestuousness. 'There's too much closeness to the chest. They came to us, we found them two new sponsors but then they became almost paranoid about protecting their investment. The way we operate as a company isn't to set things up and walk away, but the attitude of Del Simmons and his board was: We invited you in, we needed your help, now please piss off.

'This is a private club, almost, making its own rules, keeping its own purse, doing its own PR, issuing its own judgements and participating in its own tournaments. Mickey Duff doesn't make the rules for boxing. The Professional Footballers' Association don't make the rules for football. You can't *be* everything in one package. It isn't possible. You can't run what is potentially a world sport in the TV age, in-house. Because it's inevitable that the vested interests will prevent its expansion.

'The WPBSA are so good at so many things they do, why do they want to do so many other things as well? Their tournament management, for instance, is outstanding. The organisation is meticulous. Everything is timed to the minute. The weakness of the sport, I think, is its strength. It was put together by people who were totally committed and totally dedicated to its success, but who now are not prepared to stand back.

'Snooker has relied on sheer cheek to get it where it is, but it has reached a plateau. The next step is critical. The whole game needs a rethink and a restructure. Above all else, sponsors have to be absolutely sure that the sport is being run objectively. There has to be no *hint* of scandal in its administration, even if there is scandal away from the table. Everything hasn't got to be money, money, money . . . There has to be more promoting and less collecting going on.'

Gill thought they could make a useful start by toning down the WPBSA's Bristol headquarters, whose knee-high Wilton and handcut crystal had left his Dulux and Mercantile clients aghast. They could also stock the WPBSA room at the major tournaments with something more run-of-the-mill than vintage champagne. The whole thing generally, he thought, had to be less totally-Del-boy-over-the-top.

Around the end of February, word started to leak out about Goya withdrawing after only one year as sponsors of the Goya Matchroom trophy. As soon as it became official, David Fisher submitted an offer to become the replacement sponsor at the same money on behalf of BCE.

9 Changing a person's life

Willie Thorne signed with Matchroom in February. The signing
went out live on national television at the beginning of the Dulux
Open and Barry made the usual ebullient noises about improving
the marketing mix and making Willie a millionaire inside five
years.

He had been watching Willie, he said, since the disaster of his
defeat by Davis in the final of the Coral UK in November,
when he crashed out in the final session after being six frames
ahead. He had watched Willie to see how he stood up after
that, and he had stood up well enough to suddenly be an interesting proposition. He hadn't lost his bum. Barry thought the Coral
had been Willie's coming-of-age.

'It was getting to where I was losing business,' Barry said.
'I'm running out of players. I'm getting full-up on Davis, pretty
well full-up on Taylor, Griffiths and Meo reasonable. But at
the end of the day I need other people. I need more back-up. So
I phoned Willie, I said I'm looking at it, and he said: "How
much d'you want?" Which is exactly the answer I look for. I
always say, "If they don't think it's a compliment me looking
after 'em, I don't want 'em either." Well, he's got his watch
now'.

It had all happened very quickly. Willie himself had had to
buy out his contract with his former manager, because Barry's
attitude is that if they don't come to him 'clean', then they don't
come. 'I wouldn't pay a ha'penny,' he stresses. 'For *anybody*.'

In fact, the day before he became a Matchroom Professional,
Willie had been on the point of signing with Howard Kruger.

Aitch later said that he thought Willie was 'a berk'; he'd offered him a better deal all across the board than Barry Hearn had. Willie had turned round and told him himself, Aitch said, that he thought that what he was doing was a mistake. 'An hour before he was due to go on television and sign with Hearn, Willie called me. "I know in my heart and in my water I'm doing wrong," he said. "I've made a mistake. And the only reason is, you've got no track record." All his friends advised him to sign with me.'

Cliff Thorburn's reaction to the news of this latest swelling of the Matchroom ranks – 'I wouldn't want to be number five. I wouldn't want to be thrown a couple of dog biscuits' – had been typical. But what other way could Willie jump? Howard Kruger had only been in snooker a few months. He was untested. The only way anybody had of judging his capabilities as a manager was to look at Tony Knowles. And Tony Knowles, in the week that Aitch was trying to persuade Willie to entrust his future to him, was hardly a picture of happiness and health.

He discharged himself from hospital to play his second match in the Dulux, got beat and returned to hospital again. He was going to pieces, physically. And many onlookers were of the opinion that there was only one man to blame. 'Howard Kruger', one of the better-read of the reptiles said, 'is to the world of sports management what Wackford Squeers was to the world of education.'

Aitch's reply to these criticisms was that, although the build-up of stress caused by the *Sun*'s 'knickers' story might be the immediate cause of Tony's problems, the deeper reason was fifteen and a half years of fast living taking their revenge. It was Aitch, after all, who had got Tony out of the knickers mess by organising a press conference and having a doctor on hand to administer a huge vitamin injection seconds before Tony went out to face 'the vultures'. As soon as he came out of hospital this time, he was going to pack Tony off to a health farm for two weeks. 'He's actually a very sensitive, insecure guy,' Aitch said.

But, his critics persisted, the night before Tony's semi-final against Cliff Thorburn in the Benson and Hedges just three weeks earlier, Aitch and Tony had been seen at Tramp in Mayfair in the early hours of the morning. Not so, Aitch said. It had been Blondes in Albemarle Street and it had been in Tony's own best interests that they were there. It was the only sure way to relax him before a big match. 'He's the sort of person, if I say, "I want you in bed at ten o'clock," he won't sleep. He'll watch the video till four in the morning. So I take him out for a dinner. What can I tell you? You can't get him to change overnight.'

Aitch had got Tony a contract with Vidal Sassoon. He could walk into any Sassoon salon anywhere in the world and have his hair styled for free. One of the first things he'd done when he took Tony on was to get rid of the old 'seventies style he wore his hair in, with the high crown and the unsightly kink at the back, and replace it with something much more un-Bolton and up-to-date. Tony never did have much idea when it came to his appearance. 'Send Tony into a shop', his previous manager said, 'and you could bet your life he'd come out with the wrong thing.'

Aitch had phased out the 'Saturday Night Fever' strides and the black shirts with the divvy diamante bibs. 'TK' was looking less like Tom Jones these days and more like Aitch. 'He likes the way I dress. I know the way I should look: four hundred- to five hundred-pound suits. He does what I tell him now. He phones the office every day to ask what he should wear.'

None of this had been enough to keep Tony out of Beaumont Hospital in Bolton, though. For five months he had ignored the jokes and the sniggers and pretended that he didn't know the first thing that sprung to people's minds when he walked into a room or what people were saying about him behind his back. His results hadn't been brilliant, but they hadn't been a total nightmare either. He had done what Howard had told him to do and had toughed it out.

The week before the Dulux British Open, however, his whole body had started to erupt in huge abscesses and boils. Some of them measured as much as seven inches across and eventually had to be cut. His back and chest looked like satellite pictures of the moon, and the doctors at the Beaumont were trying to work out the cause. The circuit was abuzz with rumours that he was seriously, maybe even terminally, ill.

*

David Roe and Mark Thompson were rivals but they were also good friends. David's style, which was safe and solid, attractive but not flashy, reflected the influence of the two players he admired most, Steve Davis and Cliff Thorburn. Mark, David's regular practice partner, was a player straight out of the Alex Higgins–Jimmy White school. At 18, he had become the British Junior champion and, a year and a half later, stood two places above David Roe in the *Snooker Scene* amateur rankings.

David Roe and Mark Thompson spent the best part of every day in each other's company, mostly down at the Cue Ball Club in Derby, where the man who managed both of them had his base.

Like David, Mark Thompson had started playing snooker before he was in his teens. Unlike David, though, Mark was from what a friend of his describes as 'one of the struggling families – he was known throughout Derby as a young lad who had nothing and was coming through'. Winning the British Junior championship was his passport to 'Junior Pot Black'. Being on television was seen as a sure sign that he was on his way.

Within the snooker world of the West Midlands, Mark Thompson was regarded as the new Jimmy White. A number of local businessmen had expressed interest in backing him and, according to Mark's friend, Dave Freeman, at least one definite offer had been made: 'He often talked about a well-off person in Ashbourne who had a fun-pub with a wine bar and a couple of pool tables downstairs. He drove round in an XJS and to Mark that was his goal. Snooker changes a person's life and, to Mark, that was it then.'

Dave Freeman, who was physically much bigger than Mark and more experienced, functioned as his driver and his guide to the grown-up pleasures of life away from the table. It was in Dave's company that Mark started to go to the Pink Coconut, the Grand Casino, and the Slick Chick 'fun-drinkery', which all stood in a row next to the Pyramid snooker club in Colyear Street in Derby. It was in Dave's Capri ('He's a nut-jobber wi' car,' David Roe says) that Mark would travel to London to compete in the 'graveyard' all-nighters at clubs in Tottenham and Leytonstone.

Dave would leave his job on a construction site on the M42 at five o'clock, pick Mark up at home and be in London well before closing time. Mark would play through the night until dawn and often later, Dave would have a few side-bets on him and be back on the site before anybody had had a chance to notice that he was missing. 'He was just easy,' Dave Freeman says of Mark in those days. 'Mark Thompson, free and easy.'

One Wednesday in the middle of November 1984, Dave drove Mark the few miles from Derby to Chesterfield to play a match in the Chesterfield and District League, which he easily won. He had made half a dozen one-hundred-plus breaks in a single practice session a few days earlier. Willie Thorne was one of Mark Thompson's better-known 'scalps'.

They called in at a pub where a live group was playing on the way home, and Dave dropped Mark off at his bus-stop in the centre of Derby. They arranged to meet again at the Cue Ball Club at ten o'clock the following morning.

The following morning, Jean, Mark's mother, woke him early. It was his turn to do the pots. Afterwards he got on his pushbike and rode to a nearby supermarket to buy some pet food. He was home before eleven. Returning home later in the day, Jean Thompson went up to Mark's room. The mattress from his bed was on the floor. Mark was on it and he was dead. He had pulled a plastic bag over his head and a rope was knotted around his neck.

Some weeks later, the Derby coroner recorded a verdict of suicide. It was mystifying, he said, why a person as popular and as likeable as Mark, with everything to live for, and no record of depression, should have done such a thing. He was 19.

Fifteen months after Mark Thompson's death, his family and friends were as mystified as they had been on the day it occurred. Various explanations had been floated: he was becoming irritated at not making more money from snooker (he had won about £2,500 in the twelve months before he died); he was finding it frustrating to be beaten by steady, solid players of less talent but with more knowledge and experience than himself; he was about to be catapulted into a professional world he was uncertain he wanted to join; he was developing an anxiety neurosis about his cue – 'A Freudian psychologist would no doubt have diagnosed adolescent sexual fears from this obsession with a classic sexual symbol', Clive Everton noted in *Snooker Scene*, in an article called

'How pressure killed'. But none of them made it any easier to come to terms with the simple facts, which were these: one day Mark Thompson was alive and apparently happy, and the next he was dead.

David Roe's reaction had been to give up playing for what was a long time for him, two weeks. 'But I wasn't there — really there — for two months. I was rubbish. It done me head in . . . It's the biggest mystery I'll ever know.'

Dave Freeman thought it was 'some kind of big game going off' when he first heard. When he realised it wasn't, he went out to the Pink Coconut and got drunker than he'd ever been. 'I couldn't understand if there was something wrong with him why he didn't come to me. If we were that close. I got blown out my head. There were two rooms in the club, one with funky music and one slow. And going from one to the other, one to the other, made you feel really weird. A crazy feeling that was. Me and another friend of Mark's, we cried together.'

The final of the 1986 Dulux British Open was between Steve Davis and Willie Thorne. It was a re-run of their Coral UK final of three months earlier.

David Roe was one of the many in Derby who would have liked to have gone, but there were no tickets available. Instead he got into his father's car and travelled to Huntingdon to play in a competition there.

That same Sunday of the Dulux final, the Derbyshire Amateur Championships were being played in the Derby branch of the Breaks chain of snooker clubs, which was situated in a recently up-graded neighbourhood on the edge of the city centre.

Dave Freeman was one of the competitors. Out of work for the time being, he said his girlfriend had paid his entry fee. If he could win this, he said, he had a sponsor ready and waiting to come in. It was much harder getting sponsorship in the West Midlands than in London, and therefore the competition was much fiercer; Midlands players were much keener to win, he said. Dave Freeman's was the only black face in Breaks.

Also competing in the county championship that Sunday was a slight, slightly hunched man in beige trousers with a white open-necked shirt under his beige pullover. Geoff Thompson was Mark Thompson's father. He had taught Mark to play at Derby Mechanics Institute, where he had learned to play himself as a boy, and had coached Mark until Mark had outgrown him at around the age of thirteen.

Geoff Thompson's version of his son's last night differed slightly from Dave Freeman's. Instead of dropping Mark off at his bus-stop, Geoff Thompson said that both boys joined him at the Pink Coconut and stayed there drinking until about 2.00 am. He said that Mark had got into the habit of going to bed late and getting up late, usually not much before lunchtime.

Geoff Thompson didn't live with Mark's mother any longer. They had split up the year before Mark committed suicide, after being married for twenty years. Dave Freeman said that Mark found it embarrassing when he walked into the Pyramid Club and found his father there with his girlfriend. But nobody was suggesting that that had been enough to make him go into his bedroom at half past ten on a Thursday morning and pull a plastic bag over his head.

Geoff Thompson didn't have an any more plausible answer than anybody else's for the terrible thing that was still a presence in all their lives. 'Mark didn't suffer from nerves. He was in the mood or he wasn't. If he was in the mood, nobody could beat him. If his play went off, he'd take a week away and go fishing,' he had told a reporter in the immediate aftermath of Mark's death. But now he said he wasn't so sure about Mark's ability to handle pressure. There was the occasion of his 'Junior Pot Black' appearance in 1983. Mark was embarrassed about the make-up the TV people made him wear to blot out the perspiration. And he had embarrassed himself by going all to pieces in his semi-final.

The winner of that semi-final had gone on to win the tournament. Now Geoff saw young John Parrot on the television trading one-liners with David Vine. 'I would've backed our Mark eight times out of ten,' he said, 'but Parrot was always inclined to be in the right environment at the right time with people who could push him on. His dad had a table. There was a bit of money from somewhere floating about. It goes a long way in this game.'

Geoff had gone out of the Derbyshire championships, which

were still continuing upstairs at Breaks, in the last eight. As well as playing snooker to county standard, he coaches and referees. He was sitting among the rattan furniture and potplants in the 'family area' at the club, pouring himself a pot of tea, relaxing, when the doors opened and David Roe and his father came in.

David had qualified to turn professional in the season which would begin in just a few months' time. He had also qualified for the final rounds of the competition he had been playing in that afternoon, but the Roes seemed reluctant to talk about David's success at Huntingdon in front of Geoff Thompson, as if it was in poor taste.

'You get them there and they don't want to know you. They don't even get you a cup of tea,' David's father said to Geoff, who chuckled and nodded his head. There was a silence then between the two men in which the pop music which had been playing all the time on a tape in the background suddenly sounded very loud. Their faces were reflected dimly in the glass panel which separated the playing area and the lounge: two fathers whose lives had seemed destined to run in tandem as they followed the achievements of their sons but whose meetings now were full of awkward silences like this.

Dave Freeman had also gone out in the quarter-finals of the county championship at Breaks. He wasn't a natural player, he confessed, not like Mark. But he liked performing in front of people. You didn't feel the pressure when you were hungry to win. He liked 'the glamour' of the snooker world.

Dave had taped Mark's one appearance on television and he had played it a lot in the last fifteen months. He had freeze-framed it and rewound it and stared at it without blinking, trying to find out what happened? Why? What forces propelled him from there to here?

'I like to be reminded of him and his mannerisms. Everybody's got these little characteristics of his own,' Dave Freeman said.

10 *Where the clean-cut came from*

Whoever won the Dulux Open (Steve won it), Matchroom had been sure of bagging their biggest–ever winnings from a single tournament – £111,000.

Davis had beaten Higgins in the semi-finals on the day that it had been announced that, after a rocky, ten–year relationship, Alex was finally leaving Del Simmons to join Howard Kruger. This was only a few days after the Hurricane had sauntered into the press room and made the dramatic announcement that he felt his days in snooker were numbered.

'I'm not going to be at the top for much longer – three or four years and that will be it,' he'd said. 'I don't like the hassle any more. I'd like to have a good hard four years at snooker and then quit the game and get on with life.'

Nobody, of course, had believed a word of it, any more than they believed that Alex was going to change the habits of a lifetime and become a reformed character now that he was under new management. An illustration of the up–hill nature of the task that Aitch and, on the PR side, Greg, had set themselves was the man who staggered into the VIP section to watch Alex play Steve Davis in the Dulux just hours after the brave new dawn of his career had been announced.

A friend of Alex's, he was like Arthur Haynes or Jimmy James playing their celebrated variety–hall drunk. He wasn't as old as either of the two comedians in their heyday, but his props – the shapeless suit, the flapping soles, the cigarette dribbling ash down his tie – could have been on loan. The seats he was attempting to reach were on a platform at the side of the scorers' desk, but they might as well have been at the summit of Ben Nevis.

In order to sit down, he had to negotiate three wooden stairs. He got one foot on the first stair but, before his other foot could join it, staggered backwards, slopping the beer that was in the pint glass in his right hand over the television cables and his shoes. In his left hand he was clutching a tumblerful of whisky which made it even more difficult for him to climb the stairs and remain upright. After trying to get past the first step several more times and failing, this realisation seemed to suddenly hit him: carefully placing the whisky on one side of the step and the lager on the other, he moved forward on his hands and knees.

Once seated, he hooked a pair of national health glasses with one arm missing over one ear, watched Steve Davis string together a few shots, squinted at the scoreboard, muttered, belched and exited stage-right, forgetting to use the stairs. A few seconds later the doors re-opened and he re-appeared flashing his 'Player's guest' badge at the officials: he'd left his drinks on the floor under his chair and he was insisting on reclaiming them.

Everybody had told Howard Kruger he was a fool to get involved with Alex Higgins. 'How much did Del pay you?' they'd asked him at the press conference. But, three weeks later, he seemed to be bearing up under the strain. So far, Aitch said, Alex hadn't been giving him any aggravation. The opposite, in fact.

'I was very, very tough', Aitch said, 'the first time I met with Alex, because I wasn't sure then whether I wanted an involvement with him or not. But what can I tell you? I'm used to dealing with artistic-stroke-temperamental people. Pop stars. And that's what he cried out to me. That he wanted to be treated correctly, which he has never been in the past. I wouldn't try to knock the rough edges off Alex. He's real. But he's got to put it together now. He's been screwing around long enough.'

Aitch said he'd got Alex the Vidal Sassoon freebie, same as Jimmy and Tony. Greg had just got him a double-page spread in *Ritz*, the glitterati-type gossip magazine. 'I have a lot of people in the City,' Howard said. 'The chairmen of big public companies.

Merchant bankers. Leisure Investments. Pleasurama. Alex has just spent four days with me rubbing hands with City people, and he arrived on time, drank in moderation, came one hundred per cent suited up. He looked fantastic. He handled it like a true pro.

'"Everything I do", I told him, "is professional. Everything you do is now a reflection of me," With me now it's all yes-sir no-sir. He calls me boss. It works.'

Alex was representing Ireland 'A' in the World Team Championships. Jimmy and Tony were playing with Steve Davis in the England Team, and they were all together in the foyer-sized hospitality suite in the Conference Centre which reared above the amusement arcades, souvenir shops and wind-lashed palm trees on Bournemouth seafront.

Alex looked better than he had all season: alert, well-groomed, scab-free. 'I've renounced the devil,' he said. Tony had been out of hospital for a fortnight and all the physical symptoms of his illness – the boils and abscesses – had disappeared. Jimmy, affable as ever, was heavily fancied for the World Championships, which were less than a month away. Everything seemed to be on the up-and-up for 'Framework', as the snooker arm of the Kruger Organisation's multi-interest entertainment group was now called. There was only one small cloud on the horizon: the *Sunday People* was due to start running a new series of 'disclosures' as part of their world championship build-up, and the first one was scheduled to appear the following day.

Geoff Lomas – 'The man who knows all the secrets of the wild stars of snooker' – had acted as an agent for Alex, Jimmy, and Tony, as well as for Kirk Stevens and other players, at some point in the past. Since his contractual ties had been dissolved, he had repeatedly sold his reminiscences and 'exclusives' to the popular papers. It was Lomas who Tony Knowles still suspected of being responsible for the content of the 'Superstud' articles in the *Sun* in 1984, which he claims he was just recovering from when the 'knickers' accusations appeared and sent him reeling back to square one.

On this occasion, however, Tony believed he had something which he had never been able to claim before: a manager who was on the ball, and the strength of numbers. It was his conviction that he, Alex and Kirk had been the butt of all the scandalmongers because they had been out on their own. Barry

Hearn, on the other hand, had always been able to threaten collective action should anything damaging to himself or any of his players appear.

'The papers will pick on anybody who can't retaliate,' Tony said, 'and they've been taking advantage for years. But notice they haven't taken advantage of Hearn if his players have done anything wrong. I could tell you plenty which would make his pretty-boys look . . . You've got to have a lot of bargaining power to stop things like that. You've got to be able to go in mob-handed.'

'If somebody had been there in the past to slap wrists for Alex', Howard said, 'and sue the papers, not a lot of that stuff would have got out. Like this particular time, this crap that's going on tomorrow, we've subpoenaed the paper and now they're double-checking all their facts. Simply because they know that a lawyer's involved. It might just stop that little odd comment that could be the one everything hinges on. All I know is that it's going to be shitty tomorrow, and double-shitty next week.'

Whether because of the pressure that Alex's new management had been able to bring to bear, or because their source was beginning to dry up, 'the paper that shakes out the real stories' the following morning served up a number of warmed-over tales about 'gangsters' threatening to smash Alex's fingers, his antics on his stag-night and his 'punch-ups' ('Lynn flew at Alex, claws out') with his wife.

'Same old bloody nonsense' an elderly man rumbled early that morning as he crossed the foyer of the Carlton Hotel in Bournemouth, heading for the exit and his waiting car. He was wearing a pair of beige, slightly raised snakeskin shoes with gold tags across them, from which the trees had been removed at the last minute; a 'golfing' sweater covered in a geometric design of pink and grey; a cashmere jacket, grey razor-creased trousers and the sort of parboiled, crusty expression that only men of his age and eminence seem able to get away with. As he strapped himself into the seat next to the driver, an agreeable disgruntledness and a musky-sweet aroma enveloped him.

Ted Lowe is 'The Voice of Snooker'. But even without opening his mouth, his formality of manner and the immaculateness of his turnout suggests the world of smoke-room stewards and grand hotels and the quiet and civility of the Leicester Square Hall of which he was general manager throughout the 1940s and 50s. The Voice of Snooker is now resident in a house called Autumn Lodge in a retirement resort further along the coast from Bournemouth, and he brings a little bit of the De la Warr Pavilion, Bexhill-on-Sea, with its lilting organ music and its chinking tea-drinkers, with him, wherever he goes.

'It seemed clear to me that once an English person had reached Bexhill-on-Sea he had no intention of going any further,' Paul Theroux noted during his journey around the perimeter of Britain at the beginning of the decade. 'This was, so to speak, the edge of the cliff . . . Another Surbiton-on-Sea, the solidest London suburb grafted onto the solidest stretch of the south-east coast, the best of both worlds . . . [It was] the quintessential England . . . secretive, rose-growing, dog-loving, window-washing, church-going, law-abiding, grumpy, library-using, tea-drinking, fussy and inflexible England.'

It is possible that this is what the voice of 'whispering' Ted Lowe – like the voices of Dan Maskell in tennis, and John Arlott in cricket – embodies for many of the snooker-addicted millions. By turns sonorous and sentimental, laced with malapropisms and ancient locutions, redolent of dog-baskets and antimacassars over uncut moquette, it is a voice which the Queen Mother would be pleased to entertain to tea.

'I made it respectable by insisting that they wear evening-dress from day one of "Pot Black" in 1969,' Ted stoutly maintains. 'The same as at Leicester Square, I stipulated that every player must sign a contract by which they were obliged to wear a dark suit during the day and a tuxedo in the evenings. Clark McConachy, for instance, (World Professional Billiards finalist, 1932; world champion, 1951) once wanted to go on as he was, but I made him change. We used to have dinner-parties after the finals at which full evening dress was obligatory for every male attending.

'And by insisting on these same standards at 'Pot Black' from the beginning, I gave snooker the up-market image it has today. That's where the clean-cut came from and where the old ladies came into it. *I* brought the women and the children and all the other people who had never *thought* about watching a game of snooker, whatever your Barry Hearns and the rest of them might claim today.'

Needless to say, Ted Lowe is the declared enemy of the forces of lasciviousness and greed which he believes are gnawing away at the fabric of snooker; he is the scourge of the bad-boys and their followers who, for reasons unknown to him, seem hellbent on dragging snooker through the dirt. Ted personally got Alex Higgins banned from 'Pot Black' for five years, for threatening to walk out in the middle of recording the 1973 series and for other behaviour unbecoming of a sportsman and a gentleman. 'He had three girls in his dressing room, black as the ace of spades, straight off the streets of Birmingham,' Ted said, his jowls quivering, still aghast at the memory.

To Ted, the Hurricane is the epitome of everything that could eventually bring the house of snooker crashing to the ground. He thinks it's outrageous, for example, that Higgins, on the strength of some doctor's letter, gets away with not wearing a tie. 'Part of their job is to entertain the public, and to do that they should *dress* the part. Steve Davis, of course, always dresses impeccably, acts correctly and is constantly straining for perfection in everything he does. You've got Ray Reardon, who's an ambassador of the sport. You've got Dennis Taylor, who's a personality in the game . . .

'But when you come to the other end of it, what d'you see? They're walking around in jeans, dirty shirts, not turning up on time. They don't even put in an appearance at the sponsors' parties, which is a common courtesy, as far as I'm concerned. But perhaps that's today's world. You look at these chat shows and see the state of some of these so-called stars who come on. Open shirts showing all their bellies. Necklaces. Medallions. *Plimsolls*, for Christ's sake. Can you imagine walking into a boardroom and facing your chairman dressed like that? I think it's disgraceful. No wonder the youngsters of today are so undisciplined.

'I personally couldn't wear a pair of blue shoes with brown trousers, and vicky versee. Everything has to match, even the braces. This is the kind of example the younger players should be setting. But it comes too *easy* – as it does in many other things of course – for too little. Every player I talk to now, he's got his manager. People I've never heard of. Howard what's-his-name. These are the things I'm not too sure about, creeping into the game.'

The errand which Ted was on his way to fulfil this Sunday morning was much more the kind of thing he thought the papers *should* be writing about. A couple of weeks earlier, 'Jim'll Fix It', the ratings-topping television programme in which Jimmy Savile plays fairy godmother to the nation's young-at-heart, had swung into action and made good the wish of a young spina-bifida sufferer to play Steve Davis at snooker. A small (Riley) table had been set up in the Matchroom, David Vine had been on hand to make the introductions and all that was needed now was one of Ted Lowe's 'whispering' voice-overs to lend the final patina of authenticity. He had two hours to do this at the BBC's studios in Southampton before he was due back in Bournemouth to begin his commentary of the afternoon's World Team Cup final.

'We all go out of our way to help a sad little chappie like this. But do you read about it in the papers? You do not,' Ted said as the car approached a fortess-like building near the docks. 'But if Steve had slept with some girl off the street, they'd write about that, wouldn't they? Bet your life on it. The world's upside down.'

BBC Southampton was more or less deserted, but a young producer from 'Jim'll Fix It' and several technicians were waiting on an upper floor. The item had been allocated a running-time of twelve minutes, and they ran it on a monitor a couple of times, earmarking a few places where it might be useful for Ted to come in, before he retired to a sound-studio to do the recording.

He acquired his famous technique at Leicester Square Hall in the early 'fifties when, sitting in the audience with a lip-mike, he was obliged to talk in a low rumble so that the players wouldn't hear him. 'If somebody so much as coughed in those days', he said, 'the play would stop and you'd be looked at. And there was no drinking, no fear.'

Ted sat in one half of the studio with 'cans' on, the producer sat on the other side of a glass partition, adjacent to him, and they communicated via a microphone. Ted followed the action on a small monitor on the table in front of him and extemporised a few comments around what was happening. He couldn't get into the swing of it at the beginning, though, until he suddenly diagnosed the reason: he was talking into an open mike, when he was used to addressing his remarks to the kind that clamped over the lower half of the face like a muzzle. Once one of those had been run to ground, the hesitancy disappeared and he was his usual gravel-and-molasses, No-Orchids-For-Miss-Blandish self.

'Okay,' the young producer, who was quite frank in admitting his ignorance of snooker and all its workings, said to somebody in another room. 'Are we in a go state, Neville? . . . Right, give us something at the top of that, if you would, Ted.'

'And is there a sign of nerves creeping in?' Ted breathed, as the subject of the film, whose name was Simon, rolled his wheelchair up to the table. A close-up of Simon's hands on the half-butt also provided a tight-shot of the 'Riley' logo, considerably increased in dimensions for the occasion.

'A "double-kiss", is that what you say, Ted? Oh that's marvellous,' the producer encouraged him. 'Excellent. Okay then, once more with feeling. Um, just one thing, Ted. That ball that you're calling blue, is actually red.' He shut off his microphone. 'I never thought of a colour monitor,' he confessed.

This was this particular producer's last piece for 'Jim'll Fix It'. He was about to jump on another bus, as he put it. He was moving over to sit-com. As a swansong, though, he couldn't have hoped for a better, more human interest-packed item. 'Look at that face', he said as, on the screen, Simon grinned up at Steve Davis after potting a long black, and Robbo's voice could be heard in the background going 'Yaaays!' 'He's really into this snooker.'

'A *happy* Simon Fricker,' Ted emphasised in his cubicle next door. The camera pulled back from Simon's face then to take in the whole set. This was the 'master-shot', the shot that appeared on the screen most often, and the central image in it was a giant, triangular 'Matchroom' toiletries logo. Eat your heart out, David Fisher!

The BBC's man admitted that the plug was 'rather blatant' and, in the circumstances, perhaps in less than the best of taste. But they needed the facilities and they needed Davis and, with the kind of budget they were running on, this was the only way they were going to get them. 'We couldn't begin to pay Davis's fee, we needed a club and therefore we couldn't have done it without Hearn. But I don't see that it's *that* bad. It's good news for Riley, good news for Goya and Matchroom, good news for the Beeb and very good news for the boy, of course.'

It wasn't the first time Steve had helped 'fix it' for somebody less fortunate than himself. He had appeared on the programme a few years earlier and as a result of that appearance, Barry later boasted, he had added 14p to a client's share price.

Barry was equally unqueasy about the implications of this latest caper. '*Good* piece! Good *piece!*' he beamed, some time after the piece had gone out without causing any ripples. 'I'm a professional in what we do. And my game is to *maximise* the involvement of my players, my products and my clients. I'm a business animal.'

Didn't he think that, at least on this occasion, he had pressed his advantage too far? Didn't he think it was a good enough commercial for Davis as it stood? Without the extra plugs for Goya and Riley? Didn't there come a point when enough was enough? He laughed. He dismissed this as a hopelessly sentimental notion.

'What is enough? Who's judging the enough? We supply the club, we close the club down all day, we strip the table down, we let 'em make so much mess I can't begin to tell you. There was thirty-seven technicians in the club that were fed all day . . . I'm *entitled*. I'm entitled to say I would like this, I want that, I want so many close-ups, so many probes, so many verbal mentions . . . Because that's part of the deal. That's the package. Now, I mean, I'm commercial enough. I could've done without it. But why should I? If it's there to be had? I mean, I think it's just natural.

'The fact is, we bent over backwards to put on the best show we could put on. Nobody could've put on a better show than that. It was a super slot for the boy, and he had everything created for him . . .

'I don't see why I should do all this without . . . I don't see why I should supply everything for everybody all the time and be the good-guy, if there's not value on both sides. And that's

170

how the world gets on. It's an I'll-scratch-your-back, you-scratch-my-back world we live in. I mean, we do TV *all* the time. And d'you know the reason they work with us? The reason they work with us is that *it always happens*. We're *very* professional.'

Barry stopped there. He was getting too serious. Serious isn't Barry's style. He slapped his palms on his desk. He laughed. 'It's not the *Merchant of Venice*', he said, the laughs coming from his belly now, 'but it's close.'

11 *The commercial risk*

At the end of the final programme of the final series of 'Junior Pot Black' in 1983 – the programme in which Mark Thompson made his only television appearance – a small boy stepped forward to receive a 'personality' award which had been especially created for him.

He was spotty, shy, and slightly awkward, but eclipsing all that was the openness and obvious appetite for life that had made the programme's producers want to mark his contribution to the series. The dove-grey shoes that he wore with his dark, off-the-peg three piece were a sure sign that he had all the makings of a 'personality' (read 'bad-boy') player.

Although he looked younger, he had been fourteen when he made such a hit with the viewing audience. In between times, he had become Scotland's youngest amateur champion and, at the age of sixteen, the world's youngest full-time professional. Now, in March 1986, he was poised to become the youngest ever winner of the Scottish professional title and, providing he won the series of qualifying matches which started ten days later, the youngest player ever to compete in the world championships at Sheffield.

At seventeen, Stephen Hendry was still recognisable as the chubby boy in the pale grey winklepickers. He was taller and the chubbiness had drained away leaving the familiar desiccated, blue-tinged pallor. But the pudding-basin haircut was the same, same fashionable footwear (white-socks-and-loafers), same full, rather fleshy mouth. What was different about him was less easy to pin down.

He was well-dressed, well-mannered, friendly and articulate.

Where once he had been irrepressible, however, he was now guarded and reserved. The sparkiness that had been rewarded by the producers of 'Junior Pot Black' had been replaced by a coolness and slightly spooky self-possession. 'Frightening', Ann Yates, the WPBSA's press officer, would call his performance at his first press conference during the world championship qualifying rounds. 'They kept at him, but he said nothing wrong. Not a flicker of an eyelid out of place,' she'd say. 'Nothing. It was frightening. It frightened me. It can't be natural, not for a seventeen-year-old.'

A year earlier, Stephen hadn't performed as well as expected at the world amateur championships in Dublin. This had been put down to the break-up of his parents' marriage. And, although he was still close to both of them – he lived with his mother and brother in Edinburgh; his father was his driver – his parents' separation did in some way account for his new, sober approach to life.

The biggest single influence on the development of his personality, though, was the Glasgow businessman who had become his manager a few months earlier. Ian Doyle had never met Barry Hearn, but he had read the Barry Hearn Handbook; A Romford Way of Knowledge repeatedly, cover-to-cover, and seemed intent on following it to the letter. When he said that Stephen was going to be 'the new Steve Davis' (which he did at least three times per interview) he didn't mean it journalistically. He meant it in the literal sense. Where Steve had led, Stephen was to follow.

Ian Doyle's first act on signing Stephen had been to register him as a company. Gordon, Stephen's father, became Stephen Hendry Snooker Limited's first (and so far only) employee. Stephen, as far as Ian Doyle was concerned, was as much a business as the pots-and-pans wholesalers that had earned him his first million, and his rate of growth and expansion would be plotted along similar, business-like lines.

Win the Scottish Championship in two years, the World Championship in four. That was the plan. Rather, that *had been* the plan. Three-quarters of the way through his first season as a professional, Stephen seemed about to take the Scottish championship at his first attempt. It was no coincidence that BBC Scotland were televising the final live for the first time.

*

'Archie Macpherson's here! . . . Have you seen, Archie Macpherson's here'. The word spread like wildfire around Marco's Leisure, in Grove Street, in Edinburgh, that Archie Macpherson, the Mr Big of television sport in Scotland, was in attendance. Archie unbelted his trenchcoat in the centre of the packed family-area at Marco's and shucked it off his shoulders as nonchalantly as if he was in his own living-room. Also in attendance, but causing rather less excitement, was Ted Lowe, who had been flown in to certify that Stephen Hendry versus Matt Gibson was a major snookering occasion.

The Scottish National Championship had in fact only been revived in 1979. It was an example of how close snooker had come to extinction that the only Scotsman ever to have won the world title, Walter Donaldson, turned the billiard room at his Buckinghamshire home into a cowshed and broke up the slates of his table to lay a path, in the mid-'fifties.

The dominant figure in Scottish snooker since the boom had been Murdo Macleod, a former baker, in his thirties, who suffered the considerable disadvantage of choking every time he appeared on television. Stephen Hendry had beaten Macleod, the holder, in the quarter-finals of the Scottish Championship and now the only thing between him and the title was a roly-poly, totally bald man whose head blinked like a motorway crash warning signal under the accentuated TV lighting.

Stephen, in contrast, remained as dry as parchment and apparently as nerveless as the piece of wood he held in his fingers. It was this 'killer' quality, combined with a playing style as fast and almost as intuitive as Jimmy White's, that had first brought him to Ian Doyle's attention. In addition to his ironmongery business, Ian Doyle and his partner had diversified in the early 'eighties and opened a snooker centre, Spencer's, in Stirling. There was a table reserved for Stephen's exclusive use at Spencer's and, when not out on the road taking part in competitions, it was here that he practised for seven to eight hours every day.

A firm believer in the old-fashioned virtues of hard work and self-reliance – 'God helps those who help themselves' is the maxim which has ruled his life – Ian Doyle has drummed it into Stephen that a single-minded dedication comparable to that of Steve Davis's is the only way he is going to make any headway in the game. He has laid competition-quality cloth on the table at Spencer's and erected a TV-style lighting rig above it, and he calls the club at eleven every morning to make sure Stephen has clocked in.

Ian Doyle will himself have already been at work for several hours by then, and he feels it not unreasonable that Stephen should follow his example. 'Business is my life,' Doyle says. 'I love business. Business is the biggest part of my life by a long way. If my wife ever wants to see me she knows where she's got to come: to work. And it wasn't difficult getting it over to Stephen that, if he wants our lifestyle – the Bahamas, America – then he's got to graft. It's like a house: if you don't have a foundation, your house is going to blow down. Most of these young players live in a fool's paradise.'

Stephen had actually signed up with a south-east of England promoter when he was still at school. Ian Doyle had bought out that contract with twelve months still to run, and had immediately put him into a series of money matches against Scotland's top professionals to get him competition-tough.

'Barry Hearn brought big names down to Romford before Steve turned professional. We've done it the other way about. We've sent Stephen out to the public halls to play players on their own tables. The home guy is always the one the folks in the club are supporting, so you go in and find the atmosphere faintly hostile. They're all betting their own man. After two or three frames, though, the hostility seems to disappear. They're right behind you as you go out the door, because they know they've seen a player. Steve Davis at the same age had maybe forty per cent of the ability Stephen does. There's nobody outside Higgins and White who reads the game as instinctively. The boy has such an elegance round the table. He's got this magnetic appeal.'

Stephen Hendry was born in 1969, the year 'Pot Black' sparked the renaissance of snooker. He has grown up watching the game on television and the medium for him seems to hold no mystery. His only hobby away from the table is watching videos, and the first requirement of any hotel his manager books him into is that they have plenty of videos 'on tap'.

The afternoon before his two-session, best-of-19-frames Scottish Championship final, Stephen had gone to the local video hire shop with his father and taken out *Birdy* and another tape whose title, even a day later, he wouldn't be able to remember. Now, as he stood in a corner of the bar at Marco's Leisure, confirming a few biographical facts and figures with Ted Lowe, he looked like a schoolboy about to face an interview with the careers' master rather than a sportsman whose image was soon to be projected onto the large screen just a few feet away from him, as he played the most important match of his career.

The matchroom at Marco's was a scaled-down version of the cabaret clubs that prospered in the North of England in the 1970s, with small lamps and velvet-covered tiered banquettes. Any sense of intimacy, however, had been dispelled by the television lighting and the conference seating and by a sort of hi-tech tree-house, complete with electric fan and anglepoise lamp, where Ted Lowe perched, lip-mike at the ready. Any hopes the players might have had of producing their best on the day disappeared the minute they broke off.

'Oh and that's a pity. He's got a slight angle that takes the cue-ball away from the reds,' the unmistakable tones informed not only the viewing millions but also the dozens who were watching the match live. They oozed out of the perspex commentary box like marmalade out of a broken jar. 'Ohhh, dear', Ted groaned as Stephen missed what looked like an easy yellow. 'Gibson's having a go at this, a bit cheeky . . . Beautiful! Just this black or pink now to leave young Stephen Hendry requiring snookers . . .'

To the players, it must have seemed as though they were suffering a disorder of the inner ear. Every time they completed a shot, a disembodied 'whisper' told them what they were about to do next. The audience, for their part, felt like eavesdroppers at a confessional. It was a measure of the maturity that he had already acquired that Stephen was able to block it out, as he had been repeatedly taught to do, and dedicate himself to the task in hand. Tall, erect, immaculate, he looked and even moved like a competitor in the old-time section of 'Come Dancing': stopping and turning at the corners of the table, he locked his heels together and swivelled delicately on the balls of his shiny, leather-shod feet.

His opponent, meanwhile, tattooed, brawny, bedecked in sovereign rings, laboured and sweated as profusely as if it was a pick-axe he was wielding rather than a cue. A couple of inches below the royal-blue satin backing of his waistcoat was a darn as big as a bathroom plug.

At two frames all, Stephen made a break of 86 in the fifth which would stand as the highest break of the tournament. He ended the first session leading 6–3 and returned to his manager's hotel in the interval for a shower and a shave ('Which one?' his mother asked him, running a finger over the fluff on his chin). An hour later, surrounded by aunts, uncles, grandmothers, friends and other wellwishers, 'this young man from Dalgety Bay, now domiciled in Edinburgh', as Ted repeatedly called him, returned to take four of the next six frames, and the title.

After he had 'donned the crown making him the youngest ever Scottish professional champion and, with it, the £4000 first prize', Stephen was a model of good manners, modesty and discretion in his interview with Archie Macpherson. No, he didn't have a girlfriend (hoots from his pals in the audience). Yes, his ambition was to become the youngest ever world champion. His parents were his inspiration.

'We'd gone through all that beforehand,' Ian Doyle emphasised at the sponsor's reception immediately afterwards. The reception was on the floodlit squash court next door to Marco's matchroom, where drinks came courtesy of the Canada Dry girls in their knee-socks, bow-ties and hot-pants. 'A lot of women are now watching snooker. Their husband's out having a couple of pints, and they like that coming from a young boy of seventeen. It's the right image. I've already got him a Cirocco with "Stephen Hendry" written across the back, through a friend in the motor trade. I'll phone up now and get him an Audi deal tomorrow.'

Conspicuous among the members of the Hendry family, and Stephen's 'mental mates', as Ian Doyle called them, and the bamboozled-looking older Scottish professionals who had found themselves superseded in the space of a single weekend, was a grey-haired, distinguished-looking man who turned out to be the promotions manager of Riley. Impressed by Stephen's performance, by his parents and by the efficiency of the Doyle operation, he had just been on the phone to his MD, he said, and they had definitely decided to go ahead and make a commitment. This would take the form of a cue endorsement, which, with Scotland currently coming on-stream as one of the biggest growth areas in the home market, could be worth £100,000 to Stephen over a period of three years.

He said he sensed another Steve Davis in the making in Stephen, and possibly another Barry Hearn in Ian Doyle: 'Steve's not a puppet in the sense that when Barry tells him to jump, he jumps. But I've seen him walk through a party, click his fingers and say 'smile' to him, which Steve does, immediately.'

Ian Doyle assured him that, for the time being at least, he was taking exactly the same tack with Stephen. 'I'll make him go get a cup of coffee or what-have-you for me, like my own son the same age. You don't *ask* them to do something, you *tell* them.

'Some of the professionals in here tonight,' Doyle continued, 'you'll hear effing and blinding. Stephen won't say a bad word – an under-the-counter word – anywhere near me or his mother or father. He's a public figure now, and I've sat him down and had this out with Stephen. See, Stephen's here' – he took one of the six-by-eight glossies he'd had taken of the new champion and held it adjacent to his own ear. At the same time, he held another of the pictures at waist-level. 'And his pals are doon here. They're on a different plane. A different plane altogether. I think that's just starting to dawn on Stephen.'

Later, when the Canada Dry girls had packed up the free bar and the celebration party had drifted away, leaving only the regular members, a familiar face slipped into Marco's. John Spencer, whom Alex Higgins had beaten in the world championship final in 1972, had regained the title five years later. That, however, had been his first and last appearance in a final at the Crucible. The combination of his business interests and persistent double-vision had seen him sliding down the world rankings. He had started the current season ranked number 20, but was going to end it outside the top 32. This meant that, for the first time in his career as a professional player, he was going to have to qualify for the televised stages of all the major competitions.

'Eliminated, eliminated, eliminated, eliminated,' Barry Hearn had said one day, running his finger along the entries next to Spencer's name in 'the oracle', the handwritten record of players' performances which he keeps on his desk in front of him at all times. 'This is what would define who is worth the money. It's the most important chart we have. And as far as Spencer goes, forget it. He was a good player. But Spencer's the old breed that's been softened up. He *talks* about "If I played like I played in '77 . . ." In '77 he was a great player. Tremendous. But it's not really fair to discuss him. He's gone. It's a shame.'

'It's a sad slump', Steve Davis commented in his autobiography, 'because at his best Spencer is a joy to watch. He has developed a very awkward cue-action and is probably past his peak. He is far from dedicated and thinks more about playing golf and running his snooker club than he does of getting back to the top.

'Motivation is vitally important,' Davis continued. 'Once a player loses the will to compete, his game can collapse overnight. This happened to Spencer and is happening to others . . . I dread the day when I fall in a rut and have no desire to win.'

Spencer, a trim, young-looking fifty, was in Edinburgh for a few weeks trying to get himself 'up' for the world championships which started in mid-April. He spent much of his time playing money matches, and three of these had been against Stephen Hendry. Stephen won the first two 6–4, at £500 each. Spencer suggested playing the third as-they-were, instead of in suits, and this time Stephen was beaten, 4–6. Afterwards he told his father that he thought it had been a set-up. 'He knew that if I was dressed casually', he said, 'I'd play casually.' He was determined it would never happen again.

Spencer detached himself from the crowd who'd claimed him as soon as he'd walked into Marco's, and ordered a drink. Standing at the bar, he idly picked up one of that morning's papers and let his eye run down a story about the Scottish welterweight champion, Steve Watt. Watt was on a life-support system after being knocked out by Rocky Kelly at the London

West Hotel, Ealing, on Friday night, Spencer read. He had been taken to Charing Cross hospital for an emergency operation to remove a blood-clot, where his condition was said to be 'stable but comfortable'. He laid the paper down, halved it, then quartered it. He shook a cigarette out of its packet, lit it and exhaled a powerful plume of smoke. Things could be worse.

The preliminary rounds of the World Championship were held at Preston Guildhall, where the Coral UK had taken place four months earlier in the depths of winter. Despite its name, the Guildhall is a building of modern design, incorporating a small, indoor shopping precinct at ground level. The difference between being in the precinct, with its litter and bustle and choral muzak, and being inside where the snooker was happening was the difference between being above water and below it. The vaulted auditorium in the Guildhall had all the eery calm and swimming silence of an aquarium.

There was simultaneous play on six tables, each table occupying its own cell of padded grey felt, which seemed to both amplify and muffle the click and clack of the balls and the sound of the scores being shouted. Viewed from the gallery, the cells looked like a giant waffle-iron.

The Guildhall, like the locations of all the other top tournaments, had been found for snooker by Mike Watterson, the promoter who the 'player-power' putsch organised around Del Simmons had gradually eased out of the sport. Watterson had recently resigned his place on the board of the World Professional Billiards and Snooker Association. Now virtually his only contact with professional snooker was as a player. After being beaten 10–1 by one of the workhorses of the game at the 1986 World Championship qualifiers, Watterson decided that even his playing days were over.

'That's *it*,' Watterson said to Fred Davis, brother of the more famous Joe, when he came off the table. 'That is it. That was absolutely bloody disgraceful. I can't call meself a professional player after that exhibition. Jeezus! Did you see it? Every time I got straight on the black, I jumped. I've got miscueing on the black down to a fine art. Well, that's knocked it on the head for me. Never again. I'm done.'

Watterson, a middle-aged man in a frilly red shirt and big black bow-tie, was whippet-thin. There was a fringe of fine hair framing his face and black circles running round the hollows under his eyes. He hadn't been able to get to sleep the night before, he said, and had fallen out of bed twice when he had. He had arrived for his match feeling 'fogged', and this was the result. Well, he reiterated for the umpteenth time, that was it now. Curtains. 'I think today's the worst snooker I've ever, ever played since I first picked up a cue,' he said, as he downed the first of several Remmys in the 'Star Bar' at the Guildhall. 'It's like being put through a mincing machine. I couldn't go through that again.'

Hypnotists, psychotherapists, hypnotherapists, aromatherapists, acupuncturists, clairvoyants – Watterson said he'd had them all in the last few years, and none of them had been able to do anything for him. His nerves were all still shot to hell. He still ended up playing like a pillock.

July, 1979. That's when all his troubles started. That was the year Del Simmons forced the formation of a 'new WPBSA' with his players' backing, and became the contracts negotiator for WPBSA Promotions, forcing Watterson – 'Harry Grabbit – out into the cold. Watterson traces all his troubles back to the events of 1979. He had a nervous breakdown in the summer and, in the next few years, saw all the tournaments that he had inaugurated slowly slip out of his control.

'Who had to take all the commercial risk?' he said. 'I did. All they had to do was turn up with their fuckin' cues and play. I've done my bollocks in in some events and they said I was making millions. But when *I* was selling the game, you couldn't give it away.

'I'm sickened by the dirty, underhand and disgusting manner in which I was treated in my last two years in the game. To see Del Simmons lying on the top like slaked lime on clear water now really pisses me off.'

In addition to his promoting activities and sitting on the board of the WPBSA, Watterson managed Cliff Thorburn and Kirk Stevens for a time and owned the snooker monthly, *Cue World*. He had been given the magazine by Barry Hearn, who was incurring losses on it of £1,500 a month, and had sold it on to Clive Everton two years later with the circulation running at around a healthy 20,000. As a result, he said, Hearn had 'had his knife into my ribs ever since'.

Given his time again, he said he'd do what Barry Hearn was doing now: he'd take on all the key players and stitch the whole show up. At the top of his list would be the Scottish boy who was still in the process of completing his match, outside in the hall. 'Stephen Hendry', Mike Watterson said, 'if he's left alone by the ponces and flash managers, in three years will be the best player the game has ever seen. The greatest player. In my mind there is no doubt of that at all. But he's got to be kept away from the sharks and ponces. He's got to be protected.'

The further down the rankings a player is, the more matches he has to play to qualify for the final, televised stages of the World Championships at the Crucible. Being in his first season, and therefore without a ranking, Stephen Hendry had to beat four other players in the qualifying rounds at Preston in order to earn his first major appearance on television.

The youngest competitor in the history of the event, he struggled in his first three matches against players ranked 92nd, 61st and 49th in the world, but eventually made it through to face a young New Zealander who himself was only in his second season as a professional.

Dene O'Kane had leapt from nowhere to number 32 in the world largely on the strength of reaching the quarter-finals of the 1985 Dulux Open. He had won £18,000 in his first eight months on the circuit. In his second eight months, he'd won less than half of that but, nevertheless, with his gold watch-chain and electric-blue sunglasses, his velvet-collared topcoat draped casually over his shoulders, he managed to cut something of a dash.

'Deno', as he was to his friends Jimmy and Alex, was six years older than Stephen Hendry, which still only made him twenty-three. Physically, in the slightness of their build, their hair-styles and taste in clothes, there were striking similarities between the two of them. But, whereas Stephen's confidence and stability seemed natural outgrowths of his personality, Deno's gave every appearance of having been grafted on to his.

One of the Irish players, Tommy Murphy, had brought his

hypnotist along to Preston. Deno hadn't actually brought his guru, Guru Maharaji, but he was there in spirit. He had started the meditation system known as 'Knowledge' five years earlier and had found that, besides his snooker, it was 'a rejuvenating experience' which helped him 'just in my life as a person here on planet earth'.

'It gives you the feeling that you've got *love* in your life', Deno explained. 'It's like there's a space there, and you are you, and your problems are just something you've got to sort out. Like, I used to get extremely, extremely uptight playing snooker. I was much more manic. The frustration I used to feel I had to release somehow. Not only have you got to sit there and watch your opponent stick it up you, but you're in a highly-charged, enclosed environment, and there's no emotional release. I used to smash cues. I reached the stage where I wanted to give up snooker, but there was nothing else for me to do.'

Deno spent a lot of the first five frames of his match against Stephen Hendry sitting in his chair with his eyes closed in meditation. He spent a lot of the first five frames in his chair, period, as Stephen sprinted into a five-nil lead. The trouble was it was a morning session and, like his friends the Hurricane and the Whirlwind, Deno is never at his best before dusk.

He had pulled back to just three behind, however, by the afternoon interval and, when they reconvened, hauled himself to within one frame of victory with a 9–8 lead. He lost the next but went 41 points in front in the decider, only to underestimate his opponent's determination and powers of recovery. Stephen scraped together a break of 32 out of nothing and eventually ran out the winner by eighteen points.

The papers were happy because they had a story: the youngest ever competitor in world championship history. The BBC were happy because they had a new face.

'We've never doubted his bottle,' Ian Doyle said later.

'I knew I had the bottle,' Stephen said.

Deno rationed his contact with Alex during the season. But now the season was over as far as he was concerned. He'd call Alex and go over and stay with him in Cheshire and have a lost weekend.

12 *Just like the normal people*

The World Championships started on April 19th, with Dennis defending his title against one of the qualifiers. On April 18th, a Friday, Barry strode into the Matchroom offices in Romford, spun the 'combo' locks on his briefcase and held up his London marathon number and the vest that he'd just had printed with the Matchroom logo.

Marathons were Barry's latest enthusiasm. He'd always run on the electric executive treadmill in his home gym, but he'd gone into serious training a couple of months earlier – roadwork, circuits, running backwards and forwards into the office every day with Robbo bringing up the rear in the Caddy, blasting out the 'Rocky' theme. The works, mate. Oh! Areyewshaw!

On paper, Barry Hearn was a man who was currently beset with problems. Goya had just made the official announcement that they were withdrawing sponsorship from 'his' tournament. The men's leisurewear deal he had been negotiating with French Connection for more than twelve months had just bitten the dust. The public flotation of Matchroom which he had been talking about all season was now looking like it wasn't going to happen, at least not in the immediate future. The Hong Kong market, so important to Riley, had, according to David Fisher, just done a belly-flop.

In addition, his back-room wrangles with Del Simmons and David Fisher at BCE had recently gone public; and he had an upstart, Howard Kruger, trawling his waters for players and sponsors. But if Barry was a man who was feeling beleaguered, he was giving a good impression of a man who had the world on a string and was sittin' on a rainbow with the string around his finger.

'Goya have decided — I think quite rightly — to pull out,' Barry started, as soon as he was ensconced in the big office, tie loosened, shirtcuffs shooting, installed behind the big desk. The walls behind and to either side of him were papered in glossy pictures of Steve and him, and him and Steve. 'Goya's business has changed, actually, in the last twelve to eighteen months', he continued. 'They've decided the tournament was six weeks too early. The Christmas turn-around period has now got to be last week in November, first two weeks in December. That's when about 80 per cent of the volume turnover in male toiletries happens. So they think their money will be better spent, in relation to their product, in TV advertising.

'Obviously it'll make us a lot more money. Because now their budget's free to do things with us, whereas before their budget was used up. Oh, Matchroom turnover this year will, conservatively, at least double on the male toiletries. At *least* double. It should be more, hopefully. It needs a TV advertising campaign. A direct campaign. We had it two years ago. Last year we did the tournament. And, to be fair, although the range was a lot bigger and a lot better, the turnover of the product line didn't change. Which showed that the TV advertising was as effective as the tournament. Now, we're doing a new TV advertising campaign. I've just come from a lunch with their managing director, and we'll be filming in June with all the players for a major TV campaign during November and December.'

So that was Goya out of the way. Everything was hunky-dory at Goya. French Connection? 'That was a sadness,' Barry said, shaking his head, 'French Connection. I would have liked a French Connection deal, because I liked the concept of doing a full range. But, God knows, if you won every battle there would be no point in going to war. As it is, we're close to a new textile deal now which will replace them probably with a couple of noughts on. Next question.'

There had been rumours, naturally, that French Connection and Goya had cut and run because of the scandals and ... 'Nothing to do with it at all,' Barry stated firmly. 'No question. Because it would've come to me. We've had a season of adverse publicity pretty well everywhere obviously – Silvino, Higgins, Kirk, Knowlsey. But in many ways we've come out of it so well as to almost have done us a favour. The bad publicity has ushered a lot of people to us that wanted to get involved with snooker. We're just, like, the *normal people*.'

In January, the 'King of the Green Baize', as they'd called him, had been featured on the cover of *Money* magazine. Inside he had talked about going public with Matchroom. 'We have three stockbrokers and three banks wanting to float us,' Barry had told their reporter, who had explained how snooker's potential abroad, both in Europe and the Far East, was massive. 'There, perhaps, lies the longer term potential of Matchroom,' he had concluded. And now?

'I'm pleased to say,' Barry said, 'that we're not doing it at the moment. When we looked at the value, I had in my mind a figure of something like £12 or £13 million for the package. And the bloke's come back and said, Well, nine or ten's a bit more realistic, and I wouldn't have accepted that. I wouldn't have done it for that amount of money.

'Obviously it would've been nice to have had the flexibility to have been able to acquire other companies to create a bigger leisure operation. Because I think if you did the public flotation you'd have to look outside snooker. I have my fruit-machine businesses and things like that already, but they're not *massive*. I would be looking at other involvements in leisure, where perhaps you do the clothing, the franchising, keep-fit, leisure centres . . . But I dunno. Things are going *so* well for us now, I'm thinking to myself, W-e-e-ll, I'm not the greatest person at working as a team member. And I'm a little concerned as to whether this is the right thing for me. I mean, I've got to be selfish as well. I don't need the money. Money's always nice, but more of it's not going to change my lifestyle. I don't *think*.'

For months, the talk in snooker circles had been about not whether, but *when*, Barry was going to 'do a Mark McCormack' and monopolise the running of snooker the way McCormack monopolised areas of tennis and golf. There were some – Mike Watterson, Tony Knowles, David Fisher among them – who thought it had already happened, and that he already did. 'The board's too weak, there's nobody to stand up to him . . .,' Fisher had said.

Now Barry had fired speculation that he was about to move to take effective control of the game by announcing that his players would not be appearing in the Langs Scottish Masters, the traditional warm-up tournament at the beginning of the season. Instead, Steve, Dennis, Terry and Tony, plus the new boys Willie Thorne and Neal Foulds, would be playing each other in Matchroom's own 'multi-sponsorship' tournament in the same week in September as the Langs. The first prize of £50,000 would be four times what Higgins, White, Knowles, Thorburn and the rest were competing for in Glasgow.

Barry couldn't disguise his delight at having pulled off this coup. In addition to Goya, Riley, Ebel, Courage, Cathay Pacific Airlines, Trans World Airlines and Camus, backing for the tournament would be coming from four new sponsors – Fabrex (textiles), CDS (computers), Just Wise (luggage) and Pirelli (footwear) – with whom he had just signed exclusive deals.

'Yes,' he said, 'we thought it was time to cut out some of the deadwood that we have to keep playing and get straight to the nitty-gritty. No, seriously though, it's an ideal way to get all our clients together on a five-day, in-house tournament. All of our related companies will be part-sponsors, and we will use it as an entertaining and salesforce-media event.

'It's my tournament. It's my money. It's my sponsors,' Barry repeated. 'It's work that my players have done. I mean, all the time my people are breaking down doors, vis-à-vis other territories and other marketing areas, and other players are strolling in and getting the advantage. Well not this time. Not here. The whole thing is quite brilliant in its concept – of course – as you'd expect.'

Having used his muscle to undermine one established tournament and substitute a tournament of his own devising, it was simply a matter of time, so backstage speculation had it, before Barry bore down on other areas of the game. He already controlled the television contracts for snooker in the Far East and was negotiating with American and European companies over the TV rights to the new 'multi-sponsored' Matchroom tournament in Southend. He was saying that he might send his players to the next BCE-sponsored competitions in Belgium and Canada, and then again he might not. This was 'the McCormack tactic', which Barry denied using. But on the McCormack tactic, his mouth said one thing and his face – mainly his eyes, which spun and sparkled – said something else, like: Come *on*. Why-the-fuck-not?

'There's the old Jewish phrase: "But what have you done for me lately?" And I'm afraid you've got to be like that,' Barry chuckled. 'That's the way it's gotta work. I mean, we went to Malaysia two years ago. Last year we didn't go to Malaysia at all. This year I got four tournaments offered in Malaysia. This year we're not going to Singapore. Next year I'll have four tournaments on offer in Singapore.

'Now Camus want to renew their Far East contract for another three years. Well we're not gonna give them the whole Far East any more. Perhaps we can talk about Hong Kong . . . My contract with them runs out on September the tenth, 1986, by which time I will know exactly who I'm going to sign with to tie up *parts* of the Far East for the next few years.

'And exactly the same with BCE. If it's commercial levels of money they're offering next year in Belgium and Canada, we're happy to play for them. If it's not commercial, we won't play. We'll just have to wait and see. Strange things happen at sea. It's a hard old world out there . . . Carol!'

Barry was pointing his nose at the ceiling and bawling at his secretary in the office next door. 'Carew! . . . Where are we in this week's chart?'

Ten days earlier, warfare had broken out on a new and unexpected front with the release of a pop record by the 'Rockney' partnership of Chas and Dave. 'Snooker Loopy' was a novelty number with, and about, the individual members of the Matchroom team, aimed squarely at the middle-of-the-road, mass market. Alex, Jimmy and Tony Knowles were rumoured to be countering with a chart-bound sound of their own in the next week or two. But, naturally, Matchroom had already gone one better and had a video made. It was a copy of this that Barry was carrying as he led the way up the spiral staircase to the private-members' club on the next floor.

Like most private-members' clubs, the atmosphere inside the Romford Matchroom is kept so that it feels like the middle of the night all day. It is a cocoon of easy lighting, deep seating, drinking, snookering, punting and men's talk. Pulsing strips of light run down the walls and along the floor, and greenery flourishes in the darkened alcoves. Although he has a comfortable snooker room in his own house just fifteen minutes down the road, Steve likes to come into the Matchroom to practise, where there's a bit of life around him.

He had been in the club every day for the last three weeks, Barry said as he handed the video to one of the bar staff to load into the machine. 'This is why Davis looks as good now. These three weeks off we've given him. I bet in the last three weeks he hasn't done three days' work. He did the video, but that was a bit of fun, a bit of relaxation, for all the boys. He did an ITV technical series, and a do with Reading Football club, all up here. He hasn't been out of the club for three weeks, and looks ... I mean, if he gets beat this year, well, don't worry about being relaxed in future, because I've never seen him so relaxed, and never seen him play so well. Jeezus, he looks strong. Absolutely buzzing.'

Even by his own exalted standards, Steve had had a good season. He had won three of the five major ranking tournaments and something approaching a quarter of a million pounds in prize money. But from his point of view it had all largely been a matter of treading water until he could win back what was rightfully his. The Embassy World Championship trophy. The ne plus ultra. The one it's all about, David. 'The big one.'

In 1985 he had thrown away an eight-frame lead and had failed to win his third World Championship title in succession at 12.23 in the morning on the last ball. He was determined there was going to be no repeat performance. This time Steve was desperate to win it, and nobody was pretending any different. But the thing was to keep it light. At this stage keeping it light was what was important. On the big, backward-curving screen in the Matchroom, Steve sung and danced with his team-mates, and mugged for the camera. 'Snooker-loopy nuts are we,' he chirruped. 'We're all snooker loooo-pee.'

'Seeya on Top of the Pops, lads,' Barry called to the few members drinking at the bar, as he disappeared back downstairs to finish off the afternoon's business.

Observers at the Benson and Hedges Irish Championships the week before had noted that Dennis looked jaded, which was hardly surprising, given the number of personal appearances, signing sessions, interviews, exhibitions, guest-shots and frames of snooker he had put behind him in the previous twelve months.

'The first year Steve won, he was never indoors,' Bill Davis, Steve's father, had said back at the beginning of the season, explaining Steve's first-round defeat by Tony Knowles in the 1982 World Championships. 'It's different for Steve now, now he's established. He doesn't have to dash about so much. It's a long-term plan. Dennis, though, he might not be the world champion this time next year. In fact I think nobody would be more surprised than him if he was. So he's got to get out there and cash in while he can. Getting out there an' securing his family's future's what it's all about.'

Dennis had put himself through the wringer in an effort to squeeze out every last drop of commercial potential that is not the least important aspect of owning the world title. He had won only one match in the four tournaments since Christmas. So it came as a surprise to very few students of form when Dennis walked out to defend his world championship looking as if his death warrant had just been signed. His colour flashed from green to scarlet and back, like a traffic-light.

A few weeks earlier, the *News of the World* had drawn great significance from the fact that Dennis's wife was spending a few days 'in retreat' at the Our Lady of Compassion Hospital in Blackburn. 'Nervous breakdown? Marriage on the rocks?' Janice Hale asked in her *Snooker Scene* 'Diary'. '"No," says Dennis. "She's there for a bit of a breather." I feel a twinge of envy at this.'

It was the sort of remark that was coming increasingly often from Janice. Like Alex Higgins, it seemed, she was nurturing a growing disillusion with the game. 'Whatever happened to the snooker world we all loved?' had been her cri de coeur in January. 'Whether because of money or something else, the fun has gone out of the game now. There is far too much whispering in corners, attempting to score petty points over other people and other signs of the malaise and complacency that success can bring.'

'The scene around the game has gone sour,' Janice repeated, in a 'Diary' entry three months later. 'The degree of hassle to which everyone is submitted sometimes makes us all just want to get out and lead a normal life. And if it's like this now, what will the World Championship be like?'

The World Championship, as Janice knew probably better than anybody, would be like it's always like: like all the other events of the snooker calendar rolled into one and pushed into overdrive. The tension would be greater, the intrigue thicker, security tighter, razzamatazz louder, drink neater, drinking sessions longer, tempers shorter, sponsorship richer, imaginations wilder, gossip rifer, prose purpler, deadlines pressinger than at any time since the players and the managers, the TV folk and PR teams, the sponsors, gofers, gamblers, gurus, hacks and groupies last collided in the City of Steel.

The Crucible was, famously, 'a pressure-cooker'. The melting-pot of men's dreams. Nerves were tested to breaking point in the white-hot atmosphere. Hard men wept. Strong men buckled. And it was just as hard on the players.

Seventeen days is a long time to spend cooped up in a concrete bunker where the only reminder of the world outside is the council flats visible through the narrow skylights. Even in a concrete bunker with a bar in the corner from which drinks are dispensed by smiling girls in tailored hostess uniforms, seventeen days is a long time. Seventeen deadlines. Seventeen stories to stitch together from somewhere.

In 1985 the big story had blown up at midnight on the first day. The early editions of the *Daily Star*, banner-headlining the long-awaited 'exposé' of the drugs scene in snooker, had caused instant pandemonium in the Crucible. This was based on the interview, taped without his knowledge, in which Silvino Francisco was alleged to have accused Kirk Stevens of being 'out of his mind on dope' during their Dulux Open final. Press conferences, briefings, an invasion of newshounds and a frantic tightening of security had followed. 'I'm looking over my shoulder all the time. There's press men everywhere,' Alex Higgins had complained after he was knocked out in the second round.

But that was off-the-table. Off the table doesn't concern the travelling retinue of snooker correspondents for the popular dailies. The frame-scores and the 'nannies' ('nanny goats' = 'quotes') is all that concerns the reptiles, whose by-lines never appear anywhere other than on the back pages. Whenever the other blows up, 'the jackals', as Janice calls them, suddenly put in an appearance, 'staying at the best hotels, running up an expense account, drinking the sponsors' booze'.

With the exception of Clive Everton, who first taught her the ropes, Janice has been reporting snooker longer than anybody else on the circuit. Inside every briefcase in the press room at the Crucible was a copy of the indispensable *Rothmans Snooker Yearbook*, which Janice edits. Janice has known Jimmy – 'little Jim' – since before he had his teeth done, and Terry since he was delivering letters around the valleys. She was a mother-confessor for Jimmy and Tony in the early days, when they were in awe of a single woman who stood at the bar and wrote for 'them papers with no pictures'. (The *Daily Telegraph* and the *Observer* until, two-thirds of the way through the season, Janice was recruited to Eddie Shah's *Today*.)

This sort of familiarity can of course have its drawbacks. Snooker players, like all professional performers, have fragile egos and long memories. 'Janice Hale described me in the *Observer* as "one of the circuit's supporting cast, a regular earner rather than a winner",' Dennis had commented tartly in the book brought out to capitalise on his championship year. 'People thereafter began to characterise me as the eternal runner-up, as a player who lost "bottle" when the chips were down.'

In general, though, her experience and encyclopaedic knowledge give Janice an authority which keeps the other (male) writers on their toes and, inevitably, breeds a certain amount of resentment. They often feel like wolf-cubs performing in front of an all-seeing, all-knowing Akela who might at any time move to expel them from the pack.

The most persistent offender against Janice's loosely proscribed code of conduct is the *Sun*'s man-on-the-spot, Alisdair Ross. 'Ally' Ross has what is usually called a larger-than-life personality. He has fierce loyalties to the Higgins–Knowles camp which tend to colour his view of events and pep up his prose. 'Rossy' had been missing for the first part of the season, charity-walking with Ian Botham, but he had rejoined the ranks just in time for the Big One.

Terry Smith, on the other hand, the *Mirror*'s man, was a no-show at Sheffield. Belts had been pulled increasingly tighter under the *Mirror*'s new proprietor, 'Cap'n Bob' Maxwell: Smith had been ordered to commute between his home in Essex and the Rothmans Grand Prix in Reading and, when he pointed out that this wasn't feasible, had been told to find himself the cheapest accommodation available. He had ended up staying at a £25-a-night boarding house instead of at the £45-a-night Rammada Inn with the players and the other snooker scribes.

In the end Smith hadn't been able to take the indignities any longer and had tendered his resignation. His replacement in Sheffield was a writer who three months earlier had used his column in the paper to sound off frankly and fearlessly against the 'snooligan' supporters who were threatening to ruin the gentlemanly image which snooker had always enjoyed. 'Snooker stands at the crossroads, fast going to pot,' he had declared, adding: 'For myself, I can't see why anyone gets so excited. I'm usually asleep by the fifth frame.'

This had hardly endeared Tony 'Stengun' Stenson to his new colleagues at the Crucible, who had very quickly made it very clear to 'The man who shoots from the lip', as the *Mirror* billed him, that he was going to have to learn to button it if he expected anything in the way of cooperation from them. The underlying hostility came to the surface early in the first week, in the bar at the Grosvenor Hotel in Sheffield whose shutters were pulled every morning just as the smell of breakfast started wafting in from the restaurant next door.

Whose turn it was to have the next round added to their bill was a constant bone of contention. And the altercation developed out of 'Stengun' accusing Rossy of the *Sun* of not digging deep enough into his pockets. Rossy was drinking with his pals Jimmy and Alex, who had breezed in around half past three looking slightly the worse for wear, and he was incensed at being accused of being a tight-wad in front of them.

What did Stenson know about snooker anyway, Rossy wanted to know. Sweet eff-ay, he claimed. He didn't know what he was doing there. He knew about personalities, Stengun protested, He was a *personality* writer. He had an insight into what made people tick that Rossy could never hope to have. Be fair. 'The man who shoots from the lip!' Alex jeered from his corner as Rossy, having been dissuaded from throwing a punch at his press room colleague, bounced a ball of tenners over the bar.

While the drinks were being pulled, Jimmy tottered across to Bill Davis and indicated he'd like a match for the cigarette that was clamped in his teeth. 'Which one should I light, Jim?' Bill Davis asked him. 'The middle one?'

'And these are the blokes who are hoping to become world champion,' Bill said, as another Crucible dawn started to come up outside.

The first big story of the championship happened on the first day when Dennis, having lost eight of the opening nine frames of the curtain-raiser to the tournament, was finally beaten 10–6 by Mike Hallett – 'Grimsby's' Mike Hallett: the prefix itself was meant to denote the extent of the miracle that had been achieved.

The second big story was Stephen Hendry versus Willie Thorne, another contest which, with Willie's history of being beaten by younger, far less experienced players, promised its own share of schadenfreude – watching the favourite get stuffed.

Not that that's what Barry Hearn thought was going to happen. 'Willie'll eat him alive,' Barry predicted. 'Every time I see something in the papers about Hendry it's doing me more and more good. 'Cause it'll get through to Willie, and Willie'll play well, I think. Oh yeh. He'll destroy him.'

In less than an hour, Hendry, who had been on the receiving end of a big media build-up, was 3–1 in front. At 3–0 down in his quarter-final against Cliff Thorburn, Willie would race round the players' room borrowing the £1000 or so in cash to place on himself in the Corals office in the foyer, in an effort to give his game some edge. He didn't do that against Hendry. He didn't need to. There was already too much at stake. At one point in the fifth it looked as if Willie was going to fall 4–1 behind, but a slip on the pink let him in and he went on to take the frame.

At the end of it, he did what he would continue to do all through the match: while the young first-timer sat quietly waiting for the referee to re-rack the balls, Willie picked up the cue ball and polished it, wandered around the arena exchanging jokes with the press benches and the scorers, whistled and sang and generally demonstrated that he was at ease here; that this sort of thing was food and drink to him; he had been here before. 'I want to make the opponent think I'm enjoying it and all that game,' Willie had said some months earlier, perched on the edge of a hotel bed in Reading. 'Let people think whatever's happening, I'm not too disappointed about it.'

He drew level with a break of 70 in the next frame and was leading 5–4 at the interval. Hopes of a major upset were revived when Hendry took three of the first four frames in the evening to leave himself needing only three more for the match. Willie, however, still whistling and singing although he admitted afterwards that he was feeling 'dreadful', dug his heels in and eventually ran out the winner, 10–8.

'I've never known pressure like it before. My brain really hurts,' he said when he mounted the podium at the end of the narrow, cruelly-lit interview room at the Crucible. 'There's not a compliment big enough for the kid,' he continued, giving good 'nannies'. He didn't think he'd ever been that nervous in a match. 'I didn't know the lad was that great. He played good.'

Good enough to have Barry round sniffing, was the general feeling. 'If Barry Hearn wanted him', Stephen's manager stated flatly, 'he couldn't afford the price.'

'I'm not in the business of looking for more players,' Barry said. 'But put it this way: if Hendry makes it, he's gonna need me if I want him.' Since Howard Kruger's appearance on the scene, Barry had started to be seen around in more casual gear — bright patterned shirts, a blouson jacket made of strips of suede and leather. 'I mean, he could possibly be *the* young player to come through. But Hendry in a *year's* time might look a better proposition.

'People don't realise that sport is the hardest thing in the world for people to do *consistently*. You'll find people that come up and have hot streaks and go, hot streaks and go . . . You've got to be pretty consistent to stay in the world's top eight, and that's where everybody's got to aim to be.

'It just depends on how things develop. If he starts doing *really* well, if Hendry starts winning majors, right, they would be doing business with me anyway. Because I would be booking him or I would be doing this or I would be suggesting things, where they work, in some way or the other. It all depends.

Sometimes their progress does a steep 'up' and then levels out for a long time. Sometimes it goes up again. Sometimes it just ducks away. You never know.'

Thanks to regular air-play and to the tape being shown on 'Top of the Pops' as well as to the blanket, and now traditional, 130 hours' television coverage which the World Championships themselves were being given, 'Snooker Loopy' entered the Top Twenty at the end of the first week of the tournament. Two days earlier, the Kruger camp had launched their bid for a piece of chart action with a champagne–finger–buffet–cum–photo–opportunity at a discreet hotel in the industrial suburbs of Sheffield.

Alex was staying at the Charnwood, mainly because it was the only hotel left in the city that would take him. But Alex was exactly the sort of celebrity guest that the Charnwood, a new enterprise, was hopeful of attracting. The City of Steel's answer to the Chateau Marmont in Los Angeles or the Portobello Hotel in London, the Charnwood's aim was to combine all the intimacy of a family home with all the conveniences of international jet-set living.

In a small beach–front–style bar overlooking a street of red-brick terraced houses, 'Four Away' — Alex, Jimmy, Kirk and Tony Knowles — were sipping champagne cocktails before moving downstairs to the conservatory to face their public. Puzzlingly, given their name, the full–colour bag accompanying 'The Wanderer', their single, featured only three players on a beach playing air-guitar with their cues. Although they swore he was on the record, Kirk, it seemed, had been unavailable at the time of the picture session.

The Charnwood was Greg-country. And, sure enough, Greg was in charge, directing operations in the conservatory. Greg was everywhere, overseeing the deployment of the ham–mayonnaise sandwiches and the paella, marshalling the lensmen and the hacks, keeping a weather-eye open for gatecrashers. There was, Greg explained when everyone was assembled, an added embellishment. This, it turned out, was to be a joint promotion. Also present in addition to the snooker players, for some reason, were two members of the headbanger band, Status Quo, making a comeback from their latest 'farewell' appearance. 'The Quo' themselves had once had a hit with 'The Wanderer'. That was the tenuous link.

'But, first, ladies and gentlemen . . .' Four Away's version of the song, which had been playing over and over on a tape-loop, was turned off, only to be replaced by the real thing. 'Well, I'm the kinda guy who will never settle down . . .' Alex was wearing big pop star 'shades' and leading the others towards the waiting chairs. 'With our balls on the table', he warbled, 'and our fingers in our hair.'

The idea for the record had come from Alex. 'The Wanderer' had been Alex's choice of song as well. 'I had no idea the rival camp had done that "Loopy" or whatever it's called,' he said. 'But we've got more up our sleeves than they have, in more ways than one. "Oh we roam from town to town . . ."'

Alex was wearing a pair of new shoes but in a curiously old-fashioned style. The reason became apparent, though, when he stood up to be photographed and his platform-heels almost put him on a par with Tony Knowles, who's six-foot-two. The two 'Quos' were wheeled on, and they were all separated from their glasses long enough to be photographed poking cues at a marble-sized ball on a spindly toy table that had been set up in the middle of the room.

'Wozzit they say?' one elderly photographer asked nobody in particular. 'Never work with kids an' animals. You've got a combination of both here.' In the absence of any kind of cutlery, a number of his colleagues had been driven to eating the paella with their fists.

When the picture possibilities had been exhausted inside the Charnwood, the posse moved outside to the carpark, where they mimicked strumming their cues like guitars. Alex, Kirk and Jimmy all seemed to be suitably loosened up, but Tony seemed awkward and ill-at-ease. He had a match to play that evening and therefore was laying off the drink.

In many ways it was like old times. Three or four years earlier, Alex, Jimmy, Kirk and Tony had all shared a manager who, like Aitch, was basically a show-biz impresario. Harvey Lisberg had discovered Herman's Hermits in the early 'sixties and had done very-nicely-thank-you on the strength of it. Twenty years later,

Kennedy Street Enterprises, his company, had its own office-block in the centre of Altrincham, a select suburb on the outskirts of Manchester; and from there Harvey observed the goings-on in the snooker world with a mixture of frustration, exasperation and benign tolerance. He didn't give Howard Kruger a cat in hell's chance.

'Jimmy will go to Barry Hearn,' Harvey stated matter-of-factly. 'He'll come back to me and I'll do a deal for him. With Barry Hearn there are disadvantages, but compared to the rest . . . The only threat to Barry Hearn is Jimmy White.'

Although he'd walked out on him the previous summer, a percentage of everything Jimmy had earned still came to Harvey Lisberg under the terms of an out-of-court settlement. It was Harvey who'd had Jimmy's teeth done and put him into nice suits and generally banged on at him about the importance of cleaning up his act. Three years of it. The boy is like a son to him. And what happens? Jimmy does a runner.

'I did a wonderful job on Jimmy White. I lost Jimmy White because the law didn't protect me, so three years' work went down the tube,' Harvey said. 'Without Jimmy I wasn't in a position to be powerful. Jimmy White just took it away from me, and I think it's disgusting, I must tell you. Unbelievable. Totally unbelievable.'

Harvey still believes he was good for Jimmy. He's still fond. 'I think I did a very good job in *limiting* the disasters. *Controlling* the disasters. And there were many. I can't see anybody else caring that much.

'I mean, no way he's going to roll up and be a good product for a sponsor to take on. He isn't going to start selling Horlicks, never in bed before five. If he'd been a fit person he'd have won the World Championship eight times. As it is, with his excesses, he'll be lucky to win it at all. I was hoping Nastase was going to win Wimbledon once, but did it happen? It never happened.'

Harvey feels a similar ambivalence about Tony Knowles, a player who he thinks proved, when he beat Davis in '82, that he has a killer instinct in him. 'But he needs help obviously. He's got a lot of problems, Tony Knowles. His head needs completely curing of a lot of things he's got in it. He needs to get over a lot of nonsense he either believes or he keeps trotting out. For instance, the excuses every time he gets beat. There's never a reason other than the other bloke's better than you. His attitude is completely wrong. But if you surround yourself with certain types of people they're going to feed your ego, and you're going to end up believing you're better than you are.

'I have a theory about how to cure Tony Knowles. Charity work. You know what I'm saying? Maybe a walk like Botham's. The boy–next–door image. Get him thinking about other people for a change, instead of himself. I phoned him up with this idea and it was immediately followed by a call from Kruger telling me that if I wanted to talk to Tony Knowles in future, it should be through him. I said I would talk to Tony personally when he was no longer his manager. In other words, in about six months.'

But if Harvey is torn in his attitude towards Tony and Jimmy, there are no two ways about how he feels on the subject of Alex Higgins. The best thing that ever happened in his life, he says, was the day Higgins turned around and walked out of it. 'I can't print what I think of the man. The girl on my switchboard refused to take calls from him because of the language. A loud-mouthed, horrible man . . .'

Lisberg was drawn to snooker in the first place, he said, for the insight it gave him into a side of British life that he had previously known nothing about. 'The nearest I'd been to it was the new Tony Christie, who was doing all the nightclubs in the early 'seventies. Wakefield Variety. Blazers. Talk of the North. That scene disappeared and snooker seemed to take its place.

'Snooker just had a magic at the time I came into it, around '81. It was like pop music in the 'sixties. I got more publicity in six weeks representing Jimmy White than in twenty years representing world superstars. You go on a train with Jimmy White, you get a hundred people asking for an autograph. You go on a train with a rock star, you get two. They're immediately identifiable. They're the people next door.

'*Were* perhaps I should say. Snooker's existing now purely on *phenomenal* finals results which almost appear to be staged, but aren't. It's over now. It's gone.'

Alex had removed his dark glasses and was rubbing the light out of his eyes. The press reception at the Charnwood was over and there was a hiatus between that and the next event on the day's programme. Greg had been appointed press officer for Sport Aid, the sports arm of Bob Geldof's fund-raising appeal for the victims of the Ethiopian famine, and Alex and Jimmy were going to be filmed wearing their 'I ran the world' T-shirts in the practice room back at the Crucible. The shots would be included in the official Sports Aid video and, as a result, Greg hoped, start to change the public's perception of them. But for the moment, there was nothing to do but wait.

Alex said that killing time between matches was the worst part of the World Championship. It could be days in the early stages. He'd thought about going home to Cheshire, but the house was big and empty and he had ended up hanging about. You couldn't get any sense of rhythm.

His regular practice partner during the first week had been Stephen Hendry, who he saw as the game's Boris Becker; he'd be world champion by the time he was 21, Alex was convinced. They'd been playing for £5-a-frame and Alex had tried to persuade Stephen to stay in Sheffield and practise with him after he was knocked out by Willie Thorne. But his manager was having none of it. Stephen had travelled back to Scotland in the safe-keeping of Ian Doyle and his father, where he'd arrived to a hero's welcome. 'It's a big, bad world we live in and it can be dynamite, what with the drugs and drinks scares. You can't be too careful,' Ian Doyle said.

Dennis Taylor, Tony Meo and Neal Foulds had all gone out in the first round at Sheffield. After the semi-finals had been completed Steve would be the only one left to carry the Matchroom flag. Willie was beaten in the quarters by his old friend, Cliff Thorburn. And, after leading by three frames with only four to play and looking a certainty to progress to the next round, Terry was eliminated by the number 16 seed. Simply by virtue of his having got this far, and human-interest stories being thin on the ground, the number 16 seed was turning into something of an item in the press and on television.

Joe Johnson wasn't a glamorous figure but – ex-gas-fitter, six kids, part-time singer with a pop-group, born and brought up in Bradford, which almost made him a local boy – he was good for a certain amount of mileage. But there was another angle that had led to a good deal of press room speculation – his race. Joe had steadfastly maintained that he was the white son of 'white, one hundred per cent English parents'. A strong body of opinion among the reporters, however, believed that Joe was 'definitely tinted', and enquiries were proceeding.

As long ago as the Dulux at the beginning of March, Steve Davis had said that the winner of his World Championship quarter-final with Jimmy White, assuming they both got that far, would almost certainly go on to take the title. 'Whoever wins out of the two of us, which will be a war,' he'd said, 'the confidence alone will win you the world championship . . . I don't fancy anybody else, to be quite honest.' There had been speculation at the time that this was a piece of gamesmanship designed to put pressure on Jimmy. If it was, it soon showed every sign of bringing home the bacon.

What everybody had predicted would be 'the match of the championship' turned out instead to be a limp affair in which Jimmy performed as if both his brain and the balls were furred with dust. Davis started with a 134 clearance in the opening frame and rarely dropped below that standard. Jimmy – chain-smoking, fidgeting, craning his neck to see what was happening – was left looking like somebody waiting at a country bus-stop.

This produced problems for the BBC directors who had been instructed by their bosses to immediately cut away from any player lighting up and to keep the 'Embassy' logo out of shot as much as possible. In one random half-hour of the White–Davis match, 'Sheffielder' in the local evening paper logged 'nine close-ups of the logo, three long shots, six shots of part of the word "Embassy", and one anxious blur'. This compared with 79 shots of the logo an hour, some as long as thirty seconds, totalling nearly seven minutes an hour, at the Benson and Hedges tournament in January.

Anticipating this development some years earlier, Embassy had moved away from what the Head of Sponsored Events of Imperial Tobacco called 'the Chapel of Rest look' – potted plants, herbaceous borders. The emphasis now was on 'colour association': in other words, Embassy's distinctive maroon and red striped logo had become the dominant motif. The set looked like one of Richard Smith's early pop paintings and the matches all seemed to be taking place inside a box of Number One King Size.

'That is one mountain I have climbed, leaving two to go,' Steve, never a laureate of the 'nannies', volunteered after he had wiped the floor with Jimmy, 13–5. He added that he couldn't be more pleased with the way he was playing.

The second 'mountain' he had to climb was Cliff Thorburn. It wasn't the first time that Davis and Thorburn had met in a world championship semi-final, and the atmosphere between them had been distinctly chilly since the famous incident, described by Steve in his autobiography, which had marked their first encounter. It happened in 1981 at the Crucible, when Davis claiming a frame as his own before his opponent had formally conceded it, almost resulted in fisticuffs.

'Thorburn, the great ice-cool grafter . . . unbelievably broke,' he wrote. 'When a man of Thorburn's calibre snaps like that, it explains better than anything else all the pressures players have to suffer under the lights, in front of crowds and before the cameras . . . I vowed to beat him next day. If he had known me better, he would have hidden his feelings inside. I am not physically violent, but I channel it all in psyching myself up. I prefer to let the talking be done on the table.' Davis had won the match and, 'proud to think that I had proved to everyone that I was hard enough to win the championship,' had gone on to take that year's title.

In 1986 the atmosphere between Davis and Thorburn, on the surface at least, was more cordial. Both remained stony-faced throughout the long, brain-bursting bouts of safety-play which characterised all four sessions. But as he walked away from the table to take a 'comfort break' after taking a decisive two-frame lead at 14–12, Steve let the mask drop for precisely the time it took him to cross the no-man's-land between the bright lights of the set and the crowded backstage area.

It was a darkened strip of floor about four-feet wide which it took him no more than a couple of strides to cover. But for the moment that he was in it, his face lost its familiar blandness and paleness and became contorted and suffused with colour, as if reflected in a bashed tin or an ancient mirror, before very quickly becoming quiet and composed again. It was like a cloud crossing the sun, or a curtain billowing, and was over just as swiftly.

He took the next two frames comfortably and qualified for his fifth final in six years. Opposing him was the 150–1 outsider who had summarily disposed of Tony Knowles in his semi-final and whose ethnic origins were still a source of fascination, if not to the snooker scribes who had watched him steadily climb the rankings over the years, then to their editors in London. 'Snooker Rupee' was one of the several spoof headlines suggested should Joe Johnson pull off the impossible and defeat the Romford Robot.

'Never hit the ball hard when you can hit it soft ... Hit the ball on the centre line ... Relaxed muscles, relaxed body, a slack grip and a smooth delivery ... Stillness ... Smooth and slack ... relaxed but solid ...' Terry had kept reminding himself of the basics during his quarter-final against Joe Johnson, but it hadn't made any difference. Johnson, especially in the final four frames, which he won in under an hour with two century breaks and four breaks of thirty and over, seemed to be listening to voices of his own.

'There was a kind of power, a kind of brilliant co-ordination of mind and of skill, that could give him as much pleasure, as much delight in himself and in the things that he did, as anything else in the world,' Walter Tevis wrote in his 1950s pool-playing classic, *The Hustler*. 'He loved the hard sound the balls made, loved the feel of the green wool cloth under his hand, the other hand gently holding the butt of his cue, tapping leather on ivory ... Things of that kind, things that simple, can be forgotten easily – especially in all the questions of money and gambling, talent and character, born winner and born loser – and they can come as a shock.'

It may have been a chemical composite he was tapping, but it seemed reasonable to suppose that, in the final minutes of his quarter-final, Joe Johnson would have found something to identify with in those lines. 'That were when I knew I were a good player,' Joe would later say. 'When I beat Terry.'

Terry felt that Joe reminded him of himself when he won the

championship at his first attempt in 1979. But Joe Johnson had more in common with another Matchroom player, Dennis Taylor, the outgoing champion. They were both homely, chubby, modest, unassuming men, who had always been regarded as having very secure futures as spear-carriers in snooker's classic dramas. It went without saying that, like Dennis in 1985, Joe Johnson would walk out the popular favourite.

Joe Johnson had a manager called Wally Springett who was a club-owner in Yorkshire and wore his hair in a blue-tinged Liberace bouffant, and mohair suits. Wally Springett took two-inch display ads in the snooker monthlies advertising Joe's availability for competitions, exhibitions etcetera. All that summed up the small-town, small-timeness of the whole Joe Johnson thing for many people. 'I can just see Wally Springett negotiating million-pound contracts' was typical of the remarks to be overheard around the Crucible.

But the thing that was becoming clear about Joe Johnson as the competition proceeded was that he had no interest in pumping himself up and turning big-time. At the end of his matches, he adjourned to neither the back-slapping of the hospitality lounges nor the seclusion of a suite at the Grosvenor, but to the public bar and, later, to an Indian take-away and his own bed in the modest semi where he lived with his second wife and six children, 25 minutes down the motorway from Sheffield.

The mundanity of this existence was regarded as unusual enough to make a story. And 'Ordinary Joe' – 'Sometimes I think I'd like to be an ordinary gas man again, playing the game for fun' – was the angle most of the papers went for on the first morning of his two-day shot at the title. When he went 3–1 down inside an hour 'ordinary' seemed an apt description. Davis had made consecutive centuries in the third and fourth frames and appeared to be flying. Johnson took the next three frames, however, Davis the next four, and so the match proceeded, like a millepede, with both players taking frames in clusters, until they stood level at the end of the second session, eight-frames-all.

The next day was a Bank Holiday Monday and Johnson

bounced down the stairs into the arena looking festive in har-lequin-patterned shoes of red, pink and white patent leather. Steve was currently appearing in a series of ads for Riley in which he wore a pair of tweedy, old-man's slippers with his evening suit. The slippers had been painted in over his normal shoes and the shoes that Joe was wearing with his otherwise conventional grey-green waistcoat and trousers gave the im-pression of having been similarly touched in by an art director. They glinted and sparkled in the lights and looked like shoes from a fantasy story which are believed to be imbued with magic, talismanic qualities.

Steve, too, had chosen to wear new shoes for the occasion whose soles were as virgin as their uppers. These shoes, though, were of a deepest black, which absorbed rather than reflected light. They were made of ostrich skin and were heavily pocked where the bird's quills had been removed. They were old-fashioned, high-fronted shoes and, with the bible-black suit he was wearing and his usual bloodless complexion, gave him an unmistakable funereal air. What was he? Distanced from the hoopla of the Crucible, the internment director of a chain of top-of-the-market funeral parlours would have been a fair guess.

Joe Johnson was overweight but, unlike Dennis, say, didn't seem self-conscious about it. He seemed comfortable with himself and with his body and this was reflected in the way he played. From the beginning of the third session he played an open game full of flair and daring and the length-of-the-table, long-potting which had been so characteristic of Steve Davis in the days when he was still making his name. Davis in comparison appeared tight and inhibited, automatically turning down adventurous shots in favour of safe ones designed to keep the cue-ball returning to baulk.

Johnson took the first four frames to put himself 12–8 in front. After the interval, Davis went down to break, stood up and approached a man on the press benches who was in his direct line of vision. 'You couldn't do us a favour, mate,' he said. 'That pink shirt . . .' Play then reverted to the previous day's pattern, with Davis taking three of the next four frames, the last with an impressive break of 100.

Bill Davis had been watching the play on a monitor in the press room, the colour in his neck rising and falling as his son's fortunes ebbed and flowed. It was ridiculous, he was coming round to thinking, that the world championship title should hang on the outcome of a single match, even a match played over thirty-five frames. Consistency should be the determining factor, of which there was no better proponent than Steve.

Joe Johnson might have been 'potting them off the lampshade', as Jimmy White put it, but Bill remained unmoved. 'They say Steve is boring to watch,' he said round the side of his cigar. 'That's because he plays snooker. He pots the ball with the minimum of effort and gets the white ball in position for the next shot. Now Higgins or White or Johnson here will do the same thing, but they'll run it along the rail, side-screw it off the lampshade and make it do a figure-eight. But it's still the same shot. They still do the same thing in the end. Of course the audience goes bananas for that stuff. The bawling and the shouting. While Steve just taps them in.'

Steve was in his dressing room, resting before the final session. 'Well, I better give him a shout,' his father sighed, looking at his watch.

'To get that title back. Since last year, that's the only thing he's wanted in life,' Frank Callan, Steve's 'guru', said when Bill had gone. Frank and Bill Davis had been giving each other a wide berth. 'He was humiliated. Are you with me? He's been living for this match.'

Davis desperately needed the first frame of the final session but missed an easy red to allow Johnson to clean up and go three frames in front. Johnson looked like making it 15–11 with a fluent 51 in the next, but Davis fluked a red and went on to win on the black. By the interval, however, Johnson was four in front at 16–12 and needing only two frames for the match and the title.

'It's just another game to Johnson,' Clive Everton said, passing somebody in a corridor. 'Davis is thinking about posterity and the record books. He's frozen. It's re-opened all last year's scars.'

Something in Davis had gone. He was still coming to the table, chalking his cue and aiming a white ball at a ball of a different colour. But there was no rhythm. He could remember the words but he had forgotten the tune. It would come back to him in snatches and, like a tennis player suddenly finding the centre of the racquet, he'd make the balls run for him. On making contact they would ring like bone china rather than pot clay.

But just when he thought he had it, the tune would go again, swallowed up by the static. His elbow would jut at an uncomfortable angle, he'd pause either too long or not long enough at the end of the backswing, the follow-through would be ragged and he'd find himself on the long walk back to his chair.

As the dead frames banked up against him like leaves in a gutter, he spent more and more time in his corner, and showed less and less inclination to leave it. 'Whites of the eyes!' was the instruction that went out from the BBC scanner vans anchored to the forecourt of the Crucible at times like these. A red light clicked on on one of the cameras on the floor of the theatre and the face in the viewfinder, hazy at first and without definition, swam into focus. Like an over-familiar poodle, the camera nuzzled the famous features trying to locate the tell-tale signals – exaggerated puckerings of the lips, perspiring, involuntary tics – which would help the watching millions decide if, and to what extent, Davis was cracking.

In the early days – in the days when he became world champion for the first time – he would betray his eagerness to be back at the table by leaning forward, chin on fists, elbows on knees, willing his opponent into the mistake that would let him back into the game. Now, a sixth sense telling him when camera-3 was homing in, he sat straight-backed, curtains-drawn, unflinching, turned in upon himself.

Joe Johnson, meanwhile, was giving no indication of being 'under the cosh'. Just two frames away from the title that nobody had believed him capable of winning, he was showing none of the signs of choking that had kept so many potential winners nearly-men. His arm was doing exactly what his brain instructed it to do, without any kicks, jumps, jerks or stammers interrupting. There was no tension – there was a palpable lack of tension – in his cueing arm. Asked at that minute to thread a needle or draw a perfect circle, you felt that he would have been able to do both without blinking.

The balls were clipping into the pockets as if that's what they were meant to do. They made a deep, clean sound as they hit the leather wadding. He was getting position on the cue ball, it seemed, without hardly trying. It was the sort of form, if he could sustain it, that was going to end up making him the world champion.

Johnson's game was so big by this time it couldn't be contained. There was something about it, as somebody wrote of another player in another game at another time, that suggested a very large aircraft beginning its descent.

A break of 46 in the twenty-ninth frame left Davis needing snookers. Another frame and it was all over, the audience booming their approval as Johnson, running on automatic-pilot by now, clipped, stroked and banged the last balls home.

'It was terrific playing Steve. His ability is second-to-none and he's the perfect gentleman inside snooker and out,' were the first words the microphone picked up from the winner's lips. They brought tears rushing to Willie Thorne's eyes, and he dabbed at them where he was standing, off to one side. Behind the dull glass window of the commentary box, tears glistened on John Spencer's face. 'I don't think he gets the recognition he deserves,' Joe was still saying as the cheers and the photographers' requests for him to hold it high, Joe, over here, Joe, give her a kiss, Joe, drowned him out.

'What's the worst that can happen? I can lose,' Joe Johnson said cheerfully before the start of the final. 'That's the worst that can happen.' He'd go home to Bradford and pick up the threads of his life where he'd dropped them a fortnight earlier.

For Steve Davis, though, there were no threads to pick up. His life started and ended on the table, Snooker *was* life for him. 'If you're not a winner, you're nothing.' Wasn't that what Barry had always said? So where did that leave him? To lose one final was unlucky. To lose two was starting to look like carelessness. Something was going wrong.

Last year, after missing a thin cut to lose on the last ball to Dennis, he looked nauseous, delirious, as if somebody had just kneed him in the stomach. How did it feel? How did it *feel?* they kept asking, until at the party afterwards Barry had had to head-butt a reporter who asked the question one time too many.

This time, though, Steve didn't look devastated or 'gutted'. None of that. He looked simply bemused, disbelieving, like somebody who had just watched an accident and the accident had turned out to be himself. The leg had been removed but the foot kept on aching. He could see the blood but couldn't feel the wound.

He edged his way through the crush of photographers and let himself be hugged by Susan, who was dressed for a victory party. He gave the loser's cheque to her husband, who slipped it into the side-pocket of his jacket without a second glance.

'It's just that Joe played better on the day, Tex,' Steve said in tones of heavy irony, speaking at idiot-speed into the *Mail* man's detested cassette-recorder turning on the desk in front of him. An air of disquiet hung over the proceedings in the packed interview room. Janice was being haunted by a line 'from the new musical, *Chess*', she would later reveal in her Crucible Diary: "There's not much between despair and ecstasy". Everybody was fighting a natural tendency to gloat.

At the press conference Barry stood with his hands in his pockets and his cheek against the cool of the concrete wall. Nothing had been worked up in advance this time. Nothing had been prepared. He didn't know what Steve was feeling this time because he didn't know what he was feeling himself.

'Tonight was a very important night in somebody's life,' Barry said many hours later. He had been dancing and perspiration ran out of his hair and into his eyes. It ran in rivers down his chest which was mottled and red. 'It was a turning-point.' His eyes opened wide, as if he hadn't had the thought until he heard it spoken out loud. 'The disappointment wasn't there.'

By lunchtime the following day, Steve was on his way to his next engagement, a 'Celebrity Snooker Challenge' for Courage breweries in Reading. 'Please welcome', the master-of-cere-monies would say, 'the game's biggest money-earner, the game's number-one seed . . .' And Steve would step into the pool of light and do the short bows from the waist he perfected in the Far East. He'd smile and he'd wave to the people high up in the balconies to whom he was just a blur. Tonight would be a very important night in somebody's life, but not his.

Postscript

Two days after the end of the World Championships, the *Daily Star* revealed in a front-page exclusive that Joe Johnson's natural father was an Asian, Malik Farooq, who had been dead for twelve years. 'But Joe was still a child when he was adopted by Ken Johnson,' the *Star* reported, 'the man who introduced him to snooker.'

Joe Johnson signed an agency contract with Howard Kruger but said 'no' to most of the commercial enticements which flooded in. Privately, he was known to believe that becoming world champion was both the best and the worst thing that ever happened to Dennis Taylor. 'Even in the first week', Johnson said, 'my wife, my friends and my family were treating me different. I don't want to be treated different.'

He did not accompany the Matchroom players to the Far East. It was the first time the reigning world champion had been missing from one of the Barry Hearn–organised summer tours.

Jimmy White did go, and signed a £200,000 cue-endorsement contract with Riley. Cliff Thorburn signed a £125,000 endorsement contract with BCE.

BCE replaced Goya as sponsors of the first major tournament of the season, and renewed their sponsorship of the Canadian

Masters. BCE were scheduled for a late October launch on the Unlisted Securities Market.

Joe Johnson and Stephen Hendry were among the eight players invited to play in the Langs Scottish Masters in mid-September, replacing the Matchroom players who were taking part in their own 'multi-sponsored, in-house' tournament.

'Jimmy now would be very, very wrong for me,' Barry Hearn had said in May, 'and I think my credibility in the industry would suffer if I was with Jimmy. Things are going *so* well for us now that I would really question taking on anything that is even a *potential* liability.' On September 10, just before the opening of the new season, Hearn announced that Jimmy White had become the seventh member of the Matchroom team. There was a picture of Barry and Jimmy in the first issue of *Sportsweek*, Robert Maxwell's new sports magazine, side by side, smiling.

'Snooker Loopy' reached number 7 on the national charts on May 14. 'The Wanderer' failed to make the Top 50.

Twelve months on

The minute it became obvious that the result of the 1986 World Championship was going to be as big an upset as the previous year – the Romford Robot rubbished again – Del Simmons had advised Joe Johnson's managers to take him 'in the mattress' as soon as possible – in other words, to encourage him to disappear.

The Johnson camp had seen this as simply a case of Del being Del-boy totally-over-the-top again, but they were wrong. By defeating Davis, 'Ordinary Joe' had forfeited any claim he might once have had to his media nickname. He had become public property, a genuine popular hero of sorts, and no amount of self-effacement and 'What can I say, lads?' was going to allow him to slip back, Swampman-like, into the obscurity whence he came. The star-maker machinery – television, the popular dailies, the trade monthlies – had got its appetite up and was demanding to be fed.

'I went to his house the morning after the final, and there must have been forty pressmen squeezed into the kitchen, packed up the stairs,' Wally Springett would say many months later, when he was Johnson's manager in name only. 'There were people wandering through the house, you didn't know who they were. He only had to ask for a cup of coffee for somebody to pull a notebook out and start scribbling.'

Wally Springett was not in fact a 'club-owner', all appearances to the contrary. When the dust had settled it emerged that he was the proprietor of Springett Welding, Batley, which is what was written along both sides of the rusted-out banger that had been Joe's first reward for putting his future in Wally's hands. It was Wally who persuaded the new champion to sign an exclusive contract with the *Star*, spelling out the details of his parentage, although he would later admit that Joe 'was crying his heart out' as he did it.

In the weeks and months following the euphoria of Sheffield, Wally Springett found himself being gradually eased out of the picture, and control of Johnson's career passing to a man who was happy to sit in his accountants' office in West Yorkshire and, like Joe, eschew the celebrity hobnobbing and limousine riding to which Wally was showing signs of becoming addicted.

'I tried to get him to cash in, to get what he can, *when* he can, but he didn't want to know,' Wally said in April 1987, still unable to conceal his exasperation. 'He doesn't want what he sees as the phoney people at the top end who are only after an angle. He decided to earn his living on the table, not singing, not book-writing, not as a commercial commodity.'

'When I won the championship I knew how to react to the people of Bradford,' Johnson himself said, 'but not worldwide. When I fly to somewhere like Hong Kong and there's press and television everywhere, it blows my mind.'

It would take the best part of the season for Johnson to regain any sense of equilibrium, by which time he was slipping back towards the number-sixteen place in the rankings that he had occupied in the run-up to becoming world champion.

'Joe had the chance to have it off,' Barry Hearn said with characteristic bluntness, 'and he fucked it up.'

The 1985–86 season had ended with Del Simmons accusing Hearn of stabbing him in the back by going public with his criticisms of the 'Mickey Mouse' way Simmons was running the WPBSA. The beginning of the 1986–87 season found the two of them still locked in a power struggle, with neither prepared to give ground.

In September, Hearn went ahead with his £100,000 'multi-sponsorship, in-house' Matchroom tournament at the Cliffs Pavilion in Southend. This was in direct opposition to the £40,000 Langs Masters being played in Scotland. In Southend 'everyone from sponsors to players to press to officials mingled freely,'

Snooker Scene reported wistfully, 'recreating the feeling of times gone by when the game's every step forward felt like a leap.'

At the beginning of October, the WPBSA sent invitations to the world's top sixteen players for the second annual BCE Belgian Classic. A week later, with a keen weather eye on the proposed phasing out of all tobacco sponsorship of sport on television, Barry Hearn announced 'the most exciting development in snooker since colour television' – the new 'live', untelevised 'Rothman's Matchroom League'.

This committed his own seven players, plus 'guest star' Cliff Thorburn, to a twenty-eight match series at various venues all over the country, starting in January and continuing until early summer. The dates conflicted, in other words, with the Belgian Masters in March. In addition to this, the Matchroom players were already committed to playing in a Kent cigarettes-sponsored tournament, with a potential viewing audience of 127 million, in Peking that month.

'I only received the dates of the Belgian tournament from the WPBSA ten days ago,' Hearn said, as his players posed for photographers outside the Albert Hall with the Rolls-Royce Silver Spirit (value £69,000) that would go to the first player to compile a 147 maximum break in the new League. 'I really cannot believe that people could put tournament dates in a diary without checking on the availability of seven of the top sixteen players. As it stands there's no way we can be there unless they change the dates.'

In February Del Simmons was obliged to announce that the 1987 Belgian Masters had been postponed. This was particularly unfortunate coming, as it did, in the wake of the commercial chaos of the second Canadian Masters, also sponsored by his old friends at BCE. BCE had refused to hand over the $125,000 prize-money, claiming that a junior sponsor had received more 'name penetration' during the television coverage of the tournament than themselves.

'As Barry Hearn announces coup after coup for his own imaginative brand of private enterprise, disaster dogs the footsteps of Del Simmons,' Simmons's old adversary, Clive Everton, declared with relish in the March issue of his magazine. 'Hearn is now the only snooker entrepreneur with an eighteen-carat international credibility, and the most powerful figure in the overseas development of the game.'

The best demonstration of this in 1987 was in St Moritz on the July Fourth American holiday weekend. Breaking snooker as 'the classy family sport' in America still remained Hearn's ultimate objective. And the three-day, $80,000 challenge match that he mounted in Switzerland between Steve Davis and the American pool player Steve Mizerak, still 'hot' from his role in the Paul Newman film *The Colour of Money*, was his statement that he meant business.

Davis and Mizerak played each other at both pool and snooker and, through the auspices of Trans World International Inc., the television subsidiary of the Mark McCormack empire, their efforts were broadcast in a dozen countries, including the Netherlands, West Germany, Austria, Hong Kong, Japan, Australia, Britain (Channel 4) and, crucially, on ESPN, the all-sports cable channel in America. 'This', Hearn emphasised, in case anybody missed the point, 'could be the breakthrough in America that we've been waiting for.'

Meanwhile, the Rothmans would become a European League in 1988, he announced. 'The response from Europe has been overwhelming. I've had proposals from Monte Carlo, Marbella, Brussels, Amsterdam, Paris and West Berlin besides Dublin and Belfast. The phone hasn't stopped ringing with requests for League Matches for next season.' He had every confidence in the League 'going global' by the end of the decade. If they played their cards right, 'outsiders' other than Cliff Thorburn might eventually be allowed a piece of the action.

Alex Higgins started the season as he meant to continue. By the end of it he had reached a low point, even for him.

In September, he publicly accused Cliff Thorburn of 'taking bags of white powder' after Thorburn had beaten him in the Langs.

At the beginning of November three of the best-known referees submitted complaints to the WPBSA accusing him of separate incidents of 'verbal and physical abuse' following his defeat in the pretelevised stage of the Dulux British Open at Solihull. 'Some of these referees think they're superstars. But if they want to run the game and play snooker my cue is for sale to any of them,' Higgins wailed.

But it was three weeks later, at Preston Guildhall on the evening of November 24, that he finally crossed the line that he had been threatening to cross since he first styled himself the 'People's Champion', and had both press and players queueing up to bury him the next day.

After beating Mike Hallett to reach the quarter-finals of the Tennents UK Open, Higgins took advantage of the post-match press conference to once again bemoan the state of the modern game. 'Snooker is going far too commercial. For me it's lost its magic. I'm absolutely disgusted with the way the game is going. It's being devalued for the sake of sponsors and television. It's all the WPBSA's fault.'

For Higgins, the WPBSA takes human form in its tournament director, and therefore most obvious authority figure, Paul Hatherell. After the press conference, downstairs in the players' bar in the Guildhall, it was Hatherell who became the focus of all Higgins's previously unfocused rage.

'Snooker star Alex Higgins was involved in a furious punch-up last night in which a senior official was head-butted', the papers were splashing before dawn. 'The controversial Irishman could be heard screaming and swearing as harassed WPBSA board members attended the scene ...' Hatherell had been cut above his eye. A door-panel had been splintered. The police had been called.

Could this mean the end at last? Had the Hurricane finally blown himself out? Plenty of people were prepared to stand up and say that it could and that he had.

Thirty-six hours after his freak-out, however, Higgins was facing the press at the door of 'Hurricane Hall' in Mottram St Andrew, Cheshire. He was covered head to toe in half a slaughterhouse of sheepskin clearly designed to make him look like a cuddly Muppets character. On his face was the kind of sheepish grin the ex-Mrs Higgins had come to recognise from those occasions when he turned up on her doorstep with a packet of bacon, wanting to know if she would cook it for him.

In December, Higgins was fined £250 in a Preston magistrates' court. On April 6, a one-man disciplinary tribunal appointed by the sport's governing body fined him £12,000 and banned him from taking part in five tournaments (only four of which he could actually enter). These did not include the 1987 World Championships, which were then less than a fortnight away.

An hour later Higgins was on *Wogan*, shooting the breeze with Terry and renouncing the devil. Perched on the pink plush at the television theatre, the Hurricane looked as telegenic and snaggle-free as any Jeffrey Archer. The hair was freshly blow-dried and tinted; the complexion was clear; he had come 100 per cent suited up and mentioned charity walking with Botham and charity golfing with Wogan himself every chance he got. Sitting on the sofa beside him, Aitch, the man behind this latest attempt at image laundering, glowed with satisfaction.

Twitching less than usual and slurring his words only slightly, Alex said he intended to take snooker 'back to the heartlands' during his enforced sabbatical (most of which was going to fall in the close-season anyway). It was time to take snooker 'back to the people'. He seemed to mean all this most sincerely. Barry Hearn, meanwhile, declared himself horror-struck. 'Ludicrously lenient' is how he described the 'sentence'. It had made 'a laughing stock' of snooker. Higgins deserved a suspension 'of at least a year'.

As an insurance against future skeletons clattering out of Higgins's closet — and, like everybody else in snooker circles, Barry Hearn knew it was only a matter of time — Hearn took moves to distance Jimmy White from his long-time doubles partner, boozing pal and guru in much the way that he had once warned Tony Meo off Jimmy himself. For instance, it was 'highly unlikely', he said, that White would ever again partner Higgins while he remained a Matchroom player. Stephen Hendry, who had gone on to consolidate the successes of his first season and now merited serious consideration as a future world champion — cleaner than 'Super Bairn' it wasn't possible to be — was widely tipped as Jimmy's doubles partner in 1987–88.

The signs, however, were that it could already be too late. JIMMY WHITE'S SECRET SHAME, the *People* roared on the last Sunday of the World Championship. 'Snooker whirlwind Jimmy White, the blue-eyed darling of millions of mums, is hooked on cocaine,' the story started. Barry Hearn immediately said he would sue.

The Higgins farrago had been triggered by the coincidence of his name coming up for drugs testing twice in the same week. Drugs tests seemed to be the topic of the season. Behind the scenes at the Crucible in 1987 the talk sometimes seemed to be about nothing else.

The drugs in question, however, were not the illegal kind that had hooked Kirk Stevens, but beta-blockers, the nerve-steadiers that were available on prescription and that Rex Williams, the WPBSA chairman, for one, had admitted taking for years.

The International Olympic Committee and the Sports Council had both banned beta-blockers, even for those with a medical certificate, because of their widespread misuse in sports such as shooting and archery, where their properties — beta-blockers don't actually stop you from being nervous, but they do stop you being nervous about your nervousness — were felt to give the users an unfair advantage by slowing the heartbeat and reducing tremor in the playing arm.

The WPBSA, though, had not included beta-blockers on their list of banned drugs. Players were allowed to play under their influence so long as they could prove there were 'sound medical reasons'.

The ethical, moral and pharmaceutical dilemmas all came to a head at the end of the first week of the World Championship when Barry Hearn called a press conference to announce that Neal Foulds, the most successful player of the season, had been taking beta-blockers since being diagnosed as having 'tachycardia' — rapid heartbeat — nine days before.

It was open-season from then on. In a front-page headline a few days earlier — GET OUT NOW, REX! — the Star had called on the WPBSA's player-chairman to resign. The call was now taken up by Colin Moynihan, the Conservative MP for Lewisham East, who also demanded that Neal Foulds 'should lay down his cue'. Dick Tracey, the Minister for Sport, said that the WPBSA should publicly name the players who had given a positive response to drug tests which were, after all, government subsidised. There were TV think-ins, questions in the House, letters to *The Times*.

'What's it all about?' Tony Meo said one afternoon in his garden in Willesden. 'Is it right or is it wrong? I've been thinkin' an' I dunno. I tellya, it's doin' my head in.'

For Joe Johnson, his season as world champion had been a catalogue of disasters. He had gone out at the pretelevised stages of all but one of the major tournaments. His predicament, as a BBC documentary a couple of days before he started the defence of his title made all too painfully clear, was that his game had fallen victim to the burdens and pressures of fame.

He had a new house and a new top-of-the-range Mercedes, courtesy of the northern brewers with whom he had an exhibition contract. Apart from that, all he had to show by the time the 1987 Championship came round was a sense of distrust and an apparently deep-seated disillusionment. 'It's knocked his puddin' out, it really has,' Wally Springett said.

' "Joe" — it's a right northern name', John Cocker said, 'and a right northern attitude to life.' Cocker is a central figure in the Johnson camp. He opened Morley Snooker Centre in 1983 in the old woollen mill near Leeds where he himself had once worked, and hired Joe Johnson as the professional. The club has provided a bolt-hole for Johnson ever since.

He was still struggling in the days when John Cocker first met him: he was driving an old Hillman and had a hole in one of his shoes. The two of them prospered together, and Cocker remains one of Johnson's closest friends. But whereas Cocker has shown imagination and enterprise — he had recently added a whole new wing to the snooker centre and was about to build a conservatory and motel — Joe has been content, as he himself admits, 'to just plod along'.

He had started the 1986 Championships as a 150–1 outsider; and it said all that needed to be said about his year as champion that, twelve months on, the odds against him were stacked almost as high.

He surprised everybody, however, by surviving his first-round match against Eugene Hughes (just), bouncing Murdo McLeod in the next, and scraping past Stephen Hendry in the round after that. Suddenly, he was in the semi-final and singing 'Fairytales do come true . . .' to David Vine in the interview room.

A Neal Foulds still suffering from 'stress, tension and emotional things' was Johnson's next victim. And now, staring him in the face, was an action-replay of the 1986 final against the player who, when he stepped through the curtain on his *This Is Your Life*, Johnson had dropped to his knees before and salaamed at his feet.

And, essentially, this was the spirit in which he played his second World final against Davis. Any urge he might have felt to use the occasion to stick it to all those who had him written off as a one-hit wonder, was outweighed by his innate decency and sense of natural justice. Davis was the best. Johnson had said he was the best even as he himself was being presented with the Championship trophy. Now it was Davis's turn to win. Fair dos. 'It would've been a travesty,' Johnson said, 'if I'd levelled and somehow gone past him.'

Afterwards, Steve cried, Barry cried and even Robbo sniffed a bit. When Barry had stopped crying he announced his intention of making the World Championship itself part of his irresistibly expanding empire. He would be prepared to pay £12.5 million for the television and promotional rights when the existing contracts expired in 1990. 'I believe we are on the verge of a global breakthrough the likes of which no sport has seen for over a hundred years,' he croaked emotionally. 'We are setting our stall out to challenge golf and tennis. Better believe it. I am deadly serious.'

Earlier in the year, asked to comment on snooker's power struggle on *Wogan*, Hearn had simply shrugged. 'People still talk about a power struggle,' he said, glowing, grinning slyly, 'but that's been and gone.'

In August, just a few weeks before the 1987–88 season was due to begin, Barry Hearn announced the World Series, a Grand Prix tournament worth a minimum of £600,000 in prize money to be played on five continents. Far and away the most significant dates, however, were four days in mid-December. These were the days when the first official snooker tournament in the United States would take place, in Las Vegas.

Davis — 'Lean and square-jawed, his good looks and clean-cut behaviour have made him the hero of Britain' — was featured in *Time* magazine and the *International Herald Tribune*. 'We want to create millions of snooker enthusiasts in every nation on earth', Barry was inevitably quoted as saying.

After years of talking, the big push, it seemed, was about to begin. He was all set at last to have a go at cracking America.

Author's note

I've made no attempt in *Pocket Money* to provide a comprehensive history of snooker. Somebody has already done that –
Clive Everton, in *The Story of Billiards and Snooker* (Cassell,
1979). I'd like to acknowledge a debt to that book as well as the
Guinness Book of Snooker Records, of which Everton is editor, and
to his reports in *Snooker Scene*.

Other books which were useful were *Playing on Their Nerves*,
by Angela Patmore, *The Cruel Game*, by Jean Rafferty, and
Levels of the Game, by John McPhee.

I'd like to thank Barry Hearn for his generosity with his time
and for the access to his players; Ann Yates of the WPBSA, who
was unfailingly helpful, Brian Pegler of Strachan and Co., and
the various sponsors who helped me gain more than a stone.

Most of 'the reptiles' made my task easier and pleasanter,
particularly Alexander Clyde of the *London Standard* and Steve
Acteson of the PA.

I want to thank David Godwin for his invaluable encouragement and enthusiasm; Roger Smith, for unearthing J. B.
Priestley's 1932 essay, 'At Thurston's'; and Carol Gorner, without whom.

EAMON DUNPHY

A Strange Kind of Glory

Sir Matt Busby is one of the few great men produced by Britain's national game. A coal-miner's son from Scotland, he created one of the most glorious and celebrated sporting institutions in the world. Manchester United was built in his image. Busby had the grace of an aristocrat, the presence of a great actor, the cunning of a powerful politician. In an age when footballers, indeed most professional sportsmen, were serfs, he was a dignified exception to the muddied oaf of common perception.

Although his first great team, the Busby Babes, was tragically destroyed in the Munich Air crash of 1958, he created another which went on to win the European Cup in 1968. Sadly, reality has been a frequent intruder in the twenty-three years since Sir Matt realised his dream. Mention Manchester United today and the talk is more likely to be of greed and betrayal than of romance and courage. Busby survives, a witness, poignant, silent and dignified, reminding us of a glorious age which he did more than anyone to inspire.

A Strange Kind of Glory is Busby's story, told with his co-operation and from the inside by people, like Best, Charlton and Law, whose view of football, indeed of life itself, was shaped by the Glory Game. It is the story of Britain at a certain time, of Britain's national game as experienced by its most distinguished man. Perhaps the last great football man.

BILL BUFORD

Among the Thugs

In 1982, Bill Buford joined an inter-city train at a rural railway station in Wales. The train had been taken over by football supporters who were methodically destroying it, and the police could do nothing to stop them. Before reaching London, the train was taken out of service.

Bill Buford, an American living in Britain, had, until then, never witnessed this kind of football supporter – England's 'hooligan', its 'thug' – first hand. Were people *really* aware of what was taking place every Saturday? Why had no one written properly about them?

For the next eight years – the years of riots on Channel ferries, street-fighting outside Britain's football grounds, the deaths at Heysel Stadium and Hillsborough, the violence at the 1990 World Cup – Buford travelled with the supporters.

He travelled with them up and down Britain, to Italy, Turkey, Greece and Germany. He attended a National Front disco and witnessed the robbing of a pub. He saw stabbings and scenes of extreme violence – in one instance, violence that was stopped only when the army sent in a tank. He met people with names like Bone Head, Paraffin Pete and Steamin' Sammy. He befriended others, many now in jail, who were pickpockets, safe-crackers, cocaine dealers, traders in 'moody' counterfeit money, and one who bit out the eye of a policeman.

Among the Thugs is about the experience, and the attractions, of crowd violence.

DON MOSEY

Fred: Then and Now

'Fiery Fred' Trueman was the greatest fast bowler in the world, arguably England's greatest ever. He was the first man in the history of cricket to take 300 Test wickets, and his name is as widely known today – as critic, broadcaster, entertainer and TV personality – as it was when he was the scourge of Test and county cricket batsmen everywhere.

Not only was he an all-time great as a player but he was by far the most colourful and best-known character in the game – fiery, controversial, a man of strong opinions and strong words. His bowling was hall-marked by its sheer naked hostility, yet he was a fine technician. In a twenty-year career he sprinted two million yards to the crease.

Don Mosey is uniquely qualified to write this new biography of his friend, colleague and fellow Yorkshire-man, and considers both the player and the man with fairness and affection.

GERALD HOWAT

Len Hutton

Len Hutton was the first professional to captain
England, the second to be knighted and the youngest
ever to score a century for Yorkshire.

In 1938, Pudsey parish church pealed an echo to his
phenomenal 364 at the Oval – a world record beaten
only by Gary Sobers 365 twenty years later. He won
the series against India in 1952, regained the Ashes after
19 years in 1953, and retained them eighteen months
later in Australia.

Hutton was not only one of England's most successful captains, but also the most classical of batsmen.
Relaxed, deliberate, consistently precise, he was a
complete stylist with every stroke.

In this, the first full-scale study of Hutton's first-class
career, Gerald Howat brings alive the man's modesty,
dedication and humour, and helps immortalise one of
the greatest cricketers of all time.

FFYONA CAMPBELL

Feet of Clay

Ffyona Campbell was thirteen when she first dreamed
of walking around the world. At sixteen she walked
from John O'Groats to Land's End; at eighteen she set
the women's world speed record walking from New
York to Los Angeles; at twenty-one she broke the *men's*
world record by walking 3,200 miles from Sydney to
Perth. In March 1991 she began her monumental 8,600-
mile trek from the Cape to Cairo, the penultimate leg in
her round-the-world hike.

Related with rare frankness and intimacy, this is the
story of a wilfully independent young woman's journey
across Australia. Traversing some of the toughest
country in the world, she endures dehydration, tarmac-
melting heat, and blisters that outnumber the flies. Her
money runs out and her relationship with her back-up
driver alternately sustains and devastates her. Not only
a compelling adventure, *Feet of Clay* is the realisation of
a dream . . .

JOHN OAKSEY

Oaksey on Racing

For over three decades John Oaksey has been a well-known figure in British racing. As a journalist with the *Daily Telegraph*, the *Sunday Telegraph* and *Horse and Hound*, he has commanded a substantial following. As a distinguished amateur jockey he participated directly in National Hunt racing for twenty years (riding as John Lawrence before he succeeded to his father's title, Lord Oaksey) and was leading amateur twice. And as a regular presenter of racing on television – most recently on Channel Four – he has become familiar to millions.

Oaksey on Racing distils the essential Oaksey from his thirty years as 'Audax' in *Horse and Hound*, and offers a rich selection of his writings on horses, people and issues. Here are the highs and the lows of his love affair with the Grand National, including his unforgettable account of how the 1963 race was snatched from him and Carrickbeg by the outsider Ayala.

An extraordinary variety of racing personalities – equine and human – is described with John Oaksey's characteristic blend of enthusiasm and knowledge, nowhere more graphically displayed than his accounts of his own riding experience. From the controversial moments such as the 1974 Whitbread Gold Cup finish when his mount Proud Tarquin was disqualified in favour of The Dikler, or the amateurs' race at Cheltenham when he took the wrong course, to his memories of bumping round the 'gaff' tracks, John Oaksey's involvement adds a special dimension to his writing.

A Selected List of Non-Fiction Titles Available from Mandarin

While every effort is made to keep prices low, it is sometimes necessary to increase prices at short notice. Mandarin Paperbacks reserves the right to show new retail prices on covers which may differ from those previously advertised in the text or elsewhere.

The prices shown below were correct at the time of going to press.

☐	7493 0961 X	**Stick it up Your Punter**	Chippendale & Horrib £4.99
☐	7493 0988 1	**Desert Island Discussions**	Sue Lawley £4.99
☐	7493 0938 5	**The Courage to Heal**	Ellen Bass and Laura Davis £7.99
☐	7493 0637 8	**The Hollywood Story**	Joel Finler £9.99
☐	7493 1032 4	**How to Meet Interesting Men**	Gizelle Howard £5.99
☐	7493 0586 X	**The New Small Garden**	C. E. Lucas-Phillips £5.99
☐	7493 1172 X	**You'll Never Eat Lunch in This Town Again**	Julia Phillips £5.99

All these books are available at your bookshop or newsagent, or can be ordered direct from the publisher. Just tick the titles you want and fill in the form below.

Mandarin Paperbacks, Cash Sales Department, PO Box 11, Falmouth, Cornwall TR10 9EN.

Please send cheque or postal order, no currency, for purchase price quoted and allow the following for postage and packing:

UK including BFPO
£1.00 for the first book, 50p for the second and 30p for each additional book ordered to a maximum charge of £3.00.

Overseas including Eire
£2 for the first book, £1.00 for the second and 50p for each additional book thereafter.

NAME (Block letters) ....

ADDRESS..

....

☐ I enclose my remittance for ....

☐ I wish to pay by Access/Visa Card Number ⬚⬚⬚⬚⬚⬚⬚⬚⬚⬚⬚⬚⬚⬚⬚⬚

Expiry Date ⬚⬚⬚⬚